For Pat, Alison, and Charlie

Applying Moral Theories

Third Edition

C.E. HARRIS, JR.

TEXAS A&M UNIVERSITY

WADSWORTH PUBLISHING COMPANY

 An International Thomson Publishing Company

Belmont• Albany • Bonn • Boston • Cincinnati • Detroit • London • Madrid • Melbourne •
Mexico City• New York • Paris • San Francisco • Singapore • Tokyo • Toronto • Washington

Philosophy Editor: **Peter Adams**
Assistant Editor: **Clayton Glad**
Editorial Assistant: **Greg Brueck**
Project Editor: **Gary Mcdonald**
Production: **Robin Gold/Forbes Mill Press**
Print Buyer: **Barbara Britton**
Copy Editor: **Laura Larson**
Cover: **Madeline Budnick**
Compositor: **Wolf Creek Press**
Printer: **Malloy Lithographing**

Printed in the United States of America
1 2 3 4 5 6 7 8 9 10

For more information, contact Wadsworth Publishing Company:

Wadsworth Publishing Company
10 Davis Drive
Belmont, California 94002, USA

International Thomson Publishing Europe
Berkshire House 168-173
High Holborn
London, WC1V 7AA, England

Thomas Nelson Australia
102 Dodds Street
South Melbourne 3205
Victoria, Australia

Nelson Canada
1120 Birchmount Road
Scarborough, Ontario
Canada M1K 5G4

International Thomson Editores
Campos Eliseos 385, Piso 7
Col. Polanco
11560 México D.F. México

International Thomson Publishing GmbH
Königswinterer Strasse 418
53227 Bonn, Germany

International Thomson Publishing Asia
221 Henderson Road
#05-10 Henderson Building
Singapore 0315

International Thomson Publishing Japan
Hirakawacho Kyowa Building, 3F
2-2-1 Hirakawacho
Chiyoda-ku, Tokyo 102, Japan

Library of Congress Cataloging-in-Publication Data
Harris, C. E. (Charles Edwin)
    Applying moral theories / C.E. Harris, Jr. —3rd ed.
        p.   cm.
    Includes bibliographical references and index.
    ISBN: 0-534-50526-0 (text)
        1. Ethics.   I. Title
BJ1012.H318   1996   96-17204
171—dc20

Contents

Preface

This third edition carries forward the basic themes and approaches of the first two editions, with what I hope are several improvements. The primary improvements are a completely rewritten chapter on the ethics of self-interest and the addition of two appendices. Appendix I contains some directions for analyzing moral cases that supplement the text. Appendix II presents thirty unanalyzed ethical cases for student analysis and classroom discussion. In addition, I have made a number of smaller modifications throughout the text, including rewriting the introduction to Chapter 1 and the section on "Problems in Applying Moral Theories" in Chapter 4. To accommodate the additions in roughly the same space, I have slightly reduced the number of analyzed cases in several of the chapters, eliminated the charts giving a rating of the four theories, and eliminated Chapter 9. I have preserved what I believe are the essential features of Chapter 9 in Appendix I.

The basic premise of the first edition was that, in spite of the increasing interest in applied ethics, relatively little has been done to make ethical theory more accessible to students and more easily applicable to moral problems. This text still represents, in my opinion, a unique attempt to remedy this defect. Here are some of the special features of this book:

1. A common outline format is used to present each theory, facilitating comparisons.
2. Concept summaries are provided at the end of the shorter chapters and at crucial junctures in the longer chapters.

3. A checklist provides specific directions for applying each theory to moral problems.

4. Examples are used profusely throughout the text, and the checklists are followed in applying each theory to several cases.

5. The same criteria of evaluation are applied to every theory, again facilitating comparison.

6. Appendix II provides thirty cases for classroom discussion and student analysis.

The reader should keep several considerations in mind. First, this book is on moral theory, albeit oriented toward application. The discussions of particular cases are not intended to be full-scale treatments but short examples showing how the theories can be applied and illustrating some of the problems encountered in application. Their *primary* purpose is to illustrate methodological problems rather than definitively resolve difficult moral issues. Students should be encouraged to look at the case analyses critically and to identify factual, conceptual, and moral assumptions that might lead them to different conclusions.

Second, whereas the chapters on egoism, natural law, and utilitarianism present standard positions, the chapter on the ethics of respect for persons is something of an exception. The reliance on Kant is obvious, but it should not be taken as a straightforward presentation of Kantian moral theory. Many scholars would say that my use of what Kant would call the "contradiction in conception" test is not Kant's, and I do not use Kant's "contradiction in the will" test at all. My interpretation of the means–ends principle relies as much on Alan Gewirth as on Kant. I nevertheless believe the chapter gives a reasonably clear presentation of a deontological position that still owes much to Kant.

Third, the book is oriented toward normative ethical theory and pays minimal attention to metaethical issues. However, attempts to justify individual moral standards are briefly sketched, and there are discussions of ethical intuitionism, the relation of ethics to science, the attempt to base ethics on religion, and the emotivist analysis of ethical terms.

Ethical relativism is discussed in more detail because of the considerable interest students have in this topic.

I want to thank all of those who have encouraged and assisted me in the three editions of this book. Special thanks go to Kelly Zavislak and to the reviewers for the third edition: Dan Baker, Ocean County College; Brian Hilliard, Appalachian State University; and Elizabeth Radcliffe, Santa Clara University.

C. E. Harris, Jr.

1

What Is Ethics?

Patrick Thomas was in a quandary. A major customer of his company, Maine-based Bath Iron Works, had asked the boat builder to participate in a secret investigation of one of its suppliers. Thomas, the purchasing manager, knew that the customer was important to Bath's survival, but he still was not sure how to handle the request. So he went to the company's ethics officer, who discussed the problem with the chief executive. Within twelve hours Bath had decided it would not participate in the investigation unless the supplier was informed of it. The customer eventually accepted Bath's decision.[1]

This story illustrates the way many firms are introducing ethics into their corporate culture. According to a 1994 survey by the Washington-based Ethics Resource Center, 60 percent of the firms surveyed have codes of ethics, 33 percent have training in business conduct and 33 percent have an ethics office where employees can receive advice or report questionable business activities.

Observers cite several reasons for the trend. One reason is that some executives believe a common core of values can keep companies together. Global business and the diversity of backgrounds even within our own country increase the need to agree on company values. Another reason is that federal sentencing guidelines now require federal judges to take into account whether firms have strong ethics programs, when issuing sentences for corporate wrongdoing.

---

[1] "'Business Ethics' Is Not an Oxymoron at Some Companies," *Salt Lake Tribune*, April 16, 1995.

In business, government, the professions, and private life, ethics is "in." It is now more acceptable to talk about ethics than it was a few years ago. Many people, however, still find it difficult to think clearly about ethical issues. They consider ethical discussions "soft" or "ambiguous" or "nebulous"—lacking in clarity and rigor. Here is the paradox: ethics is enormously important but difficult to think about clearly and responsibly.

This book should help you overcome this paradox. When you have finished reading it, you should be able to think more clearly and responsibly about ethical questions. In the first four chapters, we shall discuss the nature and validity of ethics and the structure and evaluation of a moral theory. Then we will consider four moral philosophies that are especially influential in our society. These philosophies are (1) *egoism*, the theory that everyone should do what is in his or her self-interest; (2) *natural law*, the theory that one should do what is in accord with human nature; (3) *utilitarianism*, the theory that one should do what leads to the greatest overall human welfare; and (4) *the ethics of respect for persons*, the theory that one should act in a way that respects the equal dignity of all human beings. You will see how these philosophies are applied to particular examples, and you will receive guidelines for applying them to new situations.

This first chapter is devoted to the clarification of concepts. In applying ethical theory to moral problems, it is important to think as precisely as possible. Our discussion will move from broader issues to more specific ones. First we shall differentiate the three major issues in a moral problem: factual issues, conceptual issues, and moral issues. Then we shall focus on moral statements and distinguish them from other types of statements that express value judgments. Finally, we shall narrow the focus still further to consider some distinctions and concepts within the realm of moral discourse. We shall conclude with an example to which the concepts we have discussed can be applied.

THREE TYPES OF CLAIMS MADE IN MORAL ARGUMENTS

On January 17, 1912, Captain Robert Falcon Scott and his four companions reached the South Pole. Then, hauling their sleigh, they began the 800-mile walk back to their base camp on McMurdo Sound. They died 100 miles short of their destination, and Captain Scott's diary, found with their bodies the following spring, tells a story of heroism that still fires the imagination.

One of the men in the party, Capt. L. E. G. Oates, became frostbitten. He suffered terribly for weeks and realized he was slowing the party's march, thereby increasing their peril. On March 10, Oates asked the physician in the party, Dr. Wilson, whether he had a chance to survive. The physician said he did not know, but Captain Scott says in his diary that, in fact, Oates had no chance of surviving the march. Scott remarks that he doubts whether the party could make it to safety in any event, but he concluded that they might have "a dog's chance" if Oates were not present.

A few days later Captain Oates said he could not go on and proposed that they leave him in his sleeping bag. The party refused and finally induced him to come on the afternoon march. He struggled a few miles, and that night he was still worse. Captain Scott gives this account of Oates's death:

> This was the end. He slept through the night before last, hoping not to wake; but he woke in the morning—yesterday. It was blowing a blizzard. He said, "I am just going outside and may be some time." He went out into the blizzard and we have not seen him since.

Scott remarks a few lines later:

> We knew that poor Oates was walking to his death, but though we tried to dissuade him, we knew it was the act of a brave man and an Englishman.[2]

One of the members of the party, Edgar Evans, had already died at the foot of Beardmore Glacier. The other three members of the party, Scott, Wilson, and Bowers, died in their tent of cold and starvation, prevented by the blizzard from struggling the last eleven miles to One Ton Depot, where they would have found food and fuel.

In determining whether Captain Oates's action was morally right, you must consider three kinds of issues: factual, conceptual, and moral. They are the same types of issues that come up in most moral discussions.

Factual Issues

Some questions of fact are relevant to the case. One question is whether Oates's removal from the party would have made a significant difference in the others' chances for survival. Scott thought Oates's absence might increase the chances of survival a little, but not very much. Perhaps Oates thought that, because the party's chances for survival were virtually nil with him along, this difference was important. Another question has to do with Oates's true motives. Was his action motivated primarily by the desire to give Scott, Wilson, and Bowers a better chance at survival, or was it primarily motivated by the desire to end his own suffering? Given the strong sense of loyalty that the members of the party had to one another, we can probably say that the primary motive was the former.

Almost every moral problem raises some unanswered questions of fact that are relevant to the resolution of the problem. To decide on the morality of capital punishment, we need to know whether it deters crime. To decide on the proper distribution of wealth in our country, we must know the current

---

[2] See Ann Savors, ed., *Scott's Last Voyage* (New York: Praeger, 1975), p. 155.

distribution of wealth. We also must know how many people are poor and to what extent a policy of wealth redistribution would affect the incentive to produce wealth. To decide whether restrictions should be placed on advertising to children, we must find out whether children can distinguish between advertising "hype" or "puffery" and genuine factual claims. To decide on the morality of premarital sex, we must know whether the widespread practice of sex outside of marriage would lead to better or worse sexual adjustment and to what extent it would contribute to unwanted pregnancies and the spread of AIDS and other sexually transmitted infections.

Sometimes the major issue in what we would ordinarily call a "moral" debate is really a controversy over the facts. Two people may agree on the relevant moral principles but still reach different conclusions because they hold different beliefs about the relevant facts. For example, you and I might agree on the moral principle that reverse discrimination is justifiable if it is the only way to end the effects of past discrimination. You might believe, however, that no other method will eliminate the effects of past discrimination on women and minorities, and I might believe that an immediate end to discriminatory practices is sufficient. In this case, you and I would disagree about whether to adopt a policy of reverse discrimination, even though we agreed on moral principles.

It is important to keep in mind that disputes over the facts can be just as interminable and difficult to settle as any dispute over moral principles. One of the problems we face in determining our obligations to future generations with respect to the use of nonrenewable natural resources such as oil is that we cannot predict what the needs of future generations will be. Perhaps sources of energy yet to be discovered will drastically reduce the need for oil, but, of course, it is impossible to know the future. Similarly, we cannot know for sure what the long-term effects of the widespread practice of sex outside marriage would be. Insofar as moral judgments depend on factual premises that cannot be known with certainty, these judgments cannot be known with certainty.

Conceptual Issues

Was Captain Oates's act an instance of suicide? The answer depends on our definition of suicide. We might propose to label as suicide any action in which a person does something he knows will end his own life. But this definition is implausible because it would mean that a religious martyr who chooses to die rather than renounce her faith is a suicide, and we do not usually call martyrs suicides. Rather, we say that they held to their faith in the face of persecution and that death was an unfortunate, undesired consequence of their steadfast faith.

Can something similar be said of Captain Oates? Was his action primarily intended to increase the chances of survival of his companions, or was his death only an unfortunate and unintended (even if foreknown) consequence of his action? The answers depend on the extent to which Captain Oates's action was motivated by the desire to end his own suffering. The fact that he proposed ending his life only when he could not travel further strongly suggests that his motive was not self-interest.

The question about the definition of suicide is a typical conceptual issue. Conceptual issues have to do with (1) the meaning of a concept and (2) whether the concept applies or "fits" in a particular situation. We might consider them to be issues involving a definition and its application. Conceptual issues are important in many, but not all, moral debates.

Conceptual issues differ from factual and moral issues; they cannot be settled by an appeal to facts or moral standards. However, one can argue that one definition is better than another and whether the concept, so defined, fits a particular situation. This type of argument can appeal to many considerations, such as our intuitive sense of how a word or concept should be used or the convenience of using one definition as opposed to another. Sometimes factual and moral considerations are also relevant in arguments about definitions.

Conceptual issues are sometimes crucial in a moral debate. The debate over abortion is probably the best example. Is the fetus a person? The answer depends on how we define *person* and whether the fetus fits this definition. The issue cannot be decided by an appeal to medical facts or moral principles alone, but the answer is nevertheless crucial to the abortion debate.

When we consider the morality of bombing civilian populations in wartime, we encounter another conceptual issue. Many moralists believe it is wrong to kill innocent people directly, but this raises the question whether civilian populations are innocent. Are people innocent as long as they are not in uniform or not directly connected with the war effort? Does it make any difference whether the civilians live in a democracy, where they have some voice in governmental actions, or in a totalitarian state, where they do not?

Conceptual issues are often prominent in business ethics. We can certainly hold individual managers responsible for their actions, but does it make sense to say that a corporation is a morally responsible agent? Corporations are like human beings in some important ways: they pay taxes, they have general policies that guide their action, and they have procedures for arriving at those policies. Yet they are also unlike individuals in that they have an indefinite life, and they can only carry out their policies through the actions of individual human beings. Are they enough like human beings to be held morally accountable for their actions?

Another issue in business ethics that involves a conceptual issue is the scope of the concept of bribery. American law sometimes allows U.S. corporations to pay extortion, when it is necessary, for example, to buy "protection" of corporate property in a foreign country. But bribery is illegal and usually considered immoral. Where does extortion end and bribery begin? When an American company pays a fee so that its products will be considered for purchase (but not necessarily chosen) by a foreign government official, this behavior is often thought of as bribery; but a good case can be made that it should be regarded as payment of extortion. Again, paying a fee to a foreign official to expedite the consideration of one's application to do business might be considered bribery, but perhaps it should be considered an extortion payment instead.

Finally, recent advances in medical technology have brought forward the need for a redefinition of death. Formerly, permanent cessation of vital signs was a sufficiently reliable criterion for death. Modern technology, however, has made it possible for people to be kept "alive" in the sense that their vital organs are functioning, even though they are not conscious. What should be done with "permanently vegetative" patients depends to a considerable extent on whether we consider them "dead." A conceptual issue is thus at the center of the controversy.

Moral Issues

Some issues in a moral problem involve genuine disagreements over moral principles. If Captain Oates's action was a genuine suicide, was it morally right? Captain Scott records in his diary that Dr. Wilson had morphine in his medical supplies and that the members of the party debated whether they should end their lives with morphine or wait to die naturally. Would it have been morally wrong to have taken the morphine? The Judeo-Christian tradition has held that genuine suicide is immoral, although many acts that will almost certainly end in one's death are morally permissible. One of the traditional grounds for this belief is that life is a gift of the Creator and that a human being should not take his or her life before the Creator takes it. By contrast, some existentialist philosophers argue that the ability to take one's life is the supreme mani-festation of personal freedom. What other considerations are relevant to the morality of suicide? How would you decide the issue?

Moral questions are, of course, the most characteristic feature of moral debates. You can probably easily call to mind some of the moral issues suggested by the other examples. If the fetus is considered a person, is an abortion still sometimes permissible? If civilians are believed to be innocent, is killing them permissible if greater numbers of innocent people can thereby be saved? Does the state have a right to prohibit people from smoking marijuana, even if it is harmful, as long as they know what they are doing? Here we have arrived at the very heart of a moral discussion.

The first step in facing a moral problem is to distinguish the factual, conceptual, and moral issues. You will often find that, in a discussion of a moral problem, people are not sufficiently aware of the differences among these three kinds of issues. Thus, they are also not aware of the important differences among the methods for resolving them. Factual issues are resolved—when they can be resolved—by empirical investigation. Conceptual issues are resolved by determining the meaning and applicability of a concept. Moral issues are resolved by appealing to moral principles or standards. Now we shall look more closely at the nature of moral principles as they are embodied in moral statements.

THE NATURE OF MORAL STATEMENTS

We all have some intuitive knowledge of what ethics is. We make ethical statements everyday. We may, however, still find ourselves unable to describe ethics successfully. We shall focus on the nature of ethics by looking at the nature of ethical statements. We begin by considering a class of statements to which moral statements belong—namely, normative statements.

Normative versus Factual Statements

To understand the nature of ethical statements, we must first distinguish between normative statements and factual statements. A *normative statement* expresses a value judgment of some kind, and its correctness is determined by reference to a norm or standard. Here are some examples of normative statements and the standards used to determine their correctness:

Normative Statement	*Type of Confirmation*
"Picasso is a great painter."	Aesthetic standard
"Do not use a singular subject with a plural verb."	Grammatical standard
"It is illegal to omit this item from your tax statement."	Legal standard (law)
"You should not lie to your father like that."	Moral standard
"Stand when a lady comes into the room."	Standard of etiquette

In contrast to normative statements, *factual statements* make claims that can be confirmed or disconfirmed by experiment, observation, or research. In the following list, factual statements are paired with the type of experiment, observation, or research that could confirm them:

Factual Statement	*Type of Confirmation*
"George Washington was the first president of the United States."	Historical research
"The sun is shining."	Observation
"Water is composed of two parts hydrogen and one part oxygen."	Scientific research
"The law you are violating in omitting this income from your statement was passed by Congress in 1978."	Legal research

The distinction between the way normative statements are confirmed (by appeal to a standard) and the way factual statements are confirmed (by appeal to experiment, observation, or research) is of great significance. Indeed, the distinction leads to an important question about the justification of moral statements. Most of us feel more comfortable with factual statements because we are better able to determine whether they are true or false. But how do we confirm the standard to which normative statements appeal? Most moral philosophers think that this distinction leads to a significant truth about the justification of moral statements.

An Important Corollary

Widespread agreement exists in moral philosophy that normative statements, including moral statements, cannot be confirmed by appeal to factual statements alone. A normative statement must always be assumed along with the factual statement to produce the normative statement we are trying to confirm.

Let us take a simple example to illustrate this claim. We shall use the type of normative statements in which we are most interested—namely, ethical statements. Consider the following argument:

The wealth of the United States is at present unevenly distributed among its citizens.

An uneven distribution of wealth in a country is wrong.

Therefore, the present distribution of wealth in the United States is morally wrong.

The first sentence is a simple statement of fact. An economist could determine whether it is true by scientific means. The second sentence is an ethical statement. Most moral philosophers believe you cannot derive the second statement from the first without assuming a moral statement. So let us add the statement:

An uneven distribution of wealth in a country is wrong.

You may or may not agree with this moral statement; in fact, most people would probably not agree with it. The important point is that the statement must be presupposed in order for the argument to work, so the complete argument now is as follows:

The wealth of the United States is at present unevenly distributed among its citizens.

An uneven distribution of wealth in a country is wrong.

Therefore, the present distribution of wealth in the United States is morally wrong.

Moral philosophers have different ideas about the relationship of moral statements to factual statements, and what we have given here is an illustration rather than a proof. Nevertheless, we shall assume hereafter that a moral statement cannot be derived from a factual statement.

This assumption has important implications for ethical argumentation. You cannot justify an ethical claim by an appeal to facts alone. Therefore, if you attempt to support an ethical claim exclusively by reference to facts, something will be missing, even if the facts are relevant to the argument. You should examine your argument to find the ethical assumptions implicit in what you say. Then you should state these assumptions clearly and show why you think they are justified.

Characteristics of Ethical Statements

Now that we have distinguished normative statements from factual statements and drawn an important corollary from this distinction, we must focus more closely on moral statements. How do they differ from other normative statements, such as those in aesthetics or etiquette? How do they differ from nonnormative statements with which they have some similarities, such as those in religion? Moral philosophers have not been able to find any single characteristic that is unique to moral statements, but they have determined several characteristics that, when taken together, give a good description of moral statements.

Prescription of Conduct   Moral statements prescribe conduct. This criterion serves to distinguish moral statements from aesthetic statements. The statement that Picasso was a great painter does not explicitly give direction to behavior, whereas the statement that we should not lie to our parents does; but this criterion is not enough to distinguish moral statements from all others. For example, the statement that we should knock before entering a room also prescribes a certain type of conduct, although we would not classify it as a moral statement.

Impartiality   Moral or ethical statements are based on impartial considerations. Philosophers sometimes say that moral standards are based on the reasons that an "ideal observer" or an "impartial spectator" would accept. If we want to make a genuine ethical claim, we must not allow our personal needs to dictate what we call right or wrong. Moral statements are not supposed to advance the interests of one person or group exclusively but rather to take a universal view in which each person's interests count the same. The implied impartiality of moral statements accounts at least in part for their power. If a moral statement were a mere expression of my own interest, others would have no reason to pay any special attention to it. After all, my interests and yours might not be the same. But, if a moral judgment is genuinely impartial, it stands to reason that you should pay attention to what I say, because you should make the same judgment in the same circumstances.

Keep in mind that some apparent exceptions to this point are not really exceptions when they are properly understood. For example, a request to be treated in a certain way does not necessarily violate the requirement of impartiality. Suppose I am a clerk in a bank that is being robbed. I say to the robber who is holding a gun in my face, "You should not kill me. I don't deserve to die." Although I am making a statement about killing that applies directly only to me, I am implicitly saying that no one else should be killed in similar circumstances either. Thus, the requirement of impartiality has not been violated. Similarly, if I say, "It is wrong for you to have done that to me," I intend to convey the idea that even you would consider your action wrong if you looked at it impartially. But impartiality alone does not distinguish moral statements from most other normative statements. The rules of etiquette and grammar should be applied impartially. Therefore, we must look for other characteristics.

Overriding Importance   Moral statements are generally thought to have a particularly serious or overriding importance. Compare the moral statement "You should not lie to your father" with the other normative statements given earlier. A violation of the moral rule against lying is more important than a violation of the rule of etiquette or the rules of grammar. Similarly, a moral judgment is more important than an aesthetic judgment, and ultimately moral statements are more important than statements about law.

Most moral and political philosophers in the Western tradition have argued that laws must be evaluated by moral standards. Something is not right simply because it is the law. The belief that laws can be immoral and that moral considerations override legal ones is the foundation of the tradition of civil disobedience. But some people say that religious statements, especially the direct commands of God, override even ethical statements. When Abraham in the Hebrew Bible was told to sacrifice his son, he believed that this command superseded even ethical prohibitions against killing the innocent. Thus, some people do not see overriding importance as a unique characteristic of moral statements.

Independence of Arbitrary Authority   Moral statements cannot be established or changed by the decisions of authoritative bodies, nor can their truth be established by a mere appeal to consensus or tradition. That it is impolite to enter a room without knocking is a matter of tradition and consensus, as are the rules of grammar to some extent. But we can always question majority opinion or tradition in a matter of ethics. We can concede to the French Academy the right to determine proper French usage, but we have more difficulty imagining an institution that determines moral propriety. Even religious institutions do not claim to determine morality by decree but rather to interpret divine law, which exists independently of the institutions. But again this characteristic is not unique to morality. The validity of factual statements is also independent of arbitrary decrees. In addition, many philosophers and artists claim that it is possible to argue rationally about aesthetic judgments, so these judgments are not arbitrary either.

Thus, we see that none of the four characteristics is unique to moral statements. Taken together, however, they give a good description of the nature of ethical or moral statements or of the moral standards from which these statements are derived. We shall refer to these characteristics from time to time in the following chapters, especially in our evaluation of a moral theory. The failure of a moral theory to do justice to one of these four criteria must be taken as a mark against the theory.

CONCEPTS IN ETHICAL DISCOURSE

Before we consider additional examples, we should focus on some concepts and distinctions within ethical discourse itself. Two pairs of terms are of special importance. First, many ethical theorists see an important distinction between consequentialist and nonconsequentialist theories. They believe that all moral philosophies can be classified into one of these categories and that this distinction is vitally important in understanding the nature of ethical theories.

In *consequentialist moral theories*, actions, persons, or motives are morally judged solely according to the nature of their consequences, particularly for the production of some good. The two consequentialist theories that we shall consider are egoism and utilitarianism. Roughly, *egoism* holds that actions are to be judged in terms of the extent to which they promote a person's self-interest. *Utilitarianism* states that actions are to be judged in terms of the extent to which they promote the welfare of humanity in general. Thus, in the case of egoism, the good is self-interest; in the case of utilitarianism, the good is the welfare of humanity in general.

Nonconsequentialist theories of ethics hold that actions, persons, or motives are to be judged not directly by their consequences but by conformity to moral rules. Of course, the consequences of actions are important here too, but only as these consequences conform to certain moral rules. What these rules are depends on the particular nonconsequentialist moral theory in question. The two nonconsequentialist theories that we shall consider are natural law and the ethics of respect for persons.

In *natural law*, the supreme moral rule or standard might be stated as "Act in a way that conforms to the natural inclinations of human beings." As we shall see, these natural inclinations include the tendency to preserve one's life, produce children, be a part of a social group, and develop one's uniquely human intellectual faculties.

In the *ethics of respect for persons*, the supreme rule or standard might be stated as "Act in a way that respects equally the dignity of every human being." Respecting the equal dignity of human beings requires that actions should be judged by whether they treat human beings as free moral agents who can order their lives by their own purposes and values.

Most of us are naturally inclined to look to consequences as a way of determining the moral acceptability of an action. "What better way," we might say, "do we have of determining what we ought to do than by looking at the consequences of various alternatives?" Nevertheless, we shall see that the consequentialist approach has severe problems. Furthermore, Hebrew-Christian morality is basically nonconsequentialist, so that consequentialism is contrary to the most influential Western tradition in morality. The controversy between consequentialist and nonconsequentialist moralities is one of the most important issues in contemporary ethics.

The second pair of terms we shall define is *right* and *good*, probably the most commonly used ethical words. Two contrasts between these words are worth noting:

1. Goodness can be thought of in degrees, but rightness cannot. Something is either right or not right, whereas an action can be good, better, or the very best thing to do in the circumstances. The word *good* can denote anything from merely morally acceptable to highly morally praiseworthy.

2. *Good* refers to a wider range of phenomena than *right*. *Good* refers to actions and the motives of actions, but it can also describe persons or things. *Right*, on the other hand, refers primarily to actions. We can speak of good people and good things, as well as good actions and good intentions, but we cannot substitute "He is a right man" for "He is a good man." Nor can we say that knowledge or courage is *right*, although we can say either is *good*.

Moral philosophers have long debated the meaning of *right* and *good*. Following one influential tradition in contemporary moral philosophy, we shall use the word *good* as a general term of moral commendation. Thus, to say that a person or an action is good is to commend morally the person or action.

Right, as we have seen, usually has the more restricted meaning of "morally obligatory" or at least "morally permissible," as applied to actions. Because *right* does have special reference to actions, we shall use *right* in the formulation of moral standards, the fundamental criteria for determining what is morally permissible and impermissible for any given moral philosophy. Thus, the moral standard will usually read "Those actions are right that ..."

We have distinguished moral statements from factual statements and from other types of normative statements. We have also defined some important concepts within the sphere of ethical discourse itself. Now let us look at a case that uses the concepts we have discussed. Remember that we are concerned with identifying the issues in the case, not with resolving them.

A BURN VICTIM'S DESIRE TO DIE

In July 1973, an unmarried twenty-six-year-old man, whom we shall call James, was severely burned when he and his father set off an explosion from a leaky propane gas pipeline.[3] The father died before reaching the hospital,

---

[3] Adapted from Robert B. White, "A Demand to Die," *Hastings Center Report* 5 (June 1975), pp. 9–10. See also videotape, "Please Let Me Die," by Robert B. White. Used with permission.

and James sustained second- and third-degree burns over two-thirds of his body. He is now blind in both eyes, although he might possibly be able to recover sight in one eye. After nine months of treatment, the tips of his fingers have been amputated, his hands are useless, he cannot get out of bed by himself, and the burns are still not healed. To keep the open burns from becoming infected, James must be immersed daily in a bath of antiseptic solution. The baths are preceded by injections that make James unconscious, but the dressing of the burns after his bath is still quite painful.

James is an intelligent and articulate young man. He has persistently pleaded to be allowed to leave the hospital and go home to die. He says that he will not wait to die a natural death from the infection that would begin in the open burns but would take measures to end his own life. He has recently refused permission for further surgery on his hands.

The physicians called in a consulting psychiatrist to have James declared incompetent, but the psychiatrist has concluded that James is rational. James's argument for wanting to end his life is that he can no longer do what he most enjoys, so his life will no longer be meaningful. He has been an active person, participating in sports and other outdoor activities. He does not find enough value in living blind and as a cripple to make it worthwhile to endure the painful treatments and the problems of adjusting to a new lifestyle. James has asked the physician to help him get out of the hospital, so he can go home and die. Should the physician honor James's request? Let us apply the concepts discussed in this chapter.

Factual Issues

The physician must answer a number of factual questions before he can make a decision. One of the questions is whether James could adjust to his new lifestyle. James says he would never find life worth living as a person with disabilities, but the physician has access to histories of other victims of catastrophes and will want to determine on his own James's prospects for future happiness. The physician will also want to know the law governing these situations. What can he do legally without incurring unacceptable liabilities for himself or the hospital? You may think of other factual issues that are important in the case.

Conceptual Issues

Two important conceptual issues arise in the case. The first is whether this proposed action should be called *suicide*. Because James wants to end his life by some direct means and out of concern for his own well-being, most people would consider his action to be suicide.

The second question, which is more difficult, has to do with the concept of rationality. Is James rational enough to make such a serious decision about his own future? The physician has to have a clear concept of what he means by *rationality* before he can answer this question. Of course, factual issues can be raised here as well. The physician might have a clear concept of what it means to act rationally but still be puzzled about whether James's behavior falls under the definition. If he defines *rationality* as involving, among other things, making decisions on the grounds of all available evidence, he might still wonder whether James fully understands the degree to which he will be able to manage his own affairs at home. Nevertheless, having a clear concept of rationality is an important first step in determining whether James is rational.

Moral Issues

This case has two important moral issues. One is the morality of killing oneself. This question is especially interesting because James is not dying. Given sufficient time, the burns will heal and James will be sent home. He should be able to live out his normal life span, even though he will be handicapped. The second issue has to do with the obligations and prerogatives of the physician. Does the physician have an obligation to help James get out of the hospital? Does he have an obligation to help James end his life if he is asked to assist? Does he have the right to try to keep James in the hospital if he thinks James is not rational? Does he have the right to try to keep James in the hospital if he disagrees with James's decision to end his life, even if he believes James is rational?

Moral and Factual Statements

Recall that moral conclusions do not follow directly from the facts of the case. For example, the fact that James will recover and can eventually be sent home does not necessarily mean that taking his own life would be wrong, although this consideration is relevant to the issue. The fact that the physician is prevented by law from directly administering a lethal injection to James at his request does not settle the question of whether he should legally be allowed to do so. The fact that the physician may be opposed to all forms of suicide does not necessarily mean that he should act to prevent James from killing himself.

Characteristics of Moral Statements

The moral questions at stake seem to exhibit the four characteristics of moral statements. First, the answers given to the moral questions at issue prescribe the conduct that James and his physician should follow. The statement that it is wrong for James to commit suicide implies that James should not take any measures to end his own life. The conclusion that the physician has an obligation to help James get out of the hospital implies that he should take steps to achieve the goal.

Second, the moral statements made about this case are ordinarily made from an impersonal standpoint. If we are making judgments about the case from an observer's perspective, this impersonal standpoint can be assumed. But, even if we take the physician's standpoint, we would presumably ask what should be done based on his moral and professional obligation. Self-interest is not a legitimate consideration unless it would apply to any other physician in the same situation. If injecting James with a lethal drug would result in the physician's incarceration, that consideration would appropriately carry some moral weight. But it would carry moral weight with any other physician in the same situation.

Third, the moral issues have a serious and overriding importance. The moral issues are more important than issues of medical etiquette or the aesthetic questions regarding James's burns. They are even more important than the legal issues in the case, because we might conclude that the laws should be changed to accommodate our moral beliefs about what should be done.

Fourth, the issues cannot be settled merely by an appeal to authority, consensus, or tradition. Deciding whether it is wrong for James to take his own life or whether the physician should help him take his life involves more than taking a vote or determining how the issue would have been decided in the past.

Concepts in Moral Philosophy

We can look at this problem from either a consequentialist or a non-consequentialist perspective. An egoist would ask about the consequences of the alternatives for James's or the physician's self-interest. A utilitarian would ask about the consequences for the general human welfare. Non-consequentialists, such as natural law theorists and advocates of the ethics of respect for persons, would approach the issues differently. They would ask whether James's or his physician's actions were in accordance with human nature or the respect due human individuals. We shall leave the steps of this determination for another time; the important point is that the consequences of alternative actions are not the decisive point. For example, by the standards of natural law, James should not kill himself, even if the remainder of his life produces no benefit for him or anyone else.

Finally, in a discussion of the case, we would use the terms *good* or *bad*, intending thereby to commend or condemn the actions, motives, or people involved. We would also refer to the actions of the people involved as *right* or *wrong*, intending thereby to classify them as morally obligatory, merely morally permissible, or morally impermissible. The concepts and distinctions we have discussed in this first chapter, then, are an important part of a clear analysis of moral problems.

CONCEPT SUMMARY

An important part of ethics is making distinctions. When analyzing a moral problem, you should first distinguish between questions of fact, questions involving the definitions and applications of concepts, and questions that directly appeal to moral principles.

Moral statements themselves are a type of normative statement, as are statements in such areas as aesthetics, etiquette, law, and grammar. Normative statements differ from factual statements in that normative statements make value judgments that appeal to norms. Most moral philosophers believe that moral statements cannot be derived from factual statements. An important corollary of this belief is that moral statements cannot be justified by an appeal to facts. This point is important in moral arguments.

Several characteristics, taken together, give a good description of moral statements. Moral statements prescribe conduct, they are based on impartial considerations, they have overriding importance, and they cannot be established by a mere appeal to consensus or tradition.

To understand a moral theory, you must know whether it is a consequentialist theory (one that judges actions, persons, or motives according to their consequences) or a nonconsequentialist theory (one that judges actions, persons, or motives by their conformity to moral rules). Egoism and utilitarianism are consequentialist theories, and natural law and the ethics of respect for persons are nonconsequentialist theories. We shall use the word *good* as a general term of moral commendation and the word *right* to mean "morally obligatory."

2

Are Morals Relative?

For eighteen months Del Monte Corporation tried to buy a 55,000-acre banana plantation in Guatemala, but the government refused to allow the sale. Del Monte officials made inquiries and asked for meetings, but nothing happened. Then they hired a business consultant for $500,000. The consultant was a wealthy businessman who frequently contributed to political parties in Guatemala.

The businessman feared that disclosure of this relationship with a large U.S. company would diminish his influence in Guatemala and perhaps even provoke left-wing threats against his life. So he demanded and received company assurances of anonymity. To further protect him, Del Monte paid him outside the country. It charged his fee to general and administrative expenses on the books of several Panamanian shipping subsidiaries. His fee was entirely dependent on his ability to get the Guatemalan government to allow the sale of the plantation.

Suddenly the Guatemalan government reversed itself and permitted the sale. Now Del Monte owns the profitable banana plantation, for which it paid $20.5 million, and the "business consultant" is considerably richer.[1]

In many parts of the world, some forms of bribery or payoff are a common and accepted practice. The practice even has names: in Arabic countries it is

---

[1] Jerry Landauer and Kenneth Bacon, "Del Monte Corp. Finds a Foreign Consultant Can Help a Great Deal," *Wall Street Journal*, July 14, 1975, p. 1.

called *baksheesh*, and in Latin American countries it is called *la mordida*. Everything from large transactions requiring government approval, such as Del Monte's purchase of the plantation, to getting a small-business license or renting an apartment may require it. Many of the government officials who accept the payoffs are poorly paid, and payoffs are a legal and accepted way of augmenting their salary. Yet, in the United States and most industrialized countries, such practices are regarded as unethical and are usually illegal.

Are such practices morally acceptable? Many people—including many college students—would justify them by making statements such as "Morals are relative" or "When in Rome, do as the Romans do." It was entirely proper, they might say, for the Del Monte officials to employ the business consultant because this is the way business is conducted in Guatemala, and morals are always relative to a particular culture.

In spite of its apparent simplicity and plausibility, moral relativism is a treacherous terrain with many pitfalls. We shall explore some of this terrain by first considering the most common form of ethical or moral relativism.

CLASSICAL MORAL RELATIVISM

Herodotus, a Greek historian, relates an anecdote told about Darius, king of Persia. Darius had been impressed by the variety of customs and beliefs that he had observed. To illustrate this variety to his court, he asked the Greeks in his court what they would take to eat the bodies of their fathers. They replied that no amount of money would entice them to do such a horrible deed. Knowing that the Greeks practiced cremation, he asked some Indians, of the tribe called Callatiae, who do in fact eat their parents' dead bodies, what they would take to burn their parents' dead bodies. Predictably, they reacted in horror at the mere suggestion of such a thing. The customs of the Greeks were regarded as offensive to the Callatians, and the customs of the Callatians appeared just as barbaric to the Greeks. Herodotus believed that this illustrates Pindar's statement that custom is king of all.[2]

This story illustrates the first two claims of what I shall call *classical moral relativism*. Many people who believe in moral relativism seem to hold the following three theses:

1. People do in fact disagree in their moral beliefs.

2. The rightness or wrongness of moral beliefs can be determined only relative to the culture or moral tradition of the individuals who hold them.

3. Individuals or social groups should adopt a tolerant attitude toward other individuals or social groups that hold different moral beliefs.

---

[2] Herodotus, *The Histories*, trans. Aubrey de Selincourt (Baltimore: Penguin Books, 1955), p. 191.

To facilitate discussion, we shall call the first claim the diversity thesis; the second claim, the relativity thesis; and the third claim, the toleration thesis. Let us consider each of these three theses.

The Diversity Thesis

The first premise makes a factual claim that moral beliefs vary. The story of King Darius illustrates the thesis, but there are many other illustrations of it. Most people in our culture find infanticide morally unacceptable, but the Roman writer Seneca wrote, "We destroy monstrous births, and we also drown our children if they are born weakly and unnaturally formed."[3] Attitudes of various cultures toward the suffering of animals are also surprisingly different. In Latin America a chicken is plucked alive with the thought that it will taste more succulent. The Hopi Indians do not object in the least to their children's playing with a bird by tying a string to its legs, even though this play often results in broken legs, wings being pulled off, and usually the death of the animal. As one Hopi put it, "Sometimes they get tired and die."[4] Cultures exhibit vast differences in attitudes toward adultery, premarital sex, property ownership, violence, the expression of hostility, and many other issues.

These examples illustrate the diversity of moral beliefs in various cultures and in what we might consider different moral traditions, but even the same moral tradition varies over time. For example, the Western religious tradition has undergone some remarkable changes. Attitudes toward divorce, once prohibited except for marital infidelity, are now much more tolerant. Historian John Noonan shows that the Christian Church has completely reversed itself on the moral permissibility of usury, the taking of interest for money.[5] In the Old Testament, usury is strongly condemned as exploitation of the poor. The Christian Church encouraged this attitude until the sixteenth century and the rise of modern commercial civilization. Now taking interest on money is accepted by almost all Christians. The attitude of many religious groups toward many other moral issues, such as sexuality and the proper sphere of activity for women, has also changed or is in the process of changing.

Although there is undoubtedly variation in moral tradition over time, the issue of moral diversity is complex, because much of the apparent diversity in moral beliefs can be traced to differences in circumstances and in nonmoral beliefs. Thus, appearances to the contrary, the difference may not be a genuine *moral* difference. For example, some so-called primitive people routinely kill their parents before the parents become senile. Most of us would be inclined to call this behavior cruel and barbaric. But suppose you believed, as they do, that a person spends the afterlife in the condition in which he or she dies.

---

[3] Seneca, *De ira*, I, 15, quoted in Edward A. Westermarck, *Christianity and Morals* (London: Kegan Paul, Trench, Trubner, 1939), p. 239.

[4] Richard Brandt, *Ethical Theory* (Upper Saddle River, NJ: Prentice Hall, 1959), p. 103.

[5] John Noonan, *The Scholastic Analysis of Usury* (Cambridge, MA: Harvard University Press, 1957).

Then ask yourself whether you would rather live forever in the prime of life or in a senile, decrepit condition. If you held the same beliefs about the after-life as these people do, would you not also be inclined to kill your parents while they are in the prime of life? Perhaps both you and the primitives share a common moral commitment that might be stated as "Act so as to benefit your parents." The apparent moral difference dissolves into a difference in nonmoral beliefs.

Some apparent moral differences turn out to be based on differences in circumstances rather than differences in beliefs. Some Eskimo tribes used to leave their old people in the snow to die when they become too feeble to contribute to the group or to keep up with the tribal migration patterns. The practice at first strikes Westerners with revulsion, but perhaps this attitude would change if we bothered to learn more about the circumstances in which the Eskimos lived. They lived a subsistence existence, and the failure of one member to contribute meant that others must work much harder. Furthermore, the tribe had to move to be close to the reindeer herds and other sources of food. If an old person could not move by himself, he had to be carried by another or the tribe had to cease its migration patterns, which were essential to its survival. Again you must ask yourself whether you, if faced with these conditions, would act any differently, no matter how much you loved and respected your parents.

It is surprising how many apparent examples of moral diversity can be traced to differences in beliefs or circumstances. The change in the Christian attitude toward usury mentioned earlier may have a similar explanation. In a subsistence culture, charging your neighbor interest on a loan when his crops have failed may drive him into poverty. And if the economy is not inflation-ary, there may be no justification for charging interest on the grounds that it is necessary to ensure that the amount returned is equivalent in purchasing power to the amount loaned. Charging interest in these circumstances becomes a form of exploitation. In a commercial civilization, on the other hand, borrowed money is used to earn money, and inflation is a fact of life. Further, a creditor, in making a loan, forgoes the opportunity to make any other investment, so that interest takes on a very different moral character. One might even say that forbidding a creditor to charge interest would mean that she is exploited, not the borrower. Different circumstances mean that the same moral beliefs ("One should not exploit others") has very different implications.

Even though much of the supposed diversity in moral beliefs can be explained through differences in the circumstances in which people live and in the nonmoral beliefs that they hold, probably not all apparent moral diversity can be explained in this way. Businesspeople in Guatemala, for example, may well believe that their way of doing business is morally superior to practices in the United States, being more sociable and more conducive to genuine human relationships than the mechanical, impersonal American way. Many scholars also believe that there are genuine differences in moral beliefs embodied in the varying attitudes toward the proper treatment of animals and the conditions under which the killing of human beings is permissible.

Genuine diversity in moral beliefs, even if it is not as prevalent as we might be inclined to think, is still impressive to most people, as it was to King Darius. But what support does it provide for belief in the relativity of morals? To answer this question, we must consider the relativity thesis.

The Relativity Thesis

The second claim of relativists is that moral beliefs are true or valid only relative to principles held by some group. An important point to keep in mind is that relativists always maintain that there *are* valid moral beliefs and that there *is* such a thing as truth in morality. However, validity or truth in moral beliefs is not absolute in the sense of being universally applicable to all human beings. Instead, moral beliefs are true *in relation* to some group. Relativists do not believe that there is no truth in ethics but rather that there are many truths. Even if no absolute and universal moral truth is objectively the same for everyone, people do make moral judgments that distinguish right from wrong. Relativists believe that it is unreasonable to say that people are wrong in making such judgments. Each individual or each society should find its own moral truth and live by that truth.

Social scientists often advocate the relativity thesis. With regard to the influence of traditions (or folkways) on moral beliefs, sociologist William Graham Sumner writes:

> The right way is the way which the ancestors used and which has been handed down. The tradition is its own warrant. It is not held subject to verification by experience. The notion of right is in the folkways. It is not outside of them, of independent origin, and brought to test them. In the folkways, whatever is, is right. This is because they are traditional, and therefore contain in themselves the authority of the ancestral ghosts. When we come to the folkways we are at the end of our analysis.[6]

Unfortunately, this argument illustrates a confusion to which relativists often fall prey. What does Sumner mean by *right*? If he means morally right, then the fact that folkways have long been accepted and possess the authority of tradition (the authority of the ancestral ghosts) does not necessarily bind us to continue to accept them as morally right. If *right* merely means what we feel good about, then he is only making a psychological claim about our feelings, which may or may not have moral validity. At least part of the plausibility of relativism seems to be based on this confusion between moral and psychological claims.

---

[6]William Graham Sumner, *Folkways* (Boston: Ginn, 1906), p. 28.

Anthropologist Ruth Benedict propounds a similar view:

> We recognize that morality differs in every society, and is a convenient term for socially approved habits. Mankind has always preferred to say, It is morally good, rather than It is habitual, and the fact of this preference is matter enough for a critical science of ethics. But historically the two phrases are synonymous.[7]

Benedict's argument is different. She claims that "It is morally good" *means* "It is habitual." The two expressions are, as she says, synonymous. But if she means by *synonymous* that the two expressions mean the same thing in our ordinary ways of speaking, her claim seems to be false. In saying that abortion is wrong, regardless of what the majority in our society believe, or in saying that our society has made progress in its attitude toward women, or in praising moral reformers like Martin Luther King, we seem to be denying that the mere approval of a relevant cultural group is sufficient to determine the moral validity of an action.

Probably the most common argument for the relativity thesis, however, is a combination of the diversity thesis and moral skepticism (the belief that there is no way to establish which moral beliefs are correct). The argument goes like this:

> Human cultures reveal a variety of moral beliefs (the diversity thesis) and there is no way to establish which beliefs are correct (moral skepticism). Therefore, moral beliefs are relative to a given culture.

But neither the diversity of moral beliefs nor the supposed inability to establish which moral beliefs are correct proves moral relativism. The fact that moral beliefs differ may only show that some of them—or perhaps all of them—are false. And the fact that we have so far found no way to establish which moral beliefs are correct in a way that is conclusive and universally convincing does not show that no such method exists. It only shows that we have not yet discovered the method. Even if there is no such method, this does not establish the relativity thesis.

Consider an analogy from science. Suppose a controversy arises over whether there is life on Mars. And suppose further that people in the United States generally believe that there is life on Mars, while people in the Soviet Union generally believe that there is not. This disagreement in belief does not show that both views are equally true, relative to their own culture. The beliefs of either most Soviets or most Americans may simply be wrong. Or the nature of life on Mars may be so different from life on Earth (perhaps based on an element other than carbon) that it is not clear whether either view is right or wrong. Suppose further that there is no way, at least at present, to establish which belief is correct. Few of us would be tempted to

---

[7] Ruth Benedict, "Anthropology and the Abnormal," *Journal of General Psychology* 10 (1934), pp. 59–82.

say that this demonstrates that the beliefs of the Americans or Soviets are true relative to their own cultures. We would be more inclined to say that we just do not know which beliefs are true.

The most obvious response to this statement is to say that important differences between science and ethics are evident. For example, we can at least imagine what experiences might confirm the truth or falsehood of the statement that there is life on Mars. We could imagine a spaceship traveling to Mars carrying human beings or scientific instruments capable of detecting life. Even though we may not be able to perform this experiment, we know what it would take to show that the statement "There is life on Mars" is either true or false. No equivalent experiment or experience is possible that would verify or disconfirm the moral validity of the Hopi practice of playing with birds or the Roman practice of allowing fathers to have life-and-death power over their children.

This reply, however, is unsatisfactory. First, although we can imagine how some scientific beliefs might be confirmed or disconfirmed, this does not hold true for others. According to one account, when Einstein first proposed his ideas on relativity, he had no idea how they could be validated or refuted. Second, even if we cannot imagine confirming or disconfirming experiences, it is not clear that this should be a decisive consideration. How could one go about establishing the claim that the only ideas that should be considered true or false are those that could be at least conceivably confirmed or disconfirmed by some experience? Can this claim itself be confirmed or disconfirmed by experience? So unless the analogy between ethics and science can be more conclusively dismissed, we can say it strongly suggests that the fact of moral diversity does not establish the truth of moral relativism.

The Toleration Thesis

People who advocate moral relativism often say that one of the advantages of their position is that it provides a foundation for toleration of other cultures and their differing moral views. For this reason, the toleration thesis was included in the statement of classical moral relativism. Toleration presumably means refraining from using force to impose the moral beliefs of one's own culture on other cultures. It would not necessarily mean that a representative of one culture should not attempt to persuade members of other cultures to adopt his or her own moral beliefs.

The supposed commitment to toleration often associated with moral relativism is one of its most attractive features for many people. In an increasingly interdependent world, toleration of diversity in moral, religious, and political beliefs seems essential for survival.

It is important to see, however, that the toleration thesis does not necessarily follow from the diversity and relativity theses. If our culture has a principle of toleration, we may be obligated, according to the relativist, to be tolerant. But if our culture does not have such a principle, no such obligation follows. Or if a principle of toleration is not a part of the moral beliefs of another culture, the members of that culture have no moral obligation to practice tolerance toward us, even if we believe in toleration. So, even though many people associate moral toleration with moral relativism, no logical relationship exists between the two. Our account of classical moral relativism includes the toleration thesis because in many people's minds, it is connected with moral relativism. Now we see that the connection is not logically required.

FURTHER PROBLEMS FOR CLASSICAL MORAL RELATIVISM

We have looked at the three basic claims of classical moral relativism and found them unconvincing. These are, however, not the only reasons for doubting its validity. Several others exist as well.

First, defining the society or culture to which a moral judgment is relative poses a problem. Suppose Bertha and Barbara disagree over abortion. Bertha may be a devout Roman Catholic and Barbara an atheist. Are we to say that they are members of different societies, even though they are neighbors? Do all Americans belong to the same society? Do all members of civilizations strongly influenced by European culture represent the same society? Until we have a better understanding of what constitutes a society, we cannot have a clear conception of the community to which moral judgments are relative.

A second problem with classical relativism is that it seems to make moral decision making either artificially easy or impossibly difficult. Consider the case of abortion again. If the relativity thesis were correct and a given society (however this is defined) enjoyed a high degree of agreement on the issue, majority opinion would tell all members of the society whether abortion is right or wrong. Yet arriving at a decision on the abortion issue seems more difficult than this. If, on the other hand, no consensus existed on the issue, there would be no way to determine the truth on the abortion issue for that society.

A third difficulty with relativism is that it makes the notion of moral progress difficult to understand, much less accept. For example, our society once tolerated slavery, but people in most contemporary societies would probably find it morally unacceptable and even morally repugnant. Many people would even say that society's change of attitude toward slavery represents moral progress. But if the relativity thesis is correct, it is hard to make sense of this idea. All we can say is that at one time our society found slavery morally acceptable—and therefore it was morally valid—and now we do not find it morally acceptable—so it is no longer morally valid. But this conclusion seems unsatisfactory. Most of us probably want to say that the idea that slavery is wrong is better, morally speaking, than the idea that slavery is morally right. And, even if we do not believe in moral progress, most of us find the notion at least meaningful.

A fourth problem with the relativity thesis is that it seems to imply that moral reformers are always wrong. Martin Luther King acted contrary to the beliefs of most people in the South when he led public protests against segregation. If the truth of a moral view is determined in relation to the moral standard of one's society and we consider the South to be a society, then King acted against the truth. Yet many of us would say that King's actions were morally right, a view that is impossible to maintain from the standpoint of classical moral relativism.

A fifth problem is that moral relativism implies that if it is true, people from different societies and cultures are not really contradicting one another when they make incompatible judgments. Suppose we believe that the conduct of Hopi children who play with birds until the birds are dead is morally unjustifiable. We might express this belief in the statement "The Hopi children are wrong when they play with birds until they are dead." If the moral relativist is correct, however, all this remark really means is "According to my moral beliefs, the Hopi children are wrong when they play with birds until they are dead." Similarly, if the moral relativist is correct, all the Hopi would be saying in reply is "According to our moral beliefs, our children are not wrong when they play with birds until they area dead." These two statements are not incompatible with one another. Indeed, according to the relativist, we cannot say the Hopi are simply wrong, for we are always implicitly saying that they are wrong *according to our moral beliefs*, and people can be wrong by one set of moral beliefs and not wrong by another. So moral relativism does not agree with our usual way of understanding morality whenever some moral beliefs are incompatible with others.

Many people are comfortable taking this position on some issues. They might say, for example, that it is right for Guatemalans to accept bribes but that it is not right for citizens of the United States. But most of us would find it hard to carry out this position consistently. We have already mentioned the practice of the Hopi in playing with birds. Even more difficult to accept would be the practice of cannibals in killing and eating human beings. Or what about the Nazis' practice of torturing innocent human beings?

An important assumption in our thinking and speaking about morality is that moral judgments can be genuinely opposed to one another. Many college students say that they are moral relativists, but they are uncomfortable with saying that Hitler was not wrong when he ordered the execution of Jews or that Mother Theresa is really not more morally admirable than Joseph Stalin. Yet if moral relativism is correct, the Nazi who says Hitler was a good man and the Jew who says Hitler was a moral monster are not contradicting one another. Each is expressing a moral judgment that is true or valid in relation to his or her group, which is all that can be said about the truth of the two moral judgments.

Sixth, many critics have argued that relativism is incompatible with the *universalization principle*, which says that if something is right for you, it is also right for me, provided the circumstances are the same. Relativism seems to deny this, for if our moral principles are different, something can be right for you and wrong for me, even though the circumstances are the same. One possible answer to the problem is that moral principles form part of the circumstances themselves, so that the universalization principle does not apply when two people have differing moral principles. If, therefore, my principles are egoistic and yours are altruistic, the universalization principle could not apply to our dispute. Thus, the universalization principle would have binding force *within* a group that adheres to the same moral principles, such as a group of egoists, but not *outside* it.

Our ordinary use of the universalization principle, however, seems to be broader than this. This point becomes especially obvious when we recall that anyone could declare him- or herself a member of a different society and thereby escape the requirements of the universalization principle. Our neighbor could simply decide that he is a member of a different society and is therefore not subject to the same moral requirements as we are. Moral relativism thus seems to provide a way of subverting the legitimate requirements of the universalization principle.

Finally, classical relativism does not provide a basis for resolving intercultural conflicts. Consider the case presented at the beginning of the chapter. Although bribery is not accepted in North American society, let us assume for the sake of argument that it is accepted in Guatemalan society. Classical relativism says that the statement "People may accept bribes" is true for the Guatemalan businessperson and not for the North American businessperson. Why, then, should either the Guatemalans or the North Americans change, since they are each acting correctly by their own cultural values? How can the standpoint of classical relativism even supply any motivation for either side to accommodate the other?

When we say that some way should be found to reconcile the positions of the North Americans and Guatemalans on bribery, we are probably stepping outside the positions of either the North Americans or the Guatemalans. Jeffrey Fadiman, for example, has suggested a gift strategy as a way of responding to people in different cultures.[8] If an individual or corporation makes a gift to the community rather than individuals, the differing views on bribery might be reconciled in a way that would not do fundamental violence to either culture. These gifts need not be in the form of cash but might include trucks, food, hospitals, jobs, and other nonmonetary items, Fadiman believes. In any case, the obligation we may feel to step outside our own cultural viewpoint is difficult to explain from the standpoint of classical moral relativism. The next version of moral relativism, to be considered after a concept summary, will provide a different approach to this issue.

---

[8] Jeffrey A. Fadiman, "A Traveler's Guide to Gifts and Bribes," *Harvard Business Review* (July–August, 1986), pp. 122–126, 130–136. See excerpts reprinted in William H. Shaw and Vincent Barry, *Moral Issues in Business*, 4th ed. (Belmont, CA: Wadsworth, 1989), p. 359.

CONCEPT SUMMARY

Classical moral relativism claims that (1) people do disagree in their moral beliefs, (2) the rightness or wrongness of moral beliefs can be determined only relative to the culture or moral tradition of the individuals who hold them, and (3) individuals or social groups should adopt a tolerant attitude toward those who hold differing moral beliefs. Against the first claim, one can argue that, although there are genuine disagreements in moral beliefs, most apparent disagreement can be traced to differences in circumstances and factual beliefs. Against the second claim, one can point out that the arguments for moral skepticism on which this claim is usually based can be shown to be faulty. Against the third claim, one can show that toleration does not necessarily follow from relativism.

Other problems with moral relativism are that it must rely on ambiguous definitions of "society" or "culture" to which a moral judgment is relative, it makes moral decision making either artificially easy or impossibly difficult, it threatens to render the notion of moral progress meaningless, it implies that moral reformers are always wrong, it makes it impossible to explain how people in different societies can contradict one another, it is incompatible with the universalization principle, and it makes it difficult to explain many people's need to reconcile intercultural conflicts.

A CONTEMPORARY VERSION OF RELATIVISM

The philosopher Gilbert Harman has constructed a version of relativism that he believes escapes some of our criticisms of classical relativism.[9]

Harman and Classical Relativism

To introduce Harman's version of relativism, we shall review some of the similarities and differences between his relativism and classical moral relativism, beginning with the differences.

First, many people have found the arguments given in support of classical moral relativism unconvincing. The heart of classical moral relativism is the relativity thesis—namely, the claim that the rightness or wrongness of moral beliefs can be determined only in relation to the culture or moral traditions of the individuals who hold them. As we have seen, the reason given in support of this thesis is that human cultures reveal a variety of moral beliefs (the diversity thesis), and there is no way to establish which beliefs are correct (the

---

[9] See Gilbert Harman, *The Nature of Morality* (New York: Oxford University Press, 1977), especially Chapters 8 and 9. See also Gilbert Harman, "Moral Relativism Defended," *Philosophical Review* 84 (1975), pp. 3–22.

appeal to moral skepticism). But we saw that neither the diversity of moral beliefs nor the difficulties in establishing the truth of moral beliefs in a conclusive and universally convincing way are sufficient grounds for establishing the truth of the relativity thesis.

Is any other way of arguing for the relativity thesis possible? Harman thinks so. He believes that moral relativism is supported by an analysis of the nature of moral judgments themselves. That is, rather than making an appeal to the diversity of moral beliefs or to the difficulty of justifying moral beliefs, he appeals to what he calls a "soberly logical thesis" about the nature of at least some of our moral judgments. If his argument is valid, it should provide a much more plausible foundation for the relativity thesis.

Second, unlike classical relativism, Harman's version of relativism explains how we can evaluate moral beliefs that differ from our own. Classical relativism appears to imply that we can never evaluate the different moral beliefs of people in other societies. It also implies that moral reformers, such as Martin Luther King, are always wrong because they act against the beliefs of most people in their society. Finally, it implies that two people from different cultures are not at odds with each other when they make contradictory moral judgments. These implications of classical moral relativism appear to be contrary to our ordinary beliefs about morality.

Harman's version of moral relativism avoids these implications by distinguishing between two types of moral judgments. One type of moral judgment, which he calls an *inner judgment*, is true relative to the society in which it is made and must be evaluated in terms of that society's moral beliefs. Another type, which he calls an *outer judgment*, can be applied to societies other than one's own. By means of this distinction, Harman claims to have developed a more subtle and sophisticated version of moral relativism that enables us to understand both how moral beliefs can be true in relation to the culture in which they are made and how we can make moral judgments about practices in cultures other than our own.

Third, Harman's relativism is not subject to the criticism that relativism makes decision making in ethics either too easy or too hard. We may establish the truth of a person's inner judgments by an appeal to her motivations and beliefs, but we may not settle disputes about outer judgments in this way. Although Harman does not make it entirely clear how disputes about outer judgments are settled, it is apparently not done merely by reference to the beliefs of a given culture.

In spite of these differences between Harman's relativism and classical relativism, there are also important similarities.

First, like classical relativism, Harman's theory holds that at least some types of moral judgments, namely inner judgments, share an implicit reference to the beliefs of a community. To say that a person is tall makes sense only in relation to some comparison class. John may be tall in relation to the average person but not to basketball players. Similarly, to say that it is wrong of someone to do something often seems to presuppose a reference class of moral concepts, and this reference class is embodied in the moral beliefs of a community, as specified in inner judgments.

Second, because of his doctrine of inner judgments, Harman's relativism, like classical relativism, implies that different moral evaluations may be appropriate for the same action in different societies. An action may be right according to one set of principles and wrong according to another. We could say that Americans should not eat human flesh, though it would not be appropriate to say this about cannibals. We could say that it would be wrong of most people to commit murder for hire, even though this might not be appropriate with respect to the person raised from birth according to the ideals of Murder Incorporated.

Inner and Outer Judgments

Let us look more closely at some of the earlier examples from the perspective of Harman's relativism. When we consider our attitude toward the Hopi practice of playing with birds, we may find that we are of two minds. On the one hand, we want to condemn the practice. We want to say that what they did was wrong or morally repugnant. We might even want to condemn their society and morality for permitting such a practice. On the other hand, we may find it difficult to judge the Hopi as individuals and to say that it was wrong of them to have done what they did. They were, after all, only acting in accordance with the morals of their own society. The same observation applies to other examples of moral difference. We may think it is morally outrageous for cannibals to eat human flesh, but they see nothing wrong with it. Indeed, they think they have the best reasons in the world for doing it. Thus, we would not *blame* them for their feasting on human flesh, even though we might be horrified at their action. Roman fathers sometimes killed their children for disciplinary infractions, and we condemn their actions as morally wrong, yet we recognize that they were exercising what they believed to be legitimate parental prerogatives.

The distinction between judging a *person* and judging an *action* is, Harman believes, basic to our moral outlook. The Hopi are living by their own moral principles. They are doing what they believe is right, and saying that they ought not to do what they think is right seems inappropriate. When a person lives by her principles and does what she thinks she has the best reasons in the world for doing, it is improper to condemn *her* for her actions, even though we may condemn her *actions* as immoral. Harman calls the judgments of people *inner judgments*. They could also be referred to as *personal assessments*. They are judgments that a person was acting in accordance with whatever principles motivate her behavior. Harman believes that these principles actually take the form of goals and desires. Thus, to say that I ought to take a given course of action is to say that I have certain goals or desires and that this course of action is the best means of achieving those goals or desires. Harman believes that an inner judgment presupposes that the speaker—the one making the judgment—also accepts the principles by which the person acts. In making inner judgments, we are not only judging the person by the criterion of conformity to her own standards but also accepting those standards ourselves.

Inner judgments may be contrasted with the class of moral judgments that Harman calls *outer judgments*. They could also be referred to as *action assessments*. We can make outer judgments—judgments of the person's action—even if she does not accept the standards used in making the judgment. If, when Hitler was alive, I said Hitler acted wrongly when he ordered the extermination of Jews, I would not expect him to agree with this judgment or change his behavior because I made it. Hitler did not accept our ordinary standards of morality. My condemnation of him would be from my own perspective, not his. If beings from another planet landed on Earth and cared nothing for humans, it would be odd to make the inner judgment that they should not harm us. From our own perspective (which they did not share), it would make sense, however, for us to make an outer judgment that their actions that harmed us were wrong.

One important point must be added to the distinction between inner and outer judgments. Morality is not merely subjective but public or social. Therefore, the only judgments, whether inner or outer, that are truly moral, according to Harman, are the products of implicit agreements among moral agents. Genuine moral demands are those for which there is a shared commitment, on the part of the individual agent and others. The private principles of one person that are not shared by others do not represent the normal case of moral principles.

This account of the major distinction in Harman's version of moral relativism is sufficient to show how it might enable him to avoid some of the more obvious problems of classical relativism. By his concept of inner judgments, he can account for the relativist's claim that moral judgments are relative to the culture in which they are made. We would not, he believes, condemn a *person* in another culture for doing what is accepted in her culture as right and what she may have every reason for believing is right. By his concept of outer judgments, he can account for the fact that people in one culture do sometimes make evaluations of people in other cultures. According to Harman, when we make such evaluations, we must understand that they refer to the *actions* of people in other societies and are not judgments about them as *persons*.

We have seen that inner judgments are relative to the society in which they are made. What about outer judgments? Is there at least an implicit claim that they, by contrast, are objective or universally valid? Or are they also relative to the society in which they are made? When I make an outer judgment about the actions of people whose morality is quite different from mine, am I claiming that the judgment is valid for everyone, or does it merely reflect either my own personal values or the values of our society? Harman's theory is not committed to any particular answer to this question. When I say that the Nazis' actions in torturing Jews were wrong, I think I am making a moral claim that is really true. Perhaps, though, I am just saying something that is true or valid in relation to my own moral beliefs. In any case, Harman's theory leaves this question open. His main objective is to show that at least one type of moral judgment is relative to the moral beliefs of the society in terms of whose moral traditions it is made.

Harman's version of relativism enables us to understand the attitude Del Monte executives might have had toward the wealthy Guatemalan businessman in the case described at the beginning of this chapter. Let us assume that the businessman was acting correctly by his society's standards. We might want to say that what he did was morally acceptable by his society's standards and that we cannot call him a bad person for this reason. In speaking like this, we would be making an inner judgment about the businessman. We would be placing ourselves in his world, adopting his moral perspective, and judging him by it. We could also make an inner judgment of the American executives of the Del Monte Corporation, maintaining that they were immoral because they did things that were wrong by the moral principles that were prevalent in their society and that they probably accepted.

We could, however, judge the actions of people by moral principles that make no necessary reference to their beliefs or motivations. We could, for example, say that the Guatemalan businessman did the wrong thing in asking for the large bribe, and the Del Monte executives did the wrong thing in paying it. We could justify this judgment by pointing out that this kind of bribery tends to have detrimental effects on a country's economic and political system. In this case, we would be making an outer judgment, whose truth would not be relative to the beliefs of those about whom the judgment was made. Harman's version of relativism, then, is more sophisticated than classical relativism, because it enables us to account for the sense in which our moral judgments are and are not relative to the beliefs and motivations of the individuals whom we evaluate. The truth of inner judgments is relative to those about whom they are made. Whether this can be said of outer judgments is a more difficult question to which we shall return shortly.

PROBLEMS WITH HARMAN'S RELATIVISM

Despite its clear advantages over classical relativism, Harman's relativism contains serious flaws that have led many moral philosophers to reject it.

First, much of Harman's case for his version of moral relativism rests on the distinction between inner and outer judgments. Much of the case for this distinction, in turn, rests on his claim that it enables him to give the best available explanation of the supposed impropriety of judging a person whose moral commitments are different from one's own. But in fact such judgments do not always seem odd. Consider the judgment "Hitler showed himself to be an evil man by ordering the extermination of Jews." Now, if Harman is right, this statement should sound odd because it is an inner judgment, and Hitler and the Nazi society of which he was a part did not share our moral sensibilities. But surely there is a perfectly straightforward sense in which it is not odd. It does make sense for us to condemn not only Hitler's actions but also Hitler himself. Harman's distinction between inner and outer judgments does not therefore appear to be well grounded.

Second, even if making inner moral judgments about people whose morality differs from ours does sometimes seem peculiar, other ways of accounting for the peculiarity are possible. Sometimes the impropriety of blaming people when they could not have been expected to act differently seems to be based directly on moral considerations rather than on a distinction between inner and outer judgments If people in good conscience act according to the only moral beliefs to which they have ever been exposed, it may be improper to condemn them, even though we may condemn their actions. This explanation, which has a long history in the Western moral tradition, has the advantage that, unlike Harman's account, it explains why we sometimes are, and sometimes are not, inclined to judge harshly those who differ from us. We may want to condemn Hitler but not the cannibals. For the cannibals are more likely than Hitler to have been acting according to the only moral beliefs to which they have ever been exposed.

Another way of accounting for the impropriety of condemning people as immoral is that such condemnation may have little or no chance of success. The impropriety in this case is based on neither a logical distinction between inner and outer judgments nor the inappropriateness of condemning people for acting according to the best moral insight they possess. Rather, it is based on the practical point that it may simply be futile, that it is a waste of our time and has no chance of changing either their beliefs or their behavior. To say that Hitler showed himself as an evil man by killing Jews may be entirely too ineffectual. The only effective thing to do may be to try to assassinate him, as some Germans attempted to do.

Third, although inner judgments are the more important judgments for Harman's relativism, outer judgments may be more important from the standpoint of morality. Philosopher William Frankena has proposed a distinction between (1) reasons that are derived from a person's actual motivations and (2) reasons that are the motivations a person would have if she were moral, that is, if she were acting from reasons that were justified from the moral point of view.[10] Let us call the first kind of reasons *motivating reasons* and the second kind *moral reasons*. Of course, one's motivating reasons might be moral reasons (i.e., morally justified reasons), but they might not be. Motivating reasons would be given for inner judgments, and moral reasons would be given for outer judgments. But moral reasons are the more important reasons from a moral standpoint; they are the ones that determine whether the act is really morally justified. So the fact that inner judgments are relative to the beliefs and motivations of a person is insufficient to show that significant moral

---

[10] William Frankena, "Obligation and Motivation in Recent Moral Philosophy," in *Essays in Moral Philosophy*, ed. A. I. Melden (Seattle: University of Washington Press, 1958), p. 44.

judgments are relative. Because Harman has not shown that outer judgments are relative, he has failed to establish a significant form of moral relativism.

Several criticisms of classical moral relativism also point to the central importance of outer judgments. We saw in the first chapter that moral judgments are made from an impersonal standpoint. Moral judgments claim to be about more than one's own personal motivations, to have a more objective quality. This is the basis of many of the criticisms of classical moral relativism mentioned earlier. For example, judgments about moral progress, judgments made by moral reformers, judgments that appeal to the universalization principle, and judgments that attempt to resolve intercultural conflicts have an impersonal quality that cannot be accounted for by inner judgments. Impersonal moral judgments would appear to be, in Harman's terminology, outer judgments. This point is further evidence that the more important judgments, from a moral standpoint, are outer judgments.

CONCLUSION

In this chapter, we have considered the claim that the truth of moral beliefs is relative to a group. It is important to keep in mind that the relativist has a definite conception of truth. Nothing is especially relativistic about a theory that acknowledges that two people can be justified in their respective judgments, even when the judgments themselves are logically incompatible. Two people may make weather predictions, and both may be justified in terms of the evidence they have; but if they are incompatible, at least one of them is wrong. A relativistic position must hold not only that two people can be justified in making incompatible moral judgments but that both judgments are true, in relation to their different and incompatible moral standards.

A relativist holds that there are no universally valid moral principles but that all moral principles are valid in relation to culture or individual choice. Alice's judgment that abortion is wrong and Janet's judgment that abortion is right can both be equally true. To make this claim is much more radical than to say that Alice and Janet are equally justified in holding their positions simply because both have been equally responsible in showing how their positions follow from the facts and relevant moral considerations.

We have not found the arguments for moral relativism convincing, but we have not yet examined another closely related issue. Some philosophers believe that moral beliefs do not contain anything that could be called truth in any sense. This position is called *ethical subjectivism*. For most moral philosophers, ethical subjectivism raises more serious issues than ethical relativism. The counterpoise to ethical subjectivism is *ethical objectivism*, which holds that two contrasting moral judgments may be equally justified but not equally true. An objectivist argues that there are universal moral principles binding on all people. In the next chapter, we shall consider the debate between objectivists and subjectivists.

CONCEPT SUMMARY

One of the most sophisticated contemporary versions of moral relativism has been formulated by Gilbert Harman. This interpretation is based on a distinction between inner and outer moral judgments. Inner judgments focus on the person who is acting and ask whether she is acting in accordance with whatever principles she accepts from her society as morally right. Outer judgments are concerned with a person's actions and disregard her moral commitments. Harman's relativism centers on his claim that inner moral judgments can be evaluated only in relation to the moral commitments of the one who is judged. Furthermore, to be genuinely moral, the judgments must be shared by other moral agents.

The validity of Harman's relativism depends on the validity of the distinction between inner and outer judgments. However, the distinction poses serious problems. First, we often make judgments of a person whose moral commitments differ form ours. Second, even if it sometimes appears odd or improper to make inner moral judgments about people whose morality differs from ours, we may be able to account for this peculiarity by means other than an appeal to the relativity of inner moral judgments. Third, outer moral judgments may be more important from a moral standpoint than inner judgments, and Harman has not established that their truth is relative to the beliefs of a culture.

3

Is Morality Objective?

On July 25, 1989, the Senate Appropriations Committee voted for a five-year ban on grants made by the National Endowment for the Arts (NEA) to agencies supporting exhibitions of photographs by Robert Mapplethorpe and Andres Serrano.[1] The measure also allocated an additional $100,000 for a study by an outside party of the endowment's procedures for awarding grants. The controversial exhibitions included homoerotic photographs and photographs of a crucifix in the artist's urine.

The action of the Senate committee came after the NEA's budget had already been reduced $45,000, the amount it granted to the two exhibitions. Commenting on the action of the Senate committee, Ann Murphy, executive director of the American Arts Alliance, said, "What they have done is shocking; it makes me fearful for the country." Murphy was one of many arts representatives who criticized the action.

More recently, the NEA has received even more severe criticism, and the Mapplethorpe photographs are still mentioned. Critics of the decision of the NEA to fund the Mapplethorpe exhibition argue that the photographs are obscene and that taxpayer money should not be used to fund obscene material. But to many people, obscenity is in the eye of the beholder. What is obscene to one person is not obscene to another. The concept is too subjective to be a determining factor in public policy. Some would even go

---

[1] See Barbara Gamarekian, "Senate Panel Asks for Ban on Art Group," *New York Times*, July 26, 1989, p. C19.

further and say that all moral concepts are subjective and reflect nothing more than the feelings of the individuals who make them.

What is subjectivism in ethics? We saw in the last chapter that ethical subjectivists, unlike relativists, usually hold that ethical statements are neither true nor false. Another difference between relativists and subjectivists is that subjectivists believe moral judgments reflect the attitudes of individuals rather than a society or some larger group. Some people might think of subjectivism as the most extreme version of ethical relativism—namely, a form of relativism in which moral judgements are not relative to a group but to a single individual. However, we shall not consider subjectivism to be a form of relativism, because we shall hold that, unlike relativism, it asserts that moral statements are neither true nor false. Ethical objectivism, on the other hand, is the view that the validity of moral judgments depends on factors independent of human beings and that moral judgments are true or false regardless of what human beings think about them.

In this chapter, we shall first consider two arguments that purport to show that claims to objectivity in ethics are wrong. The first argument compares ethics with science and maintains that ethics can never have the objectivity of science. The second argument claims that ethical statements merely express the speaker's subjective emotions or attitudes. Then we shall consider three accounts of the objectivity of moral views. The first account is based on the claim that morality is known by intuition. The second account centers on the claim that morality is derived from the commands of God. The third account is based on the recent discussion of what has come to be called *moral realism*. Finally, we shall consider the possibility of a middle position between these two extremes of subjectivism and objectivism.

THE FIRST ARGUMENT FOR SUBJECTIVISM: THE CONTRAST BETWEEN SCIENCE AND ETHICS

The argument for ethical subjectivism is often made by way of a comparison with science. Science is objective in a way that ethics is not, the argument goes. We cannot see Mary's goodness in the same way that we can see her blond hair or that she is five and a half feet tall. We cannot see the wrongness of an action in the same way that we can see that it leads to the death of innocent people. I say Mrs. Jones is a good person because I believe she is kind to those in distress, she devotes herself to the care of her children, she is tolerant of those with differing views, and so on. If she did not have these characteristics or others that I consider good, I would not call her a good person. But there is an important difference between such features as caring for her children and her goodness. Although we can observe her caring for her children, we cannot observe her goodness. Her goodness may *follow from* or be *dependent on* these observable qualities (or, as philosophers say, be *supervenient* on them), but it is not directly observable.

Compare this with a scientific claim. Suppose a scientist says that an organism of a certain description causes typhoid fever. She can place contaminated water under the microscope and show us some small organisms that conform to that description, and we can observe the effects of drinking the contaminated water. We can also predict that people who drink the contaminated water will fall prey to typhoid fever, and we can verify these predictions by observation.

Unfortunately, this contrast between science and ethics is too simple, for scientists often make reference to unobservable entities. When a physicist observes a vapor trail in a cloud chamber, he may think, "There goes a proton." Protons are not directly observed, of course, and the observation of the vapor trail confirms belief in protons only in conjunction with a large body of scientific theory. Why is this not comparable to ethics? Why is belief in the goodness or rightness of certain actions not comparable to the scientist's belief in protons?

Philosopher Gilbert Harman believes there is still an important difference between science and ethics, which he puts in the following way:

> His [the scientist's] making the observation supports the theory only because, in order to explain his making the observation, it is reasonable to assume something about the world over and above the assumption made about the observer's psychology. In particular, it is reasonable to assume that there was a proton going through the cloud chamber, causing the vapor trail.[2]

The observation of the vapor trail cannot reasonably be explained by reference to human psychology. We must also make assumptions about the natural world. In contrast, Harman maintains, moral judgments can reasonably be explained by reference to the psychology of the one making the judgment.

Harman invites us to compare the cloud chamber example with the following one. Suppose you are walking along the street and see a group of young hoodlums pour gasoline on a cat and set it afire. If you say, "The hoodlums were wrong in what they did," no reference to objectively existing moral facts that are independent of your beliefs need be made to explain either your making the judgment or the judgment itself. All we need to assume in explaining your moral judgment is that *you* have some moral principles from which it follows that for *you* igniting cats with gasoline is morally wrong. It is certainly not necessary to assume that moral principles exist independently of your beliefs to explain the observation of the hoodlums igniting the cat. You also do not need to make this assumption to explain your moral judgment that what the hoodlums did is wrong. Hypotheses about objectively existing moral principles do not help explain why people observe what they observe

---

[2] Gilbert Harman, "Moral Relativism Defended," *Philosophical Review* 84 (1975), pp. 6–7.

in the same way that hypotheses about objectively existing scientific laws explain observations of the vapor trail.

Philosopher Nicholas Sturgeon objects, maintaining that moral facts are relevant to the explanation of moral judgments.[3] Part of the reason that we say the hoodlums were wrong in setting the cat on fire might be that there are objectively existing moral principles that the hoodlums violated when they ignited the cat. But reference to what might be another explanation is not a strong argument. It is not easy to determine whether the account of Harman or Sturgeon as to why we condemn the hoodlums is correct. So we must consider this argument inconclusive.

THE SECOND ARGUMENT FOR SUBJECTIVISM: THE NATURE OF MORAL JUDGMENTS

Some philosophers have made an argument for the subjectivity of morality from the nature of moral judgments themselves. The analysis confirms, they believe, that moral judgments have a function that is incompatible with the belief that morality is objective. One of the most sophisticated versions of this position has been given by the American philosopher Charles Stevenson.[4]

As a background for understanding Stevenson's interpretation of moral language, we should remind ourselves that language has many functions. For example, I use the reporting *function* of language when I say that you left your books in my car by mistake. I use the commanding function of language when I say, "Make your bed and clean up your room." I use the expressive function of language when I say, "Wow! What a hit!"

Many objectivists apparently believe that moral statements fit the reporting function, so that when I say, "Abortion is wrong," I am saying something analogous to "You left your books in my car." Stevenson, however, believes that moral language serves an expressive and commanding function, not a reporting function. Saying "Abortion is wrong" is more like saying "Abortion—yeech! Don't do it!" or "Abortion—how awful! Don't have one!"

Let us be clear about what Stevenson is and is not saying. He is saying that moral statements *express* feelings and *give* commands, *not* that they *report* feelings. An example will illustrate this important distinction. If I say that moral judgments *report* feelings or attitudes, then when I say, "Abortion is wrong," I am saying, "I don't like abortion." This is a factual claim about my own psychological state that is either true or false. If I say that moral judgments

---

[3] Nicholas Sturgeon, "Moral Explanations," in *Morality, Reason, and Truth*, ed. D. Copp and D. Zimmerman (Totowa, NJ: Rowman & Allenheld, 1984); excerpted in Louis Pojman, *Ethical Theory* (Belmont, CA: Wadsworth, 1989), pp. 437–448.

[4] Charles L. Stevenson, *Ethics and Language* (New Haven, CT: Yale University Press, 1944).

express feelings and give commands, then I am saying that moral judgments are neither true nor false. Neither expressions of feeling, such as "Ouch!" nor commands, such as "Shut the door!" can be true or false. Reports can be true or false, but the expressions of feeling and commands cannot.

The difference between reporting and expressing feelings yields an important advantage for Stevenson. Earlier philosophers, such as A. J. Ayer in his classic *Language, Truth, and Logic*, adopted the analysis of ethical language as *reportive* rather than *expressive*. But this approach has several highly implausible implications. It means, for example, that the only way I can be wrong in making an ethical judgment is to misreport my own feelings. If I say, "Abortion is wrong" and thus report that I have a negative attitude toward abortion when I really have a positive attitude toward it, my moral judgment is incorrect. But this means that incorrect moral judgments are merely instances of lying or our inability to know our own mental states. The proper way to correct error in our moral judgment about abortion, then, is not to argue over the ethical pros and cons of abortion but to train ourselves to be more honest and perceptive about what is going on in our minds. This does not seem to be a correct account of moral reasoning, and Stevenson's account does not suffer from this weakness.

A second advantage of Stevenson's account over Ayer's interpretation is that it can give a more satisfactory depiction of moral disagreement. According to Ayer, when I say, "Abortion is always wrong" and you say, "Abortion is morally permissible in some circumstances," we are each reporting our own attitudes toward abortion. If we are both honest and perceptive enough to know our own feelings, we are both correct, and our statements do not disagree. It is as if I were to say, "I have a negative attitude toward abortion," and you were to say, "I have a positive attitude toward abortion." These two statements are perfectly compatible and not in disagreement. But this perspective is at least not what we think we are doing when we make apparently contrary statements about abortion. We think we are engaged in a serious moral disagreement over an important moral issue. Unless Ayer can give us good reasons for believing that our ordinary understanding of what is going on is wrong, his account should be rejected.

Stevenson's theory of moral language is able to give a more satisfactory account of moral disagreement. When I say, "Abortion is always wrong," I am expressing a negative attitude toward abortion and advocating that you have the same attitude. When you say, "Abortion is sometimes morally permissible," you are expressing a positive attitude toward abortion in some cases and advocating that I have that same attitude. Although we are not disagreeing in *belief* about any matters of fact—and Stevenson implies that you and I could agree about all of the factual issues and still disagree about the morality of abortion—we are disagreeing in *attitude*.

Problems persist, however, even with Stevenson's more sophisticated form of subjectivism. The equation of moral judgments with feelings or attitudes does provide insight into moral language, for our moral judgments often carry strong emotions and are intended to influence others. Nevertheless, expressions of feelings and attitudes must be distinguished from moral judgments. The easiest way to see this difference is to examine how our expression of feelings toward an issue can vary independently of our ethical judgment.

Consider the following illustration.[5] Jane is ready to go to college, but her mother wants to purchase a new house with most of the money the family has saved for Jane's education. Jane's mother says to Jane's father:

> I know we ought to save our money for Jane's education, but I want that new house while you and I are still young enough to enjoy it. So let's take at least three-fourths of the money we have saved and make a down payment on a house in Memorial Forest.

Jane might agree with her mother ethically but have a negative attitude toward the idea of buying the house. She might say:

> I agree that you ought to save the money for my education, so please save it rather that spending it on the house in Memorial Forest.

Or Jane might agree with her mother both ethically and in attitude, saying:

> Although I cannot honestly deny that you have an obligation to save the money for my education, I want you and Dad to have the new house while you are still young enough to enjoy it.

Or, finally, Jane might disagree with her mother both ethically and in attitude:

> I don't believe for a moment that it would be wrong to use the money to buy a new house. After all, you and Dad have worked hard all your lives, and I am old enough to take care of myself. But I still wish you would keep the money for my education.

Jane's feelings about the proper use of her parents' savings can be different from her moral beliefs. Most moral philosophers have rejected the Stevensonian account of moral judgments as an expression of feeling, in which rational arguments have no place. When we say that Hitler was an evil man, most of us think we are expressing more than personal tastes, such as when we say "Oysters—yum, yum! Have some!" Furthermore, ethical argument is more than just trying to manipulate people's feelings, for we recognize certain standards in determining what counts as a legitimate reason in an ethical argument. Jane believed that it would not be wrong for her parents to use most of their money for a new house because she felt she was old enough to take care of herself. If she had given as her reason the fact that she was not a pretty girl, we would be puzzled. We would have a hard time understanding how this consideration would count as a reason that is relevant to her parents' belief about the morally proper use of their money.

---

[5] This argument is adapted from Kurt Baier, "Fact, Value, and Norm in Stevenson's Ethics," *Nous* 1 (May 1967), pp. 139–160.

We have considered two arguments for moral subjectivism and found them wanting. After a concept summary, let us examine several accounts of moral objectivism. These accounts are not so much *arguments for* moral objectivism as they are ways of being moral objectivists.

CONCEPT SUMMARY

Moral subjectivism is characterized by two features. First, it usually holds that moral judgments do not state truths but rather express attitudes. Second, subjectivism ties moral judgments to the attitudes or commitments of individuals rather than groups. One argument for moral subjectivism is that moral qualities such as goodness are not observable in the way that size or color are. But science also refers to unobservables. A more sophisticated argument is that in science observations are explained by assumptions about the world over and above the assumptions about the observer's psychology. In ethics, however, our moral judgments can be adequately explained merely by reference to the attitudes and beliefs of the person who makes the judgment. This argument is inconclusive, because our moral judgments might also be explained by reference to objective moral facts.

Another argument for moral subjectivism is that moral judgments can be correctly analyzed as expressing the attitudes of the speaker and directing others to have similar attitudes. But people often make distinctions between their attitudes and their moral judgments, so this proposed analysis of moral judgments is implausible.

THE FIRST VERSION OF MORAL OBJECTIVISM: MORAL INTUITIONISM

Neither the comparison of ethics with science nor Stevenson's account of moral language were successful in showing that we must give up the belief that moral judgments are objective. But is there any positive reason to believe that moral judgments are objective, that they have validity independent of human beings? In the next three sections, we shall consider three views as to how this objectivity might be given a basis.

The first view is that moral judgments are objective because a moral quality—particularly the moral quality of goodness—is just as much a part of the world as color, number, size, and weight. Since moral qualities are the subjects of moral judgments, moral judgments can claim objectivity as legitimately as judgments about such qualities as color, number, size, and weight. This claim seems to fly directly in the face of the contrast we made earlier between statements that something is right or wrong and statements that something is blue or weighs so many pounds. We can apprehend color and weight with our senses in a way that we cannot apprehend goodness or badness. How can the claim for the objectivity of moral judgments be made?

The best-known advocate of this variety of moral objectivism in twentieth-century philosophy is the English philosopher G. E. Moore. In his *Principia Ethica*, published in 1903, Moore argues that one of the first tasks of ethics is to discover the meaning of the term *good*. Now this might seem like a strange place to begin, for we use the word *good* all the time and apparently without difficulty. But the task is not as simple as one might suppose.

Moore begins by attempting to show that the word *good* cannot be analyzed into some characteristic that can be empirically observed. For example, suppose we consider Bertrand Russell's definition of *good* as that which we desire to desire. Moore believes we can apply what he calls the "open question test" to show that this definition is false. For it makes sense to ask, "Is it good to desire to desire X?" But if *good means* that which we desire to desire, the question reduces to "Is the desire to desire X one of the things that we desire to desire?" The meaning or importance of this question is, at best, no longer clear. Moore believes that this shows that it is at least implausible to define *good* as that which we desire to desire.

Consider another example. Suppose I define *good* as pleasure. I can still ask the question "Even though flogging children to death gives me pleasure, is it good?" The fact that this question makes sense shows that *good* does not *mean* the same thing as *pleasure*. Moore believes that this can be said of any other definition of *good* that I might contrive. We cannot define *good* in terms of any property or characteristic of a person, action, or event that can be observed with the senses. Goodness, then, is not a natural or observable property but what Moore calls a "nonnatural" property.

Moore agrees to a certain extent, then, with our earlier contrast between moral properties such as goodness and observable properties such as color or weight. He agrees, that is, that goodness is not measurable or identifiable with anything observable with one of the five senses. But he does not agree that goodness is not a property of any kind or that it is not knowable in any way. If goodness is a nonnatural property that cannot be detected with any of the five senses, how can it be known? Moore's answer is, By a special faculty of intuition. This reply suggests that goodness is an objective property that some people, actions, or events have independently of a human decision. Of course, humans may decide to *be* good or to *act* in a morally proper way, but it is not their action alone that makes something good.

Moore's position has problems, however. Consider the open question test again. One criticism is that its plausibility comes from Moore's failure to distinguish between *meaning* and *reference*. We can, for example, ask the question "That is the Evening Star, but is it the Morning Star?" Now, the Evening Star is, of course, the Morning Star; that is, the Evening Star and the Morning Star both refer to the same planet in the heavens. But they do not have the same meaning. The same thing could also hold true of *good* and *pleasure*. Although the terms do not mean the same thing, they could refer to the same thing, which could be the natural property of pleasure itself. Then whether something possesses goodness would be equivalent to whether it is pleasure producing, which would make goodness accessible to empirical investigation, at least to the extent that pleasure can be investigated empirically. If this were the case, goodness would not be a nonnatural or nonempirical property.

This criticism does not refute the claims of objectivism, for if good does refer to pleasure or some other property that can be investigated empirically, moral judgments would be objective. But it does show that Moore's particular version of objectivism is suspect. Now let us consider another problem with Moore's approach that does cast fundamental doubt on his objectivism— namely, his claim that intuition is a source of moral knowledge.

Moral intuitionists, such as Moore, believe that intuition is a faculty by which people can know moral truth. By the use of moral intuition, we can somehow directly see that some people or actions possess goodness. Intuitionists disagree, however, over the nature of this faculty. Some have maintained that intuitions are feelings or sentiments: a virtuous action produces in us a feeling of pleasure, and a vicious action produces a feeling of pain or uneasiness. Of course, these feelings of pleasure or pain are distinctive; they are detached and not related to self-interest or personal gain. However, other intuitionists have held that moral intuitions are more like rational knowledge than like sensations and that what we perceive through moral intuition is a certain fitness that the right actions have. Certain actions seem to be the right course to take in the circumstances. But there are difficulties with the appeal to intuition, under either interpretation of intuitions, that are hard to answer.

First, intuitionists cannot propose any procedure for choosing between competing moral principles when both claim to be based on intuition. Suppose I say that taking innocent lives is always wrong, and you say that sacrificing an innocent person might be justified to avoid some great evil. For example, if an evil tyrant were to threaten our nation with nuclear destruction unless one of his enemies (who had actually done no wrong) were handed over to him, you might say we should give into his demand, whereas I might say that giving into his demand is immoral, even if the consequence is nuclear destruction. Now, if we both defend our claims by an appeal to moral intuition, how can we determine who is right? We might introspectively examine our intuitions, and each of us might then report that our claim is right. Then what would we do? Moral intuitionism does not seem to provide what we seek—namely, a method for objectively determining right and wrong.

Second, some forms of intuitionism, including Moore's, seem to misrepresent the relationship of moral properties to nonmoral properties. Ordinarily we say that a person is good (or bad) *because* he or she has certain characteristics. For example, I say Mrs. Jones is a good person because I believe she is kind to those in distress, she devotes herself to the care of her children, she is tolerant of those with differing views, and so on. If she did not have those characteristics or some others that I consider good, I would not call her a good person. But some moral intuitionists view quite differently the process of ascribing goodness to a person or action. They believe that our moral intuition enables us to intuit directly that a person is good without any knowledge of his or her characteristics. This belief has the strange consequence that, if we consider two people who have exactly the same characteristics, we might intuit that one person is good and the other is not. Mrs. Brown could be kind to those in distress, devote herself to the care of her children, and be tolerant of those of differing views. Yet, if we did not intuit the goodness of Mrs. Brown apart from these qualities, we could not call her good, despite the fact that she has the same qualities as Mrs. Jones, whom we call good. This peculiar result of any form of intuitionism that holds we can intuit the goodness or badness of people or actions independently of their observable characteristics has led many moral philosophers to reject intuitionism.

Not only has moral intuitionism found little favor with contemporary moral philosophers, but it has probably never been the most widely accepted way of defending moral objectivism among the general population. Let us consider next the most popular defense of moral objectivism.

THE SECOND VERSION OF MORAL OBJECTIVISM: THE DIVINE COMMAND THEORY

For many people, religion is the basis of ethics. When panels of experts are formed in hospitals or by governmental agencies to render opinions on ethical questions, religious figures are almost always included and often dominant. Showing that moral judgments have their foundations in the commands of God would, for many people, provide a sufficient answer to our quest for objectivity in ethics. What could be more objective than the commands of God? Not surprisingly, this idea has been elaborated into a theory of the objectivity of ethics known as the *divine command theory*.

We must be careful to distinguish several different senses in which ethics can be based on the commands of God. One sense is psychological: the fact that God commands something could motivate either positively or negatively. As a positive motivation, the hope of reward in the afterlife or some other manifestation of divine favor can lead to morally praiseworthy action. As a negative motivation, the fear of punishment in the afterlife or some other manifestation of divine disfavor can be powerful deterrents to certain types of behavior.

It would be hard to deny that the use of religious motivation to produce ethical conduct is an important influence in many people's lives. But the psychological account of religious motivation does not answer the question about the objectivity of morality. After all, people can be motivated to do what is wrong as well as what is right. A tyrant can motivate his subjects to act in accordance with his will, but this capability would not convince us that his commands are objectively right. Or a father who is a harsh disciplinarian may be able to bend his children to his will, even if his will is often morally perverse. Children may be motivated to many actions by the desire for parental approval, but this does not show that the actions carrying parental approval are objectively right.

To find the possible religious basis of moral objectivism, we must turn to the logical sense in which ethics is based on religion. Here three positions are possible. First, one can say that God, being omniscient, always knows what is right and wrong and, being perfectly good, always commands us to do what is right and not to do what is wrong. God commands us not to commit rape and murder because they are wrong and to love others because it is right.

Now it is certainly true that knowing the commands of God would be enormously helpful to an ethically concerned person in determining what is right. If God's knowledge in other areas is infallible, His knowledge of moral truth should also be infallible. But two questions must be asked: (1) How do we know God's commands, and (2) where does God get his ethical knowledge?

Let us consider the first question. In learning about God's commands, do we look to the Bible, the Koran, or some other religious document? The religions of the world differ significantly on some moral issues, such as the legitimacy of the use of violence and the proper treatment of animals. After we decide on a source of revelation about God's commands, how do we decide on its proper interpretation? Consider how even Christian authorities disagree over the morality of such issues as war, abortion, sterilization, and birth control. If religious authorities cannot agree on what God's commands are, how much confidence can we have in them as a guide for moral conduct?

The second question serves to point out that, according to the first version of the divine command theory, God serves only as a reliable conveyor of ethical truth but not the ultimate source of ethical truth. This view shows that the version of the divine command theory cannot provide a satisfactory answer to the question about the justification of moral truth. Appealing to God as an omniscient *knower* of ethical truth is not the same thing as appealing to God as the *ultimate ground of moral truth*.

A second version of the divine command theory addresses the issue of the ultimate ground of moral truth by holding that God's commands *make* certain actions right and others wrong. What makes right actions right is that God has commanded them, and what makes wrong actions wrong is that God has prohibited them. It is, in other words, God's commands that justify our moral beliefs. On this account, we do not need to ask about the ultimate origin of ethical truth, for God's command is the ultimate origin. Though this version of the divine command theory may answer the objection to the first version, it has serious problems of its own.

One objection that is sometimes made to this version is that, if we derive our moral beliefs from divine commands, we give up moral autonomy or independence. We base our morality on superior power rather than moral conviction. Acting as a genuine moral agent involves being self-directed; a person behaves in a certain way because he or she believes that way is right. Subservience to divine commands requires replacing autonomy with mere obedience, which is morally wrong.[6]

At this point, a defender of the divine command theory could reply that we often think it is reasonable to take things on authority. When we go to the physician, we usually accept his or her directions. The scientist accepts the authority of reports of experimental work that she has not verified. Yet we do not think the patient and the scientist have surrendered their autonomy in an unacceptable way. But there is an important difference between accepting an authority on a truth that is independent of that authority and accepting an authority that establishes the truth. The second version of the divine command theory holds that God establishes moral truth, and so the analogy does not apply.

A more serious problem is that the claim that divine commands justify moral judgments seems to lead to moral arbitrariness. If God's command is sufficient to justify any action as good, then God could command me to make it my chief end in life to inflict suffering on other human beings. And it would be morally proper for me to do this. If no moral criterion is independent of God's will, He could command us to commit rape or murder, and it would be right for us to do so.

We could reply, "But God would never do this, for He is a loving God." This response is the basis of the modification of the divine command theory proposed by philosopher Robert M. Adams. The fact that something is contrary to God's commands means that it is wrong, Adams maintains, *only* if we assume that God has the character of a loving being. If God were really to command us to make cruelty our goal, then He would not have that character of loving us, and I would not say it would be wrong to disobey Him.[7] However, if a divine command must be consistent with love to be ethically binding, then love is the most important moral criterion, or at least equally as important as the fact that something is commanded by God. The criterion of love is then independent of God, and the second position becomes equivalent to the first one. Therefore, many philosophers have concluded that the second version of the divine command theory must also be rejected.

A third version of the divine command theory holds that the statement "X is good (or bad)" *means* the same thing as "X is commanded (or prohibited) by God." In this version, the divine command theory is established by definition. But again severe problems arise. First, many people do not mean (or at least do not think they mean) the same thing by "X is good" and "X is commanded by God." The divine command theory does not appear to give a definition that is plausible for many people.

---

[6] This argument has been challenged recently. See Philip Quinn, *Divine Commands and Moral Requirements* (Oxford: Clarendon, 1978), Chap. 1.

[7] Robert M. Adams, "A Modified Divine Command Theory of Ethical Wrongness," in *Religion and Morality: A Collection of Essays*, eds. Gene Outka and John P. Reeder (New York: Anchor Books, 1973), p. 527.

A more important objection, however, is that the claim that something is good *means* that God commands it seems incompatible with the language that religious believers themselves often use. Suppose I say, "Praise the Lord, for He is good." If whatever God commands is good, then I am really saying, "Praise the Lord, for He acts according to His commands." This sounds very strange indeed! We might as well praise the standard meterstick for being one meter long! This objection suggests that the word *good* does not mean the same thing as being in accord with God's commands.

It is important to see that the rejection of the divine command theory is not the same as the rejection of belief in God. Many believers are willing to recognize that logic and mathematics are valid independently of God's commands. The fact that one and one are two does not depend on God's commands. Why should the situation be any different with morality? Many major figures in the Jewish and Christian traditions would agree in rejecting the position that the validity of ethical beliefs depends on the commands of God. The Jewish scholars who wrote the Talmud did not take divine commands as the reason for action; if God commanded them to steal and murder, they would not be obligated to do so. By their nature, humans know what is right and wrong, and revelation is needed only to avoid all uncertainty over the application of moral precepts. Similarly, Moses Maimonides and other medieval Jewish thinkers refused to identify the good with the will of God.[8] The Roman Catholic tradition generally takes a similar, though more qualified, stand. According to St. Thomas Aquinas, to say that morality is determined simply by God's will is to suggest that God's will may sometimes not follow order and wisdom, and that stance would be blasphemous.[9]

The divine command theory may not be the best version of moral objectivism. Even the religious believer may find reason to hold that moral truth is independent of God's commands, just as it is independent of human beings' beliefs and wishes. We turn now to the contemporary form of moral objectivism that appeals to many philosophers, whether or not they believe in God. This position is called *moral realism*.

THE THIRD VERSION OF MORAL OBJECTIVISM: MORAL REALISM

Suppose you are looking out your window and see a tree. One of the things you probably believe about the tree is that its existence is independent of what you think about it. It is there whether or not you are looking at it, or

---

[8] See Louis Jacobs, "The Relationship between Religion and Ethics in Jewish Thought," in *Religion and Morality*, ed. Gene Outka and John P. Reeder, Jr. (New York: Anchor Books, 1973), pp. 155–172.

[9] Thomas Aquinas, *De Veritate*, 23.6, quoted in Eric D'Arcy, "Worthy of Worship: A Catholic Contribution," in Outka and Reeder, *Religion and Morality*, p. 191.

even whether you have ever looked at it. It is there even if you have never thought about it. To put the same point still another way and perhaps more abstractly, the tree's existence is not mind-dependent. Its existence is discovered, not invented. Those who adopt this position are called *realists*.

Many people have a similar view about morality: at least some moral statements are true regardless of our feelings or beliefs. Those who adopt this position are called *moral realists*. According to the moral realist, moral truth is discovered, not invented. Moral beliefs are true or false independently of any beliefs we may have about what is right or wrong. For example, most of us would probably think of the following statements in realistic terms (i.e., as true regardless of what we, or other human beings, might think about them):

Hitler ought not to have ordered the killing of large numbers of Jews.

One ought not torture people for the fun of it.

One ought not commit rape.

One ought not tell a lie without good reason.

One ought not keep other human beings as slaves.

In addition to the way we think about these kinds of moral judgments, the moral realist believes other evidence suggests that we naturally espouse a realistic view of morality. We think of some people as more morally *perceptive* than others. We speak of moral *advancement* through history, such as the increasing rejection of slavery. We might even say that Americans in the nineteenth century came to recognize that slavery is wrong, implying that moral truth is independent of their opinions. Or we might ask whether people in former times could have *known* that slavery was wrong. And we often engage in *deliberation* about moral problems, as if there were right and wrong answers to the issue.

We should keep in mind two important considerations when discussing the claims of moral realism. First, the moral realist need not claim that her own moral beliefs are correct. Rather, she need only claim that a given belief is either correct or incorrect. Perhaps no human being has any correct moral beliefs at all, as perhaps none of us has any correct beliefs about the nature of the basic components of the physical universe. Certainly at any given time we may not be sure which beliefs are correct and which are incorrect. But this does not mean that there *are* no correct moral beliefs.

A second cautionary note about moral realism is that a moral realist need not hold that all moral obligations are independent of one's personal feelings or commitments. Not every moral statement, that is, need be true or false independently of what we might think about it.

Philosopher Walter Sinnott-Armstrong has proposed an argument to support this claim.[10] Suppose Fritz has promised a professional colleague that

---

[10] Walter Sinnott Armstrong, *Moral Dilemmas* (Oxford: Blackwell, 1988), pp. 200ff.

he will finish a project by a certain date but is late through no fault of his own. He has only one day left before the deadline, but delaying the project a few days will cause no serious problems.

On the other hand, today is his daughter's birthday. He always takes her sailing on her birthday, although he has not explicitly promised to do so. He knows that his failure to go sailing with her will greatly disappoint her. Fritz is a family man for whom commitments to professional colleagues occupy a lower place in his personal ranking than fulfilling his daughter's expectations. Therefore, he decides to go sailing with his daughter.

Pedro is faced with an identical situation, except that, for him, professional commitments take priority over family obligations in situations such as this. Therefore, he decides to keep his commitment to finish the project on time and not to go sailing with his daughter.

Now, if we assume that the views that Fritz ought to have gone sailing with his daughter and that Pedro ought to have kept his commitment to his professional colleague are both true, we have two different moral judgments applying to situations identical in every respect except the personal rankings of Fritz and Pedro. Here is an example, then, of moral judgments that do depend on personal factors. Of course, we might say that these judgments are valid only because of an objective moral principle: When a person has two equal and incompatible moral obligations, he should decide what to do on the basis of his personal rankings. But the two original moral judgments are still dependent on personal rankings and do not represent moral facts that are true independently of human beliefs.

With these qualifications in mind, what can we say about the plausibility of moral realism? Moral subjectivists do not find very convincing the argument for moral realism based on the way we naturally think about morality. Philosopher J. L. Mackie, for example, admits that a belief in objective values is built into ordinary moral thought and language but still claims that this ingrained belief is false.[11] Mackie holds what he calls an "error theory"— namely, the view that the moral realism to which most people implicitly subscribe is erroneous.[12] Nevertheless, because the belief in objective moral truths is such a deeply ingrained belief, Mackie admits that good reasons must be given for rejecting it. What are these reasons? Let us consider two criticisms of the realist position.

The first criticism begins by pointing out that when we say that we ought to do something, we are doing more than merely stating a fact. We usually think that the statement is related to action in some way: it gives us a motive for action. Subjectivists believe that realists cannot easily explain the motivating aspect of moral judgments. If moral judgments merely report facts about the world, as realists maintain, why do we feel moved to action? On realist

---

[11] J. L. Mackie, *Ethics: Inventing Right and Wrong* (New York: Penguin Books, 1977), pp. 48–49.

[12] Ibid., p. 35.

grounds, we may have an obligation to *believe* that the action is wrong, but it is not as clear that realism provides grounds for an obligation to act.

Contrast the apparent difficulty that realists have with the motivating or dynamic character of moral discourse with the relative ease that subjectivists like Stevenson have with the same issue. For Stevenson, as we have seen, an essential part of the meaning of moral judgments is to express the appraiser's attitudes or commitments. People who believe that moral judgments are nothing more than expressions of emotions claim moral judgments (1) express the appraiser's approval or disapproval and (2) invite others to join in the same attitude. So it is part of the meaning of moral judgments that the appraiser holds a positive attitude toward things judged morally permissible and a negative attitude toward things judged morally impermissible, and these attitudes are motivating factors in the appraiser's conduct. In contrast to the realist, a subjectivist such as Stevenson can easily explain the dynamic or motivating character of moral judgments.

A realist is not without responses to this criticism. Philosopher William Frankena's distinction between motives and reasons is relevant here also. The realist might maintain that the proper function of moral judgments is not to supply *motives* but rather *reasons* for action and that the subjectivist cannot account for this distinction.[13] When I ask you why I should help John with his homework, you may give two different kinds of answers. You might give a motive or a reason. In the first instance, a proper answer to my question might be "Because, if you do, he will give you some money." Assuming I am motivated by a desire for money, I have been given a motive to help John. In the second instance, a proper answer to my question might be "Because you promised to, and people should keep their promises." This response is a reason for helping John, but it may not supply a motive for doing so.

A second criticism of moral realism is referred to by Mackie as the "argument for queerness."[14] The argument is that, if the realist is correct, there must be some kind of objective connection between an action and its rightness or wrongness. However, this connection must be of a rather peculiar or queer type. For example, suppose you see someone deliberately push another person down a flight of stairs just for the pleasure of seeing him suffer. The wrongness of this action must somehow be consequential or supervenient on the fact that it is an act of deliberate cruelty. But what is the nature of this peculiar and yet objectively existing relationship between an act of deliberate cruelty and its wrongness? The moral realist must give a satisfactory account of it for her realism to be plausible.

This relationship of supervenience is indeed a peculiar one. What is the relationship between the nonmoral or natural qualities of an act and the fact

---

[13] See William Frankena, "Obligation and Motivation in Recent Moral Philosophy," in *Essays in Moral Philosophy*, ed. A. I. Melden (Seattle: University of Washington Press, 1958), p. 44.

[14] Mackie, *Ethics*, p. 38.

that the act is wrong? If the moral realist is correct, the moral fact (if it is a fact) that the action described here is wrong in some objective manner follows from the description of it as causing pain just for fun. But to what fact about the world does this relationship of "following from" correspond? Would it not be simpler, Mackie argues, to say that the moral judgment that deliberate cruelty is wrong is merely a "subjective response which could be causally related to the detection of the natural features on which the supposed quality is said to be consequential"?[15]

Another aspect of the queerness of the supervenient relation is the problem of how we could know when the appropriate supervenient relationship obtains.[16] How would we find out whether the physical facts associated with causing pain for fun produce the moral fact of its wrongness? Perhaps we could know this only by a special kind of moral intuition that could apprehend the queer kinds of entities called moral facts. But we have already seen some of the problems with moral intuition. Again, would it not be easier to suppose that the wrongness of deliberate cruelty is derived from the subjective response that we make to the situation?

Philosopher David Brink proposes answers to both of these problems.[17] In answer to the argument that the supervenient relation must be a peculiar one, Brink answers that it is no more peculiar than the supervenient relation that, according to many philosophers, holds between physical states and mental states. Let us assume, as many philosophers and scientists do, that thoughts are produced by physicochemical processes in the central nervous system. For example, when I think about the party I am going to give this weekend, this thought was produced by, or somehow followed from, the physical and chemical reactions in my body. If the physical and chemical reactions had not occurred, I would not have had the thought. How can a thought—a conscious experience—follow from something as different as a physical or chemical process? What is the relationship between the two? We do not know, but many people believe a relationship exists nevertheless. If we do not understand the relationship between chemistry and thought but still believe there is one, why cannot we believe there is a relationship between actions and their rightness and wrongness, even though we do not understand it?

With respect to our knowledge of supervenient relationships, we need not suppose, Brink maintains, that they are known by a faculty of intuition. Rather, a person discovers which natural facts moral facts supervene on by appealing to moral theories. We might discover that the wrongness of deliberate cruelty follows from a moral theory that says that actions are right if

---

[15] Ibid., p. 41.

[16] Ibid.

[17] David Brink, "Moral Realism and the Skeptical Arguments from Disagreement and Queerness," *Australasian Journal of Philosophy* 62 (1984), pp. 111–125.

they contribute to human happiness and wrong if they do not. A similar situation prevails in science. For example, we know that tables are composed of atomic particles because of scientific theories about the composition of matter. Claims in both ethics and science are theory-dependent in this way.

Both of these replies claim that morality is *in no worse shape* than other areas of intellectual endeavor. However, these analogies are problematic. The relation of thoughts to chemistry is a cause-effect relationship, whereas the relationship between human actions and their rightness or wrongness is a relationship of logical implication. The fact that someone performed an act of deliberate cruelty is supposed to imply logically (or justify) the claim that the act is wrong, not give a causal account of it. With respect to the analogy between scientific theories and moral theories, there is more agreement about the truth of theories to which scientists appeal than the truth of the theories to which moralists appeal. Nevertheless, the validity of moral realism seems to depend heavily on the validity of moral theories that link observations of natural qualities with moral terms. Perhaps this fact suggests a way out of the conflict between objectivism and subjectivism.

CONCLUSION: RATIONALITY VERSUS TRUTH

The debate between subjectivism and objectivism has considerable theoretical importance. Most of us are led at one time or another to ask ourselves whether there is moral truth that is independent of human belief. But this issue is not the center of our concerns when we are wrestling with a real-life moral decision. We are interested rather in this sort of question: What is the *best* decision? Or perhaps: What is the *right* decision for me in this situation? Put more abstractly, the question is, What is the most rational decision? The question I must answer is not what decision is true in some absolute sense. After all, even the moral realist may not be sure that she possesses absolute or final moral truth. The real issue, then, is not truth but rationality.

To make the most rational decisions, two things are necessary. First, I must use the most rationally defensible moral principles available. Second, I must apply these principles in the most rational way. Because we are concerned at this point with finding the most rational principles rather than applying them in the most rational way, let us look more closely at this first requirement.

Remember, to begin with, that whatever decision we make can be seen to follow from some moral principles. The principles may be implicit rather than explicit, but they are present in some form. If we decide that we are going to cheat on a test, we may be able to justify this decision only on the basis of egoism. If we decide that we will not use contraceptives because it is immoral to do so, we may be able to justify this decision only on the basis of natural law. Sometimes, however, our decisions may be justifiable in terms of several different moral principles—egoism and utilitarianism, perhaps. In any case, the question is not whether we will have moral principles but what they are.

Given this first point, the pressing practical question is whether the principles that underlie our actions are the best or most rationally defensible ones. The only way to answer this question is to look at various moral theories and attempt to determine which one is the most rationally defensible, all things considered. The moral principles justifiable by this theory (or these theories) would be the ones a morally responsible person should use. Whether these principles are true in the realist's sense may be hard to answer. Whether they are the most rationally defensible principles is a more manageable question. From a practical standpoint, it is the more important question regarding the objectivity of ethics. The task before us in the next several chapters, then, is to begin the examination of the four moral theories proposed for our analysis.

CONCEPT SUMMARY

Moral objectivists maintain that moral judgments express truths that are independent of human belief about them. One version of moral objectivism is that moral statements refer to nonnatural (unobservable) properties of people and actions, such as goodness. The intuitionist believes that these non-natural properties are known by a special faculty of moral intuition. But intuitionism has several problems: it is not able to supply a decision procedure when intuitions disagree, and it misrepresents the relationship between moral and nonmoral properties.

Another account of moral objectivism is based on the view that moral truth is based on divine commands. One version of this theory holds that God, being omniscient, always commands us to do what is right. But this version of the divine command theory does not explain the source of God's ethical knowledge. A second version holds that the fact that God commands us to do something *makes* it true, but this seems to open the way for moral arbitrariness on God's part. A third version holds that "X is good (or bad)" *means* the same thing as "X is commanded (or prohibited) by God," but this view has implications for the relationship of God to morality that even many religious believers find implausible.

Moral realism, which holds that at least some moral beliefs are true or false independently of any beliefs we may have about them, is one of the most important contemporary versions of moral objectivism. Two major objections to moral realism are that it cannot account for the dynamic or motivating aspect of morality and that it cannot explain how moral qualities follow from (or are supervenient on) nonmoral qualities. An answer to the first of these objections is that the function of moral judgments is to supply reasons, not motives, for action, and that a distinction between reasons and motives for actions is also necessary to account for the phenomenon of amoralism. An answer to the second objection is that the problems of explaining supervenience are no more severe in ethics than science and that moral theories provide the link between observations and moral facts, just as, for example, scientific theories provide the link between observations and atomic particles.

Finally, one way of circumventing the problem of the impasse in the debate between subjectivists and objectivists is to emphasize that rationality, not truth, is the central issue in the question of the objectivity of ethics.

4

Moral Theories

Socrates has as much right as anyone to be called the patron saint of philosophy. Few people have represented the ideal of philosophy more forcefully or eloquently, in either their words or lives. His conception of the nature and function of philosophy is closely connected with his personal "mission" in life: to coax and cajole the people of Athens into examining their values and beliefs. Socrates would engage individuals in conversation and get them to state their beliefs on some topic. Then he would examine these beliefs, pointing out difficulties and often leading people to reformulate their beliefs or perhaps abandon them altogether. Describing how he would treat someone who claims to have the truth, Socrates says:

> I shall question him and cross-examine him and test him. If I think that he has not attained excellence, though he says that he has, I shall reproach him for undervaluing the most valuable things, and overvaluing those that are less valuable. This I shall do to everyone whom I meet, young or old, citizen or stranger, but especially to citizens, since they are most closely related to me.[1]

A little later Socrates gives what might be considered the theme of his philosophical mission: "An unexamined life is not worth living."[2]

---

[1] Plato, *The Apology*, 29–30; cited in *Euthyphro, Apology and Crito*, trans. by F. J. Church, rev. ed., introduction by Robert D. Cumming (New York: Liberal Arts Press, 1956), p. 36.

[2] Ibid., p. 38.

Socrates tried to teach people to engage in critical reflection on their beliefs and values. Critical reflection involves attempting to give reasons for one's beliefs and values, examining those reasons, and being willing to modify or even abandon convictions that do not withstand rational scrutiny. This task is often very difficult and painful, as Socrates knew all too well. Sometimes his audience would simply decide they had something better to do than listen to him. At other times they would become angry at having their faulty beliefs exposed in public. Many people also felt that Socrates was undermining the state's morals by coaxing people to question their most fundamental beliefs, and he was finally put to death on a charge of "corrupting the youth."

The kind of critical reflection that Socrates sought to stimulate is at the very center of the philosophical enterprise, and it is an essential task for anyone who wants to claim that his or her beliefs are rationally justified. Critical reflection on moral principles is the only way to determine which moral principles you want to use in making moral decisions in your own life. It is an essential component of being a morally responsible person.

In this chapter, we shall consider some conceptual tools you can use in critically reflecting on your moral principles. First, we shall outline a standard conception of the structure of a moral theory. A *moral theory*, which can also be called a *moral philosophy*, is a systematic ordering of moral principles. Second, we shall consider some criteria for judging the adequacy of a moral theory. Finally, we shall discuss some typical problems you may encounter when you apply a moral theory to a particular moral issue and some reasons that critical reflection will not always resolve ethical disagreement.

THE THREE LEVELS OF A MORAL THEORY

How does a person engage in critical reflection about moral principles? By its very nature, critical reflection about moral principles is systematic. In justifying one moral claim, you will find yourself appealing to other moral claims and then to still other moral claims, so that you might finally be forced to reveal your most basic moral commitments in justifying a single ethical claim.

Let us consider a simple illustration. Suppose you and I are sitting at breakfast together reading the newspaper. Having just read a story about the execution of a criminal, I make the statement:

1. "John McRay should not have been executed."

You then ask me for a reason for this judgment, and I say:

2. "John McRay's execution is an instance of capital punishment."

Then I add:

3. "And capital punishment is wrong."

Notice that I began with a moral claim (1), made a conceptual claim about the scope of the concept of capital punishment (2), and then made another moral claim (3).

If I were asked to justify this last moral claim, I might make the following factual claim:

4. "Capital punishment is discriminatory. That is, if you are condemned to death, you are more likely to be executed if you are poor or a member of a racial or ethnic minority group."

We have already seen that moral claims cannot be derived from facts alone; so, to justify the moral claim that capital punishment is wrong, I must add another moral claim:

5. "Discriminatory actions are wrong."

What is the basis of this moral claim? I might justify it by making a factual claim about myself, namely:

6. "I would not want to be discriminated against in this way if I were condemned to death. I would at least want fair treatment."

Even this claim does not justify my judgment that discrimination is wrong without still another moral claim:

7. "In order for a principle of action to be right, I must be willing to have the same principle applied to me in similar circumstances."

If you asked me why I believed this claim, I might say that it is a fundamental belief of mine about how one determines what is right and wrong. So an attempt to defend my beliefs about capital punishment has led me back through increasingly general principles to one of my ultimate moral commitments.

This order of reasoning from more specific moral claims to very general ones gives the outline of any moral theory. A moral theory has three levels. The first level is represented by the first statement in our progression: "John McRay should not have been executed." We shall refer to this kind of statement as a *moral judgment*. Moral judgments give moral evaluations of specific actions or individuals.

The second or intermediate level is represented by statements 3 and 5. We shall refer to these as *moral principles* or sometimes *moral rules*. They make moral evaluations of types or classes of action, such as capital punishment or acts of discrimination. They refer to many actions or individuals, not just one.

The third or highest level is represented by statement 7. It is the level that you eventually arrive at when you trace your moral convictions back to your most basic moral assumptions. We shall refer to this kind of statement as a *moral standard*. A moral standard gives the characteristic that, according to the moral theory, any action or person must have to be morally right. Rather than give evaluations of specific actions or individuals (as moral judgments do) or evaluations of types or classes of action (as moral principles do), moral standards give the *criterion* that *makes* any action or person right.

We shall discuss each of these levels, beginning with the moral judgment.

First Level: Moral Judgments

A moral judgment (MJ), as we have seen, gives a moral evaluation of individual people or actions. It represents the ultimate goal of moral reasoning: the point at which moral deliberation issues in a directive for action. By making the moral judgment "John McRay should not have been executed," I commit myself to a belief that the action was wrong. I would also have committed myself to making some attempt if the appropriate circumstances arise to reverse the execution if it had not already taken place. Because the execution has already occurred, I still commit myself to actions and attitudes that oppose similar executions in the future.

Three types of moral judgment can be made about an action, and a fourth type is sometimes relevant. Some judgments evaluate actions as *morally obligatory*—that is, they say it is right to do the actions and wrong not to do them. If the alternative to the action violates the moral standard, the action itself would be described as morally obligatory: we cannot be morally justified in refraining from performing the action. In most moral theories, the judgment that parents ought to care for their children would designate an obligatory action, because the alternative to the action (that parents need not care for their children) violates the moral standard. If you are an egoist, it is morally obligatory for you to protect your property from theft, because the alternative to the action (failing to protect your property from theft) violates your self-interest.

Other judgments designate *forbidden* or *morally impermissible* actions—those that are wrong to do and right not to do. Actions that violate the moral standard fall into this category. A valid example for most moral philosophies is the judgment that murder is morally impermissible, because it violates most moral standards. For advocates of traditional natural-law moral philosophy, using "artificial" forms of contraception is morally impermissible because it is contrary to the value of procreation.

A third category is judgments that designate *morally permissible* actions. We might also refer to. morally permissible actions as morally neutral actions, because they do not themselves violate the moral standard, nor do the alternatives to them violate the moral standard. Because morally obligatory actions are also permissible, we might refer to this class of actions as *merely* permissible actions, to distinguish actions that are obligatory (and therefore obviously permissible) from those that are merely permissible. However, for convenience we shall call them morally permissible actions.

Permissible actions can be trivial or nontrivial. *Nontrivial permissible* actions are those that have important consequences, whereas *trivial permissible* actions are those that have relatively unimportant consequences. The decision to undergo a risky operation that might prolong your life a few more months and the decision to refuse the operation and die a few months sooner may in some cases be equally permissible by your moral philosophy. For example, as an egoist, you might conclude that the advantage of living a little longer would be balanced by the pain you would suffer even after the operation. If you had no other relevant considerations, both the decision to have the operation and the decision not to have it would be nontrivially morally permissible. On the other hand, the decision to wear blue jeans rather than dress slacks to a party would in most cases be trivially morally permissible.

The final type of judgment is not usually as important as the other three, but it is essential in understanding the moral status of some actions. Sometimes moral philosophers designate an action as *supererogatory*—that is, "above and beyond the call of duty." Supererogatory acts can be acts of either omission or commission. Supererogatory acts of omission are actions that are good not to do but morally permissible to do. When a businessman refrains from demanding immediate and total payment of bills from a company in financial distress, he is doing something morally praiseworthy. However, it is still morally permissible for him to demand payment of a rightful debt. The decision not to demand immediate payment would be a supererogatory act of omission.

Supererogatory acts of commission are actions that are good to do but morally permissible not to do. It can be argued, for example, that a corporation is not morally obligated to perform such meritorious actions as contributing to the arts or helping solve the problems of inner-city unemployment and urban blight. For a corporation to perform these kinds of actions would be supererogatory. Others believe corporations have a moral obligation to do these kinds of things. Therefore, the question of whether these kinds of actions on the part of corporations are obligatory or supererogatory is often morally significant.

Acts of supererogation are commonly thought to be the actions of saints and heroes. However, some acts of kindness and generosity, although they are more than what duty requires and hence supererogatory in the strict sense, are certainly not the actions we associate with saints and heroes. Contributing small change to the Home for Little Wanderers may not be a duty, but neither is it saintly or heroic. Giving one's life in the line of duty may be heroic yet not supererogatory.

Given these considerations, we must distinguish between trivial and nontrivial supererogatory actions. *Nontrivial supererogatory* actions go beyond what is morally required and also involve the elements of risk and self-sacrifice. *Trivial supererogatory* actions do not involve the elements of risk and self-sacrifice. When an engineer risks his career to expose corruption or bad engineering in a public project in which he is not directly involved, he may not be doing something he has a positive duty to do, especially if the problems do not pose a serious threat to life. But he is certainly engaging in a nontrivial supererogatory act. Similarly, a lawyer who risks his professional career and perhaps his life by exposing and prosecuting gangsters engages in action that is risky, highly meritorious, yet not morally required. It is, then, a nontrivial supererogatory action.

Second Level: Moral Principles

The next level of a moral theory consists of general moral principles. A moral principle (MP) is derived from the moral standard, and it serves as the basis for moral judgments. Moral principles apply to a wider area of conduct than moral judgments but not as wide an area as the moral standard.

Let us consider the function of moral principles in the moral philosophy known as egoism. Using her moral standard, the egoist may derive moral principles that denote kinds of goals she should pursue to achieve her self-interest. One such principle might be as follows:

MP: I should preserve my physical health.

Physical health is a necessary prerequisite to achieving one's self-interest, however one's self-interest is defined.

This moral principle might justify specific moral judgments:

MJ: I should start jogging at least three times a week.

A moral theory has many moral principles, whereas it ordinarily has only one moral standard. A useful first step in thinking about the moral principles appropriate to your own moral philosophy is to divide them into principles for personal ethics and principles for social ethics. *Personal ethics* has to do with the relationship of individuals to other individuals. Personal ethics can be further subdivided into *duties to self* and *duties to others*. *Social ethics* has to do with the relationship of individuals to groups and of groups to other groups. Let us consider personal and social ethics in more detail.

Regarding duties to oneself, the question to be asked is, What character traits and personal goals contribute most to the realization of the ideal set forth in the moral standard? The moral principle regarding preserving one's physical health is one answer to this question. An egoist may also find that she needs to develop her capacity to look at things rationally and calmly to determine what will lead to her own self-interest. So the obligation to develop the character trait of rationality follows from the egoistic moral standard.

An advocate of natural law may find that she has an obligation to get as much education as possible to better realize the natural tendency of all humans to know and understand. This obligation may be formulated in terms of a moral principle:

MP: People should develop their rational powers through education.

Duties may be negative as well as positive. As an egoist, I have a duty not to destroy my own health or to sacrifice myself to the welfare of others.

Traditional natural-law theorists believe we have a duty not to violate our own natural tendency to preserve our own lives by committing suicide and not to practice forms of contraception that violate our own procreative function.

Some of the most important duties to others are negative. Most moral theories, for example, imply that in general we have duties not to lie to another person and not to perpetrate theft, fraud, or physical violence on others. Besides the duty not to harm others, however, some moral theories may imply the positive duties of preventing harm to others and even of doing good to others. Finally, family and sexual ethics are an important subcategory of duties to others.

Many important moral issues that all of us face as citizens fall into the category of social ethics rather than personal ethics. It is important, therefore, for any morally sophisticated person to work out ideas—consistent, of course, with his or her general moral philosophy—concerning the proper relationship of societies to one another and to individuals. The most general question to be answered is, What kind of social order is best suited to realize the goals set out in my moral philosophy? We can take two differing approaches to answering this question.

One approach, represented in its extreme form by libertarianism, advocates what one libertarian calls the *minimal state*; that is, the state should limit its functions to protecting citizens from violence, theft, and fraud and providing some mechanism for arbitrating disputes among citizens. Otherwise, individuals should be left alone to pursue their own goals with a minimum of governmental interference. Many egoists are sympathetic to the libertarian way of answering questions about social policy.

The other approach advocates a more active role for the state, one in which the state has a positive responsibility to promote the welfare of individuals or to promote some larger societal goals. Utilitarians for the most part have held that the state should take an active role in implementing policies that lead to the public's general welfare.

Third Level: Moral Standard

A moral standard (MS) is the most fundamental moral principle—the principle that provides the criterion for determining right and wrong for a theory. In the example, because we were reasoning from the moral judgment back to basic principles, the moral standard was the last moral principle stated: "In order for a principle of action to be right, I must be willing to have the same principle applied to me in similar circumstances."

Notice that a moral standard is different from both a moral judgment and a moral rule. A moral standard furnishes a *criterion* for determining what makes an action right or wrong. Rather than referring to an individual action, or even a class of actions, it designates a characteristic that all right actions must have. Consider a highly simplified version of the moral standard of egoism:

MS: Actions are right if and only if they promote the egoist's self-interest.

The criterion for the rightness of an action from the egoistic standpoint is that it must promote the self-interest of the egoist. Similar right-making characteristics can be found in the moral standard of every moral philosophy we shall discuss.

For uniformity in stating the moral standard, our phrasing of each moral standard will begin with the wording "Those actions are right that...," or "Actions are right if and only if...," or some closely analogous formula. The rest of the statement will supply the criterion that right actions must satisfy.

Each moral standard has certain terms that must be defined before the standard can be applied. In the egoistic moral standard, the crucial term is *self-interest*. Without clarification of this concept, the moral standard is useless. I cannot know which actions to pursue and which to avoid if I do not define my self-interest.

Often additional distinctions and definitions must be given before a moral standard can be used. The egoist, for example, must decide whether she will pursue long-term or short-term self-interest. The utilitarian must decide whether to evaluate the utility of every action directly (a position called *act utilitarianism*) or to evaluate only the utility of general moral principles or rules (a position called *rule utilitarianism*). The natural-law theorist must decide how to determine what is "natural" before the ethics of natural law can be applied.

An outline of the three elements of a moral theory will be helpful. The order of the outline, however, will be different from our previous discussion. So far we have taken a "bottom-up" approach, beginning with moral judgments and proceeding through moral rules to a moral standard. This is the order two people would probably follow in an argument over a moral issue. In giving a general outline of a moral theory, however, it is more logical to take a "top-down" approach, starting with the moral standard and descending through moral rules to moral judgments. From the top-down standpoint, a moral theory has the following form:

I. Moral Standard
    A. Definitions of crucial terms
    B. Other relevant distinctions and principles
II. Moral rules
    A. Personal ethics
        1. Duties to self
        2. Duties to others
    B. Social ethics
III. Moral Judgments
    A. Is the action morally obligatory?
    B. Is the action morally permissible?
    C. Is the action morally impermissible?
    D. Is the action supererogatory?

I will follow this outline in presenting the four moral theories treated in this book—namely, the ethics of self-interest, the ethics of natural law, the ethics of utilitarianism, and the ethics of respect for persons.

I will furnish a "checklist" that will help you apply the moral theory to specific cases, and I will follow this checklist in discussing the cases presented. This organization should enable you to apply the theory to other moral problems as they arise in class or in your own experience.

FOUR CRITERIA FOR EVALUATING A MORAL THEORY

Having looked at the structure of a moral theory, we are now ready to consider a set of concepts necessary to evaluate your moral beliefs—namely, criteria for evaluating a moral theory. Moral philosophers do not have an agreed-on set of standards for judging a moral theory. However, consistency is a generally accepted standard for evaluating any theory, so it seems appropriate to apply it to a moral theory as well. The other three criteria we shall employ seem especially appropriate for a moral theory. They are the adequacy of the justification of the moral standard, agreement with your prior moral beliefs, and usefulness in resolving moral disagreements.

These four criteria fall into different categories. The criterion of consistency might be called a "formal" criterion, because it has to do with the logical consistency of the moral theory. The second criterion might be described as a "rational" criterion, because it concerns the rational justification of the moral standard. The third criterion might be referred to as a "common-sense" criterion, because it compares the moral judgments generated by the moral theory with our "common-sense" moral judgments (that is, those we would make independently of the theory). The fourth criterion might be called a "pragmatic" criterion, because it asks about the practical usefulness of the theory in resolving moral disagreements.

Criterion 1: Consistency—Is the Theory Coherent?

We can usually agree that any rationally acceptable theory should be consistent, but consistency can mean many different things. In the narrowest sense, a theory is inconsistent if it contains two statements that are logically incompatible. Suppose a theory regarding the origin of a disease contains both the statement "The disease is not caused by a virus" and the statement "The disease is caused by a virus." How could a disease both be caused by a virus and not be caused by a virus? In fact, the theory would be impossible to test, because evidence that the disease is caused by a virus and evidence that it is not would be compatible with the theory.

The same thing would be true of an ethical theory. Suppose we had an ethical theory with two moral standards of the following types:

MS1: An action is right if it leads to one's own self-interest.

MS2: An action is not right if it leads to one's own self-interest.

Not only would an ethical theory of this type be inconsistent at the third level, the level of the moral standard, but these incompatible moral standards would produce incompatible moral principles and judgments as well. The incompatible moral judgments would in turn give different directives to action. So inconsistency is not only a theoretical defect but also a practical defect, for it produces mixed signals as to how we should live.

Although some people may have moral beliefs that are inconsistent in this radical sense, none of the moral theories we shall consider does. The inconsistencies that we are most apt to find in a major moral theory are more subtle. We shall use the term *inconsistency* to refer to any type of incoherence within a moral theory or an incoherence between a theory and the behavior of the person who advocates the theory.

Here is a type of inconsistency that many moral philosophers believe appears in certain forms of ethical egoism. To be ethically acceptable, ethical egoists must be impartial. That is, they must admit that each person has an equal right to pursue her self-interest. As an egoist, then, I must advocate that others follow their self-interest, just as I follow mine. But in pursuing their interests, others can harm me. Thus, in advocating that others pursue their interests, I may be acting contrary to my own.

An inconsistency or incoherence within a moral theory (an inconsistency in theory) or between moral theory and practice (an inconsistency in an overall moral position) does not necessarily mean that the moral theory should be abandoned. Perhaps no moral position is fully consistent. But the concept of consistency is an integral part of the concept of rationality itself, and we must regard an inconsistency as a significant weakness in a moral theory.

Criterion 2: Justification—How Well Can the Moral Standard Be Justified?

Every moral theorist attempts to give a rational justification for accepting his or her moral standard. We have already discussed two of the most popular ways of defending a moral standard: by an appeal to religion or by an appeal to moral intuitions. However, many other ways to justify accepting a moral standard are possible.

The method of defending a moral standard must be fundamentally different from the method of defending moral rules or moral judgments within a theory. Moral rules and moral judgments can be defended by reference to the moral standard, but the moral standard cannot be defended by referring to a higher moral standard. Thus, a strict deductive proof of a moral standard is impossible. At best, a moral philosopher can show reasons why accepting one moral standard rather than another is plausible. We shall consider some of these arguments when we analyze each of the four theories.

Criterion 3: Plausibility—Does the Moral Theory Produce Moral Judgments That Agree with Our Prior Moral Beliefs?

One way to evaluate a moral theory is to work out its implications for particular moral issues and then compare these implications with our most strongly held moral beliefs. For example, consider a moral theory such as natural law, which holds that it is always wrong to take innocent human life directly. This principle implies that administering an injection to end the life of a dying cancer patient who requests to be put out of his misery is immoral. But you may believe that such an action is not immoral and is in fact an act of mercy. If so, a conflict exists between natural-law moral theory and your own prior moral beliefs.

In the face of a conflict between natural law and your prior moral beliefs about mercy killing, you have four options: (1) give up your belief that mercy killing is sometimes morally permissible, (2) reject natural-law moral theory altogether, (3) try to show that natural-law moral theory does not really condemn mercy killing, or (4) admit that in this instance your moral theory and moral beliefs conflict. If you are strongly committed to natural-law moral theory (perhaps because you are a conservative Roman Catholic), you may be most attracted to the first and third options. If you have strong reasons to question natural-law moral theory, you may choose the second option. The fourth option involves an admission that your overall moral position is inconsistent.

Keep in mind that agreement with your prior moral beliefs is not an absolute test of a theory's validity. If a moral theory conflicts with your prior moral beliefs, it may be your moral beliefs that are wrong rather than the theory. But a conflict of this nature should at least alert you that something is wrong.

Criterion 4: Usefulness—Is the Theory Useful in Resolving Moral Disagreements?

Moral theories are of little practical use if they cannot help us resolve moral problems, either within our own thinking or between us and others. A moral theory can fail to help us achieve this goal in several ways. We shall consider two general problems here and other problems in the context of evaluating particular theories.

One way in which moral theories can be deficient in their ability to resolve moral problems is that applying the principles derived from the theory may sometimes be difficult or controversial. A moral theory may show that bribery is wrong, but it may not determine whether paying a foreign official the customary $100 with an application to do business in his country is really a bribe.

Another way in which moral theories can fail to be useful is by providing conflicting directives, without showing how to resolve the conflict. For example, a moral theory may require us to keep promises and help those in distress. But it may not be easy to determine from the theory whether we should keep our promise to take a family member to a long-awaited social event or help a friend in emotional distress.

We shall see that other types of problems also keep a theory from being as useful as it might otherwise be, but in the next section we shall offer a more detailed consideration of these two problems in applying moral theories.

CONCEPT SUMMARY

To evaluate moral principles and moral judgments, we must first place them in the context of a larger theory and then evaluate the theory. A moral theory has three levels. First, a moral standard is the basic criterion for determining right and wrong. Second, a moral principle marks a class of actions that is right or wrong. Moral principles give direction for the relationship of individuals to other individuals (personal ethics) and the relationship of individuals to groups or groups to other groups (social ethics). Finally, a moral judgment is a moral evaluation of particular actions or persons. Moral judgments can evaluate actions as obligatory, permissible, impermissible, or supererogatory.

The four criteria for evaluating a moral theory are (1) consistency, (2) the adequacy of the justification of the moral standard, (3) agreement with prior moral beliefs, and (4) usefulness in resolving moral conflict. These criteria will be applied to each of the four moral philosophies that we shall consider.

PROBLEMS IN APPLYING
MORAL PRINCIPLES

The foregoing presentation of the structure and evaluation of moral theories might suggest that moral theories can provide a simple, straightforward way of arriving at moral judgments. "Just derive moral principles from the moral standard and then apply the principles to particular situations," you might be tempted to say. Unfortunately, deriving moral principles from moral standards is not always easy. Applying moral principles to specific circumstances to yield moral judgments can be even more problematic. Most of the problems in applying moral principles fall into two groups. I shall refer to the first group of problems as relevance problems and the second group as conflict problems.[3]

---

[3] For a clear description of these two kinds of problems, see James D. Wallace, *Moral Relevance and Moral Conflict* (Ithaca, NY: Cornell University Press, 1988). See especially the introduction and the first chapter.

Relevance Problems

A relevance problem occurs when we do not know whether a moral principle is relevant to a particular situation. Usually a relevance problem can be traced to a conceptual issue. You will recall that a conceptual issue has to do with (1) the meaning of a concept or (2) its application to a particular situation. Sometimes we may not be sure how a concept such as "bribery" or "confidentiality" should be defined. At other times, we do not know what the appropriate application of a concept should be in a borderline situation.

In applying moral principles, therefore, you will find some circumstances in which they clearly apply and borderline circumstances in which their application is controversial. The clear cases in which the principle does apply we may call *paradigm cases*. The borderline cases in which application of the principle is controversial or ambiguous we may call *problematic cases*. Problematic cases give rise to *relevance problems*.

Consider the following example.[4] Most of us would agree to a moral principle or rule that says, "People should return or replace borrowed items." If we borrow a friend's car for the evening, we expect to return it the next day or as soon as possible. But what about "borrowing" a match? Does the principle that we should return or replace borrowed items apply here? Using quotation marks around the word "borrow" indicates that we may have come to an example where applying the concept of "borrowing" becomes problematic.

We could arrange examples of returning borrowed items to show the transition from paradigm cases in which the principle applies, through borderline or problematic cases, to cases in which the principle does not apply:

MP: "People should return or replace borrowed items."

1. Returning a borrowed car
2. Returning a borrowed book
3. Returning $10 that was borrowed
4. Returning borrowed money for a Coke
5. Returning a borrowed pencil
6. Returning three sheets of borrowed paper
7. Returning a borrowed match

You may find that the principle clearly applies to the first three examples, and you may also have little trouble deciding that the principle clearly does not apply to examples 6 and 7. But examples 4 and 5 may be troublesome. Should we consider these examples of borrowing, or should they be considered examples of gifts?

---

[4] For the suggestion of this example, which has been considerably modified and expanded, see Albert R. Jonsen and Stephen Toulmin, *The Abuse of Casuistry* (Berkeley: University of California Press, 1988), p. 324. Jonsen and Toulmin make a distinction similar to Wallace's distinction between relevance and conflict problems.

The most obvious thing to say is that the question whether the principle about returning a borrowed item applies is answered by determining the item's worth. This may well be the most important consideration, for it points to an obvious similarity between examples 1 through 3 and examples 6 and 7. The first three examples concern objects whose worth most of us would consider substantial, whereas the last two examples concern items that most of us would probably consider to be of trivial value. The criterion of monetary value, however, does not by itself settle the issue of where we should draw the line, any more than the moral principle itself does. Exactly how much must an item be worth before it is subject to the rule that borrowed items should be returned or replaced?

To make matters more complicated, monetary worth is not necessarily the only consideration at issue in this example. How well I know the person may be a relevant consideration. Or whether we regularly borrow from each other may be important. Or my friend may know that I have a lot more money than he does, so we may have an implicit understanding that small amounts of cash can be regularly borrowed without any need to return it. Or allowing a friend to borrow money without returning it may be a subtle way of repaying him for the help he gives me on homework.

Now let us consider a more morally significant example. In 1977, the U.S. Congress passed the Foreign Corrupt Practices Act (FCPA). The new law made it illegal for U.S. businesspersons and other citizens to "corruptly" pay, or authorize the payment, of money or anything of value to foreign government officials and foreign political parties. It was passed during the Carter administration as a result of the discovery that nearly 400 American companies had paid approximately $300 million to foreign officials for business favors. For example, Lockheed had paid $22 million to foreign politicians over five years to secure aircraft contracts, and Gulf Oil Corporation had made secret payments of $4 million to foreign politicians over the same period.

The FCPA was enacted, among other reasons, because of the widespread conviction that bribery is immoral. But it also raises the conceptual problem of the proper scope of the concept of bribery. Consider the following moral principle, with the accompanying set of examples:

MP: "It is wrong to pay or accept bribes."

1. Paying money to foreign government officials to obtain a contract from a foreign government

2. Paying money to foreign government officials so that the government will at least consider a product for possible purchase

3. Paying money to expedite the processing of an application to do business in a foreign country

4. Paying money to foreign government officials to ensure that your property will not be mysteriously destroyed by "vandals"

The first example is clearly a bribe, if we think of a bribe as paying money to a person or group for special considerations that are contrary to their role. The role of the purchasing officer is to select the best product for his government. The bribe leads the official to violate this requirement.

The second example is more problematic. Unlike paradigm cases of bribery, the payment in this case does not induce the foreign official to act contrary to his role. In fact, the foreign official should make his selection from all available products, so that he should consider your product anyhow. A second difference from paradigm cases of bribery is that the person who makes the payment does so to avoid an injustice that would otherwise accrue to himself and his company. Perhaps this payment should be called extortion rather than a bribe. Nevertheless, it has this feature in common with bribery: it gives the person who can afford to pay the fee an advantage over the person who cannot afford to pay it.

The third example usually involves small amounts of "grease money" and probably should not be considered bribery. In processing an application to do business efficiently, the government official is only doing what she should do anyhow. Furthermore, the amount of money involved would be so small that ordinarily one's competitors could afford to pay it too.

The fourth example would usually be considered an example of extortion or paying "protection money" rather than paying a bribe, because it is paying a foreign official for what he should do anyhow. Furthermore, the payment is to avoid a harm rather than to obtain a benefit. If we apply the moral principle to these examples, and if we assume that extortion payments are not wrong, we can conclude that the first action is wrong, but the other three are not. These moral judgments are possible only after we have settled the conceptual problem about the meaning and scope of the concept of bribery.

Many other examples of relevance problems are encountered in applying a moral theory. Our moral theory may generate a moral principle such as "Deception is wrong." We may still wonder whether an advertisement for a children's cereal that portrays a muscular man eating the cereal is deceptive to children, because children may be persuaded that eating the cereal will ensure that they will grow up to be strong and healthy. Or we may agree that our theory justifies the moral principle "Murder is wrong" but disagree whether euthanasia should be counted as murder. Or we may have a moral principle that condemns suicide but wonder whether the action of Captain Oates described in the first chapter should be considered suicide.

Now we can summarize several important points about relevance problems. First, relevance problems may not be resolvable by appeal to moral principles or even the moral standard. Although the moral standard and the derivative moral principles may give clear direction in the central or paradigm cases, they may not give direction in controversial cases. The relevance problem may also not be resolvable by making reference to a definition of the terms that is constructed independently of the particular context in which the conceptual problem appears. The "vertical" reasoning from moral standards, through moral principles, to moral judgments that apply in clear or paradigm cases, must be supplemented by "horizontal" reasoning that relies on analysis of similarities and differences between paradigmatic and problematic cases. We must determine when the similarities and differences justify placing an example under a particular concept and when they do not. Reasoning by analogy is thus an important tool in applying moral principles to ambiguous cases.

Second, the more ambiguous the case, the more we must know about the particular circumstances of the case to determine whether the case falls under a given concept. Whether money for a Coke should be returned may be decidable only with reference to a particular person and his or her relationship to the person who borrowed the money. Whether a payment of money is a bribe may depend on the extent to which the person accepting the money grants special favors to the person who pays the money.

Third, sometimes even the similarities and differences between particular cases are insufficient to make a convincing case for one decision rather than another. In such cases, it is often necessary to come to a general agreement on the proper scope of a concept. For example, in deciding when acceptance by a purchasing agent of gifts and amenities from vendors constitutes accepting a bribe, a company may have to stipulate that accepting a pen with the company's name on it is permissible but accepting a leather attaché case is not.

Conflict Problems

Sometimes we may find that more than one moral principle is relevant to a particular situation and that we can come up with different moral judgments, depending on which principle we think has priority. Then we have a *conflict problem*—that is, a situation in which two or more apparently conflicting moral principles are relevant.

Sometimes it is clear which of two relevant and conflicting moral principles should have priority. Suppose I promise to meet you for dinner at 6:00 P.M. Driving to your house, I pass two cars that have been in an accident. One of the victims signals for help. The police and ambulance have not yet arrived, and one of the other victims appears to have some injuries. I have some emergency medical training and might be able to help; I might even be able to save someone's life. If I do respond, however, I will be late for dinner with you. I have two conflicting moral obligations and cannot fulfill both. What should I do? Assisting someone in distress and possibly saving a life takes priority over being on time for a dinner appointment, so the resolution of this conflict is simple.

Some situations, however, are not as easily resolved. In a well-known incident from World War II, the French existentialist philosopher Jean-Paul Sartre tells of a young man who came to him for advice, asking whether he should stay with his aging mother or join the French Resistance. If he left his mother, she would probably die; on the other hand, he believed he had an obligation to participate in the struggle to free France. What should he do?[5]

Philosophers have called this kind of conflict situation a *moral dilemma*. Literature furnishes many examples of moral dilemmas. In Euripides' play, *Iphigenia in Aulis*, Agamemnon is faced with the dilemma of having to sacrifice his daughter, Iphigenia, to the goddess Artemis, to persuade her to grant the Greek ships a favoring wind on their way to conquer Troy, or losing the war. His obligations to his daughter and his soldiers are on a collision course. In William Styron's *Sophie's Choice*, Sophie is ordered by a Nazi guard to shoot one of her children, or else he will kill both of them. Finally, in E. M. Forster's *Two Cheers for Democracy*, a disagreement arises over whether it is worse to betray a friend or one's country.

We have at least two ways of deciding issues when we are faced with a situation in which both of two equally important and incompatible principles appear to conflict.

First, we may be able to find a creative "middle way" between the two conflicting principles. In his struggle for civil rights for blacks, Martin Luther King found such a creative middle way in his doctrine of nonviolent resistance. King faced a choice between his obligation to obey the law and his obligation to promote racial justice. On the one hand, he respected the laws of the United States and did not wish to destroy its legal system. On the other hand, he wanted to promote the cause of racial justice, and he believed he could not do so without breaking the law. His escape from this dilemma involved taking the path of nonviolent civil disobedience. Although he did break the law in some of his activities, he did so in a nonviolent way that involved a willingness to take the legal consequences of his actions.

In another example, which we mentioned earlier, Jeffrey Fadiman suggests a creative middle way may be available to American businesspersons facing the dilemma of whether to make payments to foreign nationals. If the payments are not made, valuable business opportunities may be lost. But if the payments are made, U.S. businesspersons may be doing something that is illegal or that violates their own conscience. Instead of yielding to either of these unattractive alternatives, Fadiman proposes the adoption of a "donation strategy." Rather than giving money or gifts to individuals, Fadiman suggests making donations to the community. A corporation might construct a hospital, for example, or it might offer jobs. In the 1970s, Fadiman points out, Coca-Cola hired hundreds of Egyptians to plant orange trees on thousands of acres of desert, thereby creating more goodwill than would have been generated by bribes made to individuals. In 1983, the British gained goodwill by assembling thousands of dollars worth of tools and vehicle parts and training Tanzanians to service the vehicles. This action enabled the Tanzanians to continue

---

[5] J.-P. Sartre, "Existentialism Is a Humanism," in *Existentialism from Dostoyevsky to Sartre*, ed. Walter Kaufmann (Cleveland, OH: World, 1956), pp. 295–296.

patrolling their wild-game preserves, an activity that had almost stopped because of the weakened Tanzanian economy. The British took this step instead of making a cash donation, which might well have been interpreted as a bribe.[6]

Second, resolving moral dilemmas can sometimes be accomplished by appealing to values that might not otherwise be relevant. Philosopher Isaac Levi provides an example of this kind of conflict resolution involving professional rather than strictly moral considerations.[7] According to a slightly modified version of Levi's example, an office manager must choose between two candidates for a secretarial position. She wants to select the person who is the best typist and the best stenographer, but, unfortunately, no single person has the highest rating on both the stenographer test and the typing test. John has 94 on the stenographer test and 90 on the typing test, whereas James has 90 on the stenographer test and 94 on the typing test. How does she decide what to do?

One option is to appeal to values that she might otherwise consider inadmissible. For example, although she generally is a staunch opponent of reverse discrimination, in this case she considers it admissible to hire John (who is black) rather than James (who is white). Or, if both candidates are members of minority groups, she might consider another value that she would ordinarily consider inadmissible—namely, the fact that James is much more handsome than John. Similarly, the debate described by E. M. Forster over loyalty to one's friends versus loyalty to one's country may be decided on the basis of personal ideals rather than moral principles. Does one want to be the kind of person who is loyal to friends at all cost or who takes loyalty to one's country as supreme?

Room for Disagreement

The first four chapters have shown that people who attempt to follow the Socratic ideal of critical reflection may sometimes disagree over moral issues for a number of reasons. People may disagree over the facts, moral standards, moral principles, and conceptual issues. We have just seen that relevance and conflict problems can also lead to different moral judgments.

Given these possible sources of moral disagreement, people who use their most careful critical reflection may sometimes come to different moral judgments, especially in borderline cases. You may sometimes come to different conclusions than I do, even when you assume the same moral principles. In reading my discussions of cases in the following chapters, you should keep this in mind. When you do disagree, you should be able, however, to isolate the precise nature of your disagreement, using the concepts we have developed so far.

---

[6] Jeffrey A. Fadiman, "A Traveler's Guide to Gifts and Bribes," *Harvard Business Review* (July–August 1986); excerpts reprinted in William H. Shaw and Vincent Barry, *Moral Issues in Business*, 4th ed. (Belmont, CA: Wadsworth, 1989) pp. 328–337.

[7] Isaac Levi, *Hard Choices* (Cambridge: Cambridge University Press, 1986), pp. 28–29.

CONCEPT SUMMARY

Two types of problems in applying moral principles are relevance problems and conflict problems. Relevance problems arise when it is unclear whether a moral principle applies in a borderline case. In resolving relevance problems, we may often find it helpful to reason from clear or paradigm cases to problematic or borderline cases by observing similarities and differences. Also, the more ambiguous the case, the more we need to know about the particular circumstances. Finally, sometimes settling where the line is drawn is impossible except by stipulation and general agreement.

Conflict problems arise in situations where there are two or more relevant moral demands, both of which cannot be complied with in a particular situation. Sometimes we can find a creative "middle way" that does some justice to both demands. Failing this, we may be justified in appealing to considerations, such as personal interests and ideals, that would not otherwise be relevant.

People who are equally committed to critical reflection on moral issues may sometimes disagree in their moral judgments. Using the concepts developed in the first four chapters, they should be able to isolate the nature of their disagreements.

5

The Ethics of Egoism

Bryan Springer has a high-paying summer job as a forklift operator, which enables him to attend college without having to take out any student loans. He is now staring at a fifty-gallon drum filled with used machine coolant.

Just moments ago, Bryan's supervisor, Max Morrison, told him to dump half of the used coolant down the drain. Bryan knows the coolant is toxic, and he has already mentioned this to Max. But Max was not swayed. He insisted, "The toxins settle at the bottom of the drum. If you pour out half and dilute it with tap water while you're pouring it, there's no problem."

Bryan was not convinced, adding that Max's solution to the problem was against the law. But Max responded even more angrily:

> You aren't one of those "environmentalists," are you? You college guys spend too much of your time in the ivory tower. It's time to get real—and get on with the job. You know, you're very lucky to have a good-paying job like this, kid. In three months you'll be back in your cozy college. Meanwhile, how many other college kids do you think there are out there wondering if they'll be able to afford to go back—kids who'd give their eye teeth to be where you are right now?

Max then left, fully expecting Bryan to dump the used coolant. Bryan knows he is in danger of losing his job and jeopardizing his chances of returning to college in the fall. He wonders what he should do.[1]

---

[1] This case is adapted from Michael S. Pritchard, ed., *Teaching Engineering Ethics: A Case Study Approach*, June 1992, National Science Foundation Grant No. DIR 8820837. The case and accompanying commentaries are on pp. 162–171.

THE PRIMACY OF SELF INTEREST

The Moral Standard

We could say that this case illustrates a conflict between Bryan's desire to promote his own interests and his desire to act in a morally responsible way. But things may not be that simple. Could it be that Bryan's moral obligation *is* just to look out for his own interests? If this is the case, and if obeying Max promotes his own interests, then Bryan should dump the coolant.

Many people believe that their actions are and should be governed by considerations of their own interests, welfare, well-being or good—terms that we shall use interchangeably, "I should do what is best for Number One," they might say. We could formulate this into the following moral standard: "Those actions are right that contribute to my interests." Unfortunately, this formulation raises a number of problems. Let us look at some of them.

First, this formulation does not provide a method for deciding which action is right when several alternative actions would each contribute to my good or well-being. Suppose one act provides ten units of good for me and another provides fifty units of good; both acts would be right by the moral standard. To consider another possibility, suppose actions A, B, and C each contribute ten units of good for me, and no action contributes more than ten units of good. In this case, actions A, B, and C should be equally desirable. Thus, an act cannot be right simply because it promotes my well-being. The course of action to be followed should be the one that produces the most good for me, or at least as much good as any alternative action.

Second, this moral standard does not take account of situations in which no available action contributes in a positive way to my good. If I am faced with several alternatives, all of which will detract from my well-being, the proper course of action is the one that will diminish my well-being the least. The moral standard should reflect this requirement.

Third, it does not have the characteristic of impartiality that we attributed to ethical statements in Chapter 1. If I should look after my well-being, why should you not look after yours? What makes me so special? Am I any more human or any more a moral agent than others? If ethics requires that I be able to give reasons for my moral beliefs, and if I can give no reason why my well-being should be respected more than others', then I must recognize the equal right of others to pursue their well-being, just as I pursue mine. The moral standard should accord everyone an equal right to pursue his or her own well-being.

Fourth, this formulation does not take account of the fact that some egoists believe that their self-interest is most effectively promoted when they follow general rules rather than evaluate every action directly by how much it promotes the egoist's interests. To make this idea clearer, egoists sometimes distinguish between act egoism and rule egoism. *Act egoism* specifies that I should evaluate every act in accordance with whether it promotes my well-being. This is the type of egoism formulated in our preliminary version of the moral standard. *Rule egoism,* by contrast, states that I should act in accordance with those rules that are themselves justified because they promote my self-interest. Rather than evaluate her actions directly by asking whether they promote her self-interest, the rule egoist evaluates her actions by asking whether they conform to certain rules. We are not yet in a position to decide what these rules should be, but they must be rules that promote the egoist's self-interest.

In accordance with these four considerations, we can formulate the moral standard of egoism in the following way:

> MS: Those actions (or moral rules) are right for a person if and only if they promote the person's self-interest at least as much as any alternative action (or moral rule) or if they harm their self-interest the least or as little as any alternative action (or moral rule).

Human Nature and Self-Interest

We have still not answered one of the most important questions that an egoistic moral standard raises: How should we define "self-interest"?

Let us begin by saying that a person's self-interest is in promoting his well-being. Although I could say that my well-being is whatever I think it is at the moment, I will probably decide that what is important is my *considered* well-being. That is, my well-being is determined by what I think is most important, after weighing the matter carefully. I must also decide whether I want to evaluate my actions in terms of their long- or short-range consequences for my well-being. Most egoists conclude that they want to promote the fullest realization of their well-being over a lifetime.

How, then, does an egoist determine his or her well-being or self-interest? Most egoists fall into two groups in answering this question, depending on their accounts of human nature.

One representative account of human nature was given by the Englishman Thomas Hobbes (1588–1679), one of the most important philosophical egoists. According to Hobbes scholar Gregory Kavka, Hobbes's account of human nature contains six elements: (1) people are primarily concerned with their own well-being and act accordingly; (2) people want to avoid death and act accordingly; (3) people are concerned with what others think of them (reputation) and act accordingly; (4) people care about their future, as well as their present well-being, and act accordingly; (5) satisfaction of one person's desires often conflicts with another person's desire satisfaction, owing to such factors as material scarcity and competing claims to the same objects; and (6) people are roughly equal in their intellectual and physical abilities.[2]

It is easy to see what account of human well-being follows from this picture of human nature. Well-being consists of survival, physical safety, and

---

[2] Gregory S. Kavka, *Hobbesian Moral and Political Theory* (Princeton, NJ: Princeton University Press, 1986), pp. 33–34.

the attainment of material goods and social status for oneself, in a highly competitive environment.

Another conception of human nature has its origins in Greek thought and is especially associated with Aristotle (384–322 B.C.). Although some passages in Aristotle's writings might suggest that he is a strict egoist, in that he believes one should always act so as to maximize one's own well-being, most scholars do not believe he should be so interpreted.[3] Nevertheless, his primary focus is on pursuing one's own good. We can summarize Aristotle's view of human nature in the following way: (1) Humans seek happiness or well-being; (2) like other things in nature, humans have a characteristic function; (3) the characteristic function of humans is their capacity for rational thought; (4) humans achieve well-being by exercising their distinctive human capacity for rational thought; (5) humans are "political animals," as Aristotle put it, in that they can most effectively exercise their characteristic human capacities in an organized society; and (6) humans seek well-being over a lifetime, not just for a short period of time.[4]

This account of human nature yields a conception of human well-being as the realization or actualization over a lifetime of our characteristically human abilities, which are connected with human rationality. Although there is some dispute about what Aristotle believed, we need not interpret him as holding that well-being is exclusively connected with intellectual activity. Rather, he probably holds that our well-being consists in the development of all of our capacities (physical, intellectual, emotional, and so forth) under the organizing power of reason.[5] Thus, well-being is self-actualization; it is the development of our distinctively human capacities in a way that is proper for us as members of the human species.

Philosopher David Norton formulates the chief moral imperative of an Aristotelian self-actualization ethics in this way: "it is every person's primary responsibility first to discover the daimon [the principle of self-actualization] within him and thereafter to live in accordance with it."[6] Like Aristotle, Norton believes that self-actualization is a project for a lifetime, usually involving several developmental stages that we will discuss later.

Despite the differences in the Hobbesian and Aristotelian accounts of well-being, two observations are worth making. First, both accounts agree that a person's primary aim should be to promote her own well-being, however it is defined. Second, the two accounts are complementary of one

---

3 For a discussion of passages in which Aristotle seems to endorse egoism, see Richard Kraut, *Aristotle on the Human Good* (Princeton, NJ: Princeton University Press, 1989), p. 115ff. Kraut nevertheless believes that Aristotle makes other claims that are incompatible with strict egoism, such as his beliefs that some people should devote themselves to politics even though the life of philosophy is more rewarding, that a friend acts for the sake of the other friend, and that governing well is not just governing to promote one's own interests. See Kraut, pp. 11, 78–86, and 103–119.

4 For documentation of this summary, see ibid. See also J. L. Ackrill, "Aristotle on Eudaimonia," in *Essays on Aristotle's Ethics*, ed. Amelie O. Rorty (Berkeley: University of California Press, 1980), pp. 15–33.

5 This view generally follows Ackrill's "inclusivist" interpretation of Aristotle's understanding of well-being. See Rorty, *Essays on Aristotle's Ethics*, pp. 15–33.

6 David L. Norton, *Personal Destinies* (Princeton, NJ: Princeton University Press, 1976), p. 16.

another to some extent. The Hobbesian account, with its focus on survival and physical well-being, points to the conditions necessary for any type of self-actualization. If you are dead or do not have the bare necessities of life, you are not going to be able to pursue the type of self-actualization that Aristotle and Norton advocate. Thus, the Hobbesian account points out the conditions necessary for pursuit of one's well-being, however it is defined. The versions of Aristotle and Norton give a more developed interpretation of the nature of human well-being.

IS EGOISM SELF-LIMITING?

We have seen that the impartial standpoint characteristic of genuine ethical statements forces the egoist to recognize that everyone has an equal right to pursue their own self-interest. Whether or not others have this right, Thomas Hobbes and most other egoists believe that people will pursue their self-interest, at least most of the time. As Hobbes also recognizes, however, my pursuit of my interests or well-being can conflict with your pursuit of yours. The fact that egoism appears to justify pursuit of self-interest even when it harms others is, in fact, one of the chief objections to it.

In response to this objection, many egoists argue that limitations on actions that harm others can be justified by the principles of egoism itself. In other words, egoism is self-limiting. Hobbes develops the self-limiting aspect of egoism in the following way. When egoists pursue their interests without restraint, the result is an intolerable state of turmoil and conflict. Whenever it suits my interests and I believe I can get away with it, I will steal and commit violent acts against you, and you will behave the same way toward me. Many of the products of civilized society will be absent, and everyone will live in a state of fear.

In a famous passage, Hobbes describes this miserable condition of war of everyone against everyone else, which he calls the "state of nature":

> In such condition, there is no place for industry; because the fruit thereof
> is uncertain: and consequently no culture of the earth; no
> navigation,…no knowledge of the face of the earth; no account of time;
> no arts; no letters; no society; and which is worst of all, continual fear,
> and danger of violent death; and the life of man, solitary, poor, nasty
> brutish, and short.[7]

Here is what we might call the *paradox of egoism*: unrestricted pursuit of self-interest produces a state of affairs contrary to the egoist's self-interest. It

---

[7] Thomas Hobbes, *Leviathan*, Chap. 13. Many modern egoists present this problem of unrestricted egoism in terms of the so called "prisoner's dilemma." For a discussion of this dilemma and the larger issue of cooperation among egoists, see Robert Axelrod, *The Evolution of Cooperation* (New York: Basic Books, 1984).

would be more desirable for everyone to limit their pursuit of self-interest in certain ways (particularly with respect to the use of violence, theft, and fraud), provided others limit themselves in similar ways. If egoists could agree on certain rules that everyone would follow, the individual egoist would be better off. These rules would limit what each egoist can do, even in the pursuit of self-interest.

Rule egoism is thus the antidote to the paradox of egoism. To promote mutual self-interest, egoists must agree on such rules as "Do not commit murder," "Do not steal," "Do not commit fraud," and many others that make a peaceful, orderly society possible. Within the framework of these rules, of course, the egoist is free to pursue her own interests, in accordance with the perspective of act egoism. Thus, I can pursue my own interests as long as I do not violate the rules that I and other egoists have agreed to accept. Act egoism operates within a framework provided by rule egoism.

This answer to the paradox of egoism has its own limits, however. If I could get others to forswear violence and still be able to use violence myself, I would be ahead in the Hobbesian war of all against all. If a little dishonesty is the only way to get something that is enormously important to my self-realization, it might seem like an acceptable trade-off.

The Aristotelian ethics of self-realization might seem to provide a better answer to the paradox of egoism. Self-actualization ethicists argue that self-realization involves the development of one's character, and character cannot be developed by violence, theft, fraud, and other actions that harm others. Thus, self-realization by means of such actions is self-defeating. However, this answer depends on a view of human nature, according to which "true" self-realization is incompatible with such actions as violence, theft, and fraud. In Chapter 6, we shall consider some of the issues associated with an ethics based on a philosophy of human nature.

CHECKLIST FOR APPLYING ACT EGOISM

____ 1. Determine the alternative actions that are possible in the situation and their consequences.

____ 2. Choose the action that promotes the egoist's self-interest at least as much as any alternative action or harms the egoist's self-interest the least (or as little as any alternative action).

       a. An action that promotes the egoist's self-interest more than any alternative action or harms it the least is morally obligatory.

       b. An action that promotes the egoist's self-interest less than an alternative action or harms it more than an alternative action is morally impermissible.

       c. If several actions equally promote the egoist's self-interest or equally harm the egoist's self-interest, they are all morally permissible.

CHECKLIST FOR APPLYING RULE EGOISM

____ 1. Determine the alternative actions that are possible in the situation.

____ 2. Determine the rule that is justified by egoism and relevant to the alternative actions.

____ 3. Evaluate the action in the following way:

    a. An action that is more consistent with the relevant rule than any alternative possible action is morally obligatory.

    b. An action that is less consistent with the relevant rule than an alternative action is morally impermissible.

    c. Actions that are equally consistent with the relevant rule are all morally permissible.

CONCEPT SUMMARY

Egoists hold that everyone should pursue their own interests, welfare, well-being, or good. An adequate formulation of ethical egoism, however, must take account of four considerations. First, sometimes several actions contribute equally to one's well-being. Second, sometimes no actions contribute in a positive way to one's well-being. Third, others have an equal right to pursue their well-being. Fourth, there is an important distinction between act egoism and rule egoism.

Philosophers who emphasize promoting one's own self-interest fall into two broad classes. Some philosophers, such as Thomas Hobbes, define self-interest in terms of survival, physical safety, and attainment of material goods. Others, such as Aristotle, define it in terms of self-actualization.

Most egoists believe that a person's self-interest can best be promoted by living in a society in which everyone agrees to rules that limit behavior that harms others, but the justification of these limits, from the standpoint of egoism, is controversial.

THE PERSONAL AND
SOCIAL ETHICS OF EGOISM

Duties to Self

As an egoist, the only direct obligations I have are to myself. All my moral obligations to others must be justified because they promote my own good, either directly or indirectly. After giving a considered answer to the question of what my well-being is and deciding whether I want to aim for its short- or long-term realization, I must come up with a strategy for achieving my well-being. What kind of lifestyle will I want to adopt? How much education do I need? What kinds of friendships should I cultivate? What kind of career do I want to pursue?

Even more basic than these concerns, however, is the question, What kind of person do I need to be to realize my goals? The kind of person I am is determined by the virtues or character traits I have. Ayn Rand, a popular writer who advocates egoism, believes certain virtues will promote a person's well-being, no matter how it is defined.[8]

One of these character traits is *rationality*. To achieve my long range goals, Rand believes, I must not be unduly swayed by emotions of the moment. I must learn to analyze the consequences of alternatives in a clear, analytical way and then decide on the best alternative. Another desirable character trait is *self-discipline*. After I have rationally determined the most prudent course of action, I must have the self-discipline to pursue it, even if this means foregoing temporary satisfactions. Still another desirable virtue is *industry*, a willingness to work hard to achieve my goals. You can probably think of other character traits that would be important in realizing the kind of egoism you find most plausible.

Although no doubt agreeing with Rand that rationality, self-discipline, and industry are virtues, Norton's focus on self-actualization leads to an emphasis on the virtues appropriate to the four stages of development: childhood, adolescence, maturity, and old age.[9] The most prominent feature of childhood is dependence on others, and the corresponding virtue of childhood is *receptivity* to the instructions of elders. Adolescence is the time when individuals free themselves from the supervision of parents and other adults and find their own mode of self-actualization. The characteristic virtue of adolescence is *openness* to new values and experiences. In maturity a person finds his or her own path of self-actualization, so the virtue of maturity is *fidelity* to one's self-development. Old age is characterized by the completion of life; the virtue appropriate to old age is *acceptance* of the life one has lived.

It is easy to understand how duties to oneself can justify these character traits. But duties to oneself can also justify actions that might at first seem incompatible with egoism. For example, occasions may arise in which I as an egoist might risk my life without violating my duties to myself. I might take risks to achieve a coveted goal. Or, if I am unfortunate enough to live in a society where the conditions necessary for achieving my interests are lacking, I might risk my life to escape or foment revolution. Similarly, if I am dying in agony of an incurable disease, I might decide to take my own life.

Duties to Others

As an egoist, I can justify many other-regarding actions that might initially seem incompatible with egoism. Suppose I am a wealthy man whose wife is

---

8 See especially Ayn Rand, *The Virtue of Selfishness* (New York: New American Library, 1964).

9 Norton, *Personal Destinies*, Chap. 6.

dying of a disease that can be cured only at great expense. I might spend my entire fortune to cure her if her life is crucial for my happiness. Similarly, my children's happiness is important to me, so I may be willing to make considerable sacrifices to ensure their education for a good career. I might also become the chairperson of a fund-raising drive for the local charity hospital because I know the publicity will help my career at the bank. I will cultivate friendships and go out of my way to help my friends, because I know that this is the only way to have friends, and friends are important for my happiness. I will refrain from theft, fraud, and violence against others, on the condition that others agree to refrain from the same acts against me.

Social Ethics: The Minimal State

In deciding on the rules of social ethics, Hobbesian egoists face the issue of cooperation with other egoists in its most acute form. We have seen that, as a Hobbesian egoist, I am willing to agree to rules that limit my ability to pursue my self-interest, as long as others agree to the same rules. This fact does not, however, settle the question of precisely what these rules should be. Insofar as I can influence the formation of these rules, I must keep in mind two considerations. First, I would like others to agree to rules that are as compatible with my own interests as possible. Second, I must realize that my ability to get others to agree to rules that promote my own interests is limited by what others are willing to accept. What kinds of rules would come out of hypothetical (or actual) negotiation with other egoists under these conditions? Two proposals seem especially interesting. One proposal results in what we shall call the *minimal state*; the other results in what we shall call the *extended state*.

The first proposal is that the state should be limited, and its function should be primarily negative. The minimal state, as it is sometimes called, would be limited to protecting individuals against physical violence, theft, and fraud. The minimal state allows me the maximum opportunity to pursue my interests freely in competition with others. It also embodies a set of rules to which other egoists might agree. This political philosophy, known as *libertarianism*, might appear to be the most obvious outcome of negotiations in Hobbes's state of nature. It provides the most basic protection from the most violent and destructive tendencies of other human beings.

Ayn Rand is probably the best-known defender of libertarianism, but philosopher Robert Nozick has given the most sophisticated recent account of libertarianism in *Anarchy, State and Utopia*.[10] Here are three characteristics of the minimal state, according to Nozick.

First, the minimal state will have two explicit limitations. There will be no enforced benevolence. Even though voluntary benevolence is perfectly permissible (and we have seen that the egoist may sometimes want to help

---

[10] Robert Nozick, *Anarchy, State and Utopia* (New York: Basic Books, 1974). Nozick does not justify libertarianism on egoistic grounds, but the libertarian state he describes can be justified on egoistic grounds.

others for her own benefit), the state has no right to tax one person to support another. Thus, few if any welfare programs will be available to aid the disadvantaged. The only possible exceptions might be programs that counter-act a clear and present danger to civil disturbance or that aid victims of natural and war-related disasters. Even an egoist might prefer to spend tax dollars on relief for the poor rather than have riots in the streets.

Similarly, the state will not engage in paternalism—that is, forcing persons to do or not do something for their own good or protection. Paternalism requires a limitation of individual freedom of action that many egoists believe is contrary to their desire to run their own lives. Because of this undesirable feature of paternalism, the libertarian state will not require people to use seat belts or wear crash helmets, even though these behaviors would be for their own protection. It will not require people to put away part of their income for retirement. However, a voluntary social security program, in which persons receive after retirement the contributions they made to the program, plus interest, would be acceptable, as long as one person's earnings were not distributed to others.

In opposing all strictly paternalistic laws, the libertarian will examine carefully the laws against the use of drugs such as marijuana and even heroin. The minimal state can prohibit the use of drugs only to the extent that they cause crime that limits the rights of others. In fact, any law must be rejected that can only be justified paternalistically.

Second, because the only justification for coercion by the state is the protection of individuals from one another or other states, the minimal state will not prohibit conduct simply because someone thinks it is immoral. Thus, no laws will be made against pornography unless legislators can show that pornography substantially increases sex crimes and thereby threatens the basic rights of others. Similar considerations apply to laws against homosexuality or other kinds of sexual behavior that some people consider immoral. Laws for-bidding certain kinds of commercial activity on Sunday must be eliminated. Laws prohibiting people from having more than one spouse would have no justification in the minimal state. You can probably think of other laws that must be eliminated for the same reason.

Third, egoists generally believe that their moral position is most com-patible with laissez-faire capitalism. Capitalism is an economic system charac-terized by private accumulation of capital, private ownership of the means of production, and a free-market system. An economic system compatible with egoism will grant maximum freedom for an individual to pursue her own self-interest in terms of profit, as long as she does not violate the basic rights of others.

Social Ethics: The Extended State

Does the minimal state offer enough protection for individuals who are intent on pursuing their interests? Even some Hobbesian egoists might conclude that it does not. Suppose I have a heart problem requiring extensive medical care or worry that my elderly parents may not have saved enough to provide for themselves in old age. These considerations might lead me as an egoist to come up with a very different set of principles to govern the social order.

An egoist who defines well-being in terms of self-actualization may also find the minimal state inadequate. David Norton believes the political order most acceptable to his own philosophy of self-actualization is "developmental democracy," according to which the "paramount function of government is to provide the necessary but non-self-suppliable conditions for optimizing opportunities of individual self-discovery and self-development."[11]

These conditions, Norton believes, are different for different stages in a person's life. Children need education; adolescents need the opportunity for new experiences; adults need meaningful work; the elderly need physical security. Citizens should have rights to those conditions necessary for self-realization. Some of these rights are "negative," such as the right to protection against physical violence, forcible intrusion into one's property or person, and fraud. Other rights, however, are "positive," such as the rights to the necessities of life, education, and the variety of experiences that a person needs to make crucial decisions about the course of one's own life.

Philosopher John Rawls has come up with several principles that an egoist advocating an extended state might endorse.[12] Two principles are especially important. The first one is the *principle of liberty*:

> Each person is to have an equal right to the most extensive total system of equal basic liberties compatible with a similar system of liberty for all.[13]

Depending on how it is interpreted, the libertarian might not have any objection to this principle. It simply assures that each egoist has the maximum liberty to pursue his own interests, that is, as much liberty as is compatible with other egoists' having the same liberty.

The second one is the *difference principle*:

> Social and economic inequalities are to be arranged so that they are both (1) to the greatest benefit of the least advantaged and (2) attached to offices and positions open to all under conditions of fair equality of opportunity.[14]

---

[11] David L. Norton, *Democracy and Moral Development* (Berkeley: University of California Press, 1991), p. 44.

[12] See John Rawls, *A Theory of Justice* (Cambridge, MA: Harvard University Press, 1971). Rawls would not consider himself an ethical egoist, but his principles of justice are arrived at by agreement among hypothetical "negotiators" who are concerned only with their own interests. Rawls specifies, however, that the negotiators operate under a "veil of ignorance," so that they do not know the circumstances of their own lives (for example, interests, abilities, intelligence, degree of health, social position). Thus, they can only negotiate to guarantee an acceptable life, no matter what their particular circumstances might be. I am assuming that a group of egoists who *know* their own condition but who must negotiate with other egoists living in very *different* conditions might agree to principles similar to the ones Rawls develops. Thus, Rawls's principles of justice are rules that at least some rule egoists might endorse.

[13] Ibid., p. 250.

[14] Ibid., p. 83.

The libertarian would not agree with this principle, because it can justify massive infringements on the liberties of individuals, to maximize the benefits to the least advantaged members of society or to ensure that the more desirable social positions are equally accessible to everyone.

As an illustration of the way the difference principle works, consider the fact that physicians have higher incomes than average citizens. According to the difference principle, this discrepancy can be justified only (1) if paying physicians above-average salaries benefits the least advantaged members of society by attracting talented people into medicine *whose services are then available to all citizens*, and (b) if everyone has an equal opportunity to become a physician. This last condition could only be met if everyone of sufficient talent had an opportunity to go to medical school, regardless of their financial means. More than likely, this condition in turn could be met only if the government, through the use of tax dollars, paid the medical school tuition of poor but talented students.

The contrast between libertarian and Rawlsian principles shows that egoism can lead to very different social principles, depending on how egoists define their own well-being, how they assess their own situation, and what principles they can negotiate with other egoists. There is no such thing as *one* egoistic social ethics. We can only point out some of the courses that egoists can take in developing their position.

CONCEPT SUMMARY

As an egoist, I have a duty to myself to develop those character traits, such as rationality, self-discipline, and industry, that enable me to pursue my well-being more effectively. I can also justify many apparently altruistic activities, such as caring for my family and being a loyal friend, because they ultimately promote my own well-being. The society in which egoists live will be determined by the rules to which I and other egoists can agree. We might agree to rules constituting a minimal state that protects us from violence and fraud by others and allows everyone the maximum freedom to pursue her own interests. We might, however, want to be protected from the worst conditions that could befall us or be assured that we will have the necessary conditions for our own self-actualization. In this case, we might agree to rules constituting an expanded state, structured according to Rawls's principle of liberty and difference principle.

APPLYING THE ETHICS OF EGOISM

Now we shall examine, from the egoist's standpoint, several cases requiring a moral decision. These examples will help you understand how an egoist would analyze a situation requiring moral choice and formulate an answer as to what he should do. We shall follow the methodology outlined in the checklist. When useful, we shall also refer to the distinctions among factual, conceptual, and moral questions and to the notions of relevance and conflict problems. Because Hobbesian egoism and the egoism that defines the good in terms of self-actualization sometimes lead to rather different conclusions, we shall sometimes use one position and sometimes another.

Case 1: Bryan's Dilemma

Let us consider the case presented at the beginning of this chapter. We shall first analyze it from the perspective of a version of act egoism, in which Bryan defines his self-interest in terms of career success.

1. The two most obvious alternatives open to Bryan are obeying Max and not obeying him. Another alternative is to try to find some middle way between these two alternatives. Bryan should consider carefully the consequences of each of these three alternatives.

    If he obeys Max, he will be able to continue his summer job. Because Max has dumped the coolant for some time without reprisals from his superiors or the law, Bryan may assume that this state of affairs will continue, at least long enough to allow him to finish his employment. On the other hand, if Max runs into trouble for his practice of dumping the coolant, Bryan might share in the blame. This outcome could cost Bryan his job or possibly result in legal fees that he cannot afford. Perhaps Bryan could defend himself by arguing that he is a junior employee who was just following orders, but this defense might not be successful in court.

    If he disobeys Max, he might lose his job. This course of action would protect him from legal repercussions, however. On the other hand, Max's supervisors may not know about his practice of dumping the coolant and might not approve if they knew. Then, if they did learn about Max's practice, Bryan's refusal to go along with it would probably increase his standing in the firm and might even help get him a permanent job there.

    The problems with both alternatives suggest that a middle-way solution might be best for Max. He might dump the liquid, because it has apparently been dumped for some time without adverse consequences to Max. If Max has suffered no punishment, Bryan probably will not either. Then Bryan might attempt to persuade Max to take a different course of action in the future. He might try to discover whether there is a cost-effective way of treating or recycling the liquid. Or he might try to convince Max that the legal consequences of continued dumping could be unpleasant, for both Max and the firm. Another option is to inform Max's superiors of Max's action, in the hope that managers would protect Bryan and perhaps place him under someone else's supervision.

2. If our analysis of the facts is correct, Bryan should try to find a middle-way solution, because both of the other options pose problems. If no

middle way is possible, Bryan should continue to follow Max's orders, if he believes that the practice of dumping the toxic material is unlikely to be discovered and punished.

Let us now look at the same case from the standpoint of rule egoism.

1. The alternative courses of action are the same three described earlier: obey Max, disobey Max, and find a creative middle way.

2. Most egoists would probably agree on the rule that everyone should obey the law, provided that others agree to a similar rule. The alternative, in which everyone disobeys (or at least tries to disobey) the law whenever it is in their interest to do so, would produce a chaotic situation close to Hobbes's state of nature. This would be contrary to the interests of most egoists.

3. Applying this rule to Bryan's situation, obeying Max is impermissible, because it requires him to break the law. Finding a creative middle way, however, would allow Bryan to promote his own interests while still obeying the law, except for the one dumping. Therefore, either finding a creative middle way (if it is possible) or disobeying Max is morally required.

If Bryan can find a creative middle way, he can act consistently with both act and rule egoism. If he cannot, he must decide whether he will act according to act or rule egoism.

Case 2: The Legalization of Homosexual Acts between Consenting Adults

In 1957, the Wolfenden Committee in Great Britain recommended that Britain's laws on homosexuality be liberalized, so that homosexuality between consenting adults would no longer be a crime. Sir Patrick Devlin, who served on the Queen's Bench, objected to this recommendation, arguing that legalizing such activities could cause the disintegration of the social order. Devlin believed that agreed-on moral values are a part of the binding force that holds society together and that the view that homosexual acts are wrong is a widely shared value in British society. Tampering with the moral consensus on such issues is tampering with the social fabric. Therefore, homosexual acts between consenting adults should not be legalized. What position would an egoist take on this issue?

We shall assume that the egoist defines his interests in a way requiring him to embrace libertarian social ethics. Libertarianism implies a rule that might be stated in a simplified form as "The state should be limited to protecting individuals against physical violence, theft, and fraud." When the egoist tries to get others to agree to such a rule or simply advocates social policies that agree with it, she will be acting in accordance with rule egoism. Therefore, we shall consider this issue only from the standpoint of rule egoism, because act egoism is not relevant.

1. The egoist has two options: either advocate legalizing homosexual acts between consenting adults or advocate not legalizing them.

2. The relevant rule is the libertarian rule stated earlier, which requires government to refrain from regulating its citizens, except when necessary to protect individuals against physical violence, theft, or fraud.

   This rule might seem to yield the conclusion that the egoist should favor decriminalization of homosexual acts. But the egoist would be concerned with Devlin's claim that legalizing homosexuality can threaten the social fabric. If legalization produces or tends to produce social chaos, the government's ability to protect citizens against physical violence, theft, and fraud will have been impaired. Therefore, the egoist will look carefully at the evidence for the view that legalizing homosexual acts would contribute substantially to social disintegration.

   Unfortunately, evidence on either side of this issue is difficult to obtain. One reason is that we cannot easily establish causal relationships between two historical events to say that one event (for example, a change to a more tolerant attitude toward homosexuality) might cause or even contribute to another event (for instance, disintegration of the social order). Another reason is that we often have difficulty distinguishing between social disintegration and mere social change. The social changes that may follow changes in moral values are not necessarily signs of disintegration.

   Given these problems, the egoist would probably conclude that the evidence is not clear enough to justify the claim that legalizing homosexual acts between consenting adults would materially contribute to social disintegration. In addition, we have seen that the libertarian egoist favors laws that allow for maximum individual freedom, as long as conduct does not limit the equal freedom of others. The only way the egoist can obtain tolerance for her own conduct is to agree to a similar respect for the liberty of others. Suppressing homosexual conduct would be contrary to the principles of libertarianism and therefore contrary to the kind of social order the egoist prefers.

3. We must conclude that the rule egoist who is a libertarian would find laws that suppress homosexual conduct between consenting adults morally impermissible.

   This conclusion does not imply that egoist libertarians favor giving adults freedom to molest children, either homosexually or heterosexually. Protecting children from harm by others is simply an aspect of the state's protection of individual liberty. Even genuinely paternalistic action can be justified, when the paternalism is exercised toward children. If we assume that children are incapable of making a free, informed decision about participation in sexual activity because of their lack of experience, cognitive development, and emotional maturity, we can easily justify paternalistic intervention on behalf of children by a libertarian state.

Case 3: Should a Lawyer Reveal the Truth?

David Spaulding was badly injured in an automobile wreck and sued the driver responsible for the injury.[15] David's examining physicians reported to his lawyer that David might have permanent brain injury from a cerebral concussion caused by the accident and recommended refusing to settle the case for one year. The driver's defense lawyer, John Zimmerman, also had his physician examine David. This physician discovered an even more serious problem, an aortic aneurism, apparently caused by the accident, that the boy's doctor had not found. The physician's report contained the following statement: "This aneurism could dilate further and it might rupture with further dilation and this would cause his death." Apparently because David was a minor and the physician was employed by the defense lawyer, the physician reported this information only to Zimmerman, not to David or his attorneys. Zimmerman realized that David's attorneys would ask a higher settlement if they learned of the aneurism. He also knew that, according to the code of ethics for lawyers, he was not required to reveal the information. His responsibility was to keep secret the information gained in the professional relationship whose disclosure would likely be detrimental to his client. If Zimmerman is an egoist, should he reveal the information?

We shall assume that the lawyer is an egoist who defines his interests in terms of self-realization. Part of his self-realization is becoming the best and most successful lawyer that his abilities will allow. His self-realization also includes developing a number of virtues in his own character, including honesty and fairness.

Whether this problem should be approached from the standpoint of act or rule egoism (or both) is not easy to decide. We could assume that one of the rules to which egoists have already agreed is the provision of legal ethics that lawyers must keep secret the information gained in the professional relationship whose disclosure would likely harm their client. If this assumption is made, the rule implies that Zimmerman should not reveal the information about David's aneurism to David's lawyer or his family.

We have seen, however, that egoists may sometimes choose to disregard even those rules to which they and other egoists have agreed, if their interests are thereby more effectively served. Is this one of those occasions? Let us look at this question from the standpoint of act egoism.

1. If Zimmerman reveals the information to the youth's lawyer, his ability to defend his client will be substantially weakened. This result may lead to his having to settle for a higher payment from his client, which will harm his standing as a competent defense lawyer and perhaps lead to fewer cases in the future. He also knows that, if he decides not to reveal the information, he has a basis for defending himself in the legal code of

---

[15] This case is based on *Spaulding v. Zimmerman*, 116 N.W.2d 704 (1962).

ethics, thus preserving his standing as an ethical as well as a successful lawyer. A consideration of these consequences suggests that he should not reveal the information.

If he does not reveal the information and the boy dies, however, his reputation as an ethical lawyer will be damaged, regardless of the provisions of the legal code. Furthermore, he may believe that preserving confidentiality in this situation compromises his personal commitment to the virtues of honesty and fairness too severely.

2. Zimmerman must carefully investigate the consequences of breaking confidentiality with his client in this case. He must also think carefully about the relationship of the two roles he occupies: as a lawyer subject to professional guidelines and as an individual who wants to manifest the personal virtues of honesty and fairness. He must also acknowledge that he would be dishonest and unfair to his client if he failed to abide by the ethical rules of his profession to which he is publicly committed.

Zimmerman will not find it easy to decide which decision would involve the most effective promotion of his interests, including his desire to protect his own personal integrity. He might conclude, however, that the rules protecting strict confidentiality force him to compromise his honesty and fairness too much and that his reputation will be compromised too much if the boy dies. In this case, he will decide that he should break confidentiality and reveal to the father what he knows about his son. Zimmerman might believe, however, that the requirement to keep secret the information gained in the professional relationship whose disclosure would likely be detrimental to clients is not a rule to which rational egoists would agree. If this were the case, he would have no obligation to obey it.

Now let us look at this issue from the standpoint of rule egoism.

1. We shall assume that the only two actions available to the lawyer are revealing or not revealing the existence of the aneurism.

2. A strict prohibition of lawyers' revealing information gained in the professional relationship whose disclosure would likely be detrimental to clients might appear to be in the interests of lawyers, so that they would mutually agree to its enforcement. The prohibition would enable the lawyers to protect their clients' interests more effectively and thereby be more professionally successful themselves. As we have seen from the discussion of the act egoist analysis, however, lawyers could experience disadvantages from adherence to the rule. In situations, such as the present one, where the rule produces unfortunate or even tragic consequences, the reputations of individual lawyers and even the legal profession could be damaged. If lawyers hold to a self-actualization form of egoism, in which honesty and fairness play a part, they may have additional reasons for rejecting this prohibition.

It is extremely difficult to decide whether accepting or rejecting this prohibition would promote lawyers' interests in the long run. But the rule invariably produces a negative reaction on the part of the public, when it leads to tragic consequences for individuals. The public standing of the legal profession should be a primary consideration in deciding which rules the egoistically oriented lawyer should support. Therefore, we shall conclude that the strict prohibition as it has been stated is not justified from the standpoint of rule egoism.

3. If these conclusions are valid, concealing the information about the aneurism from David Spaulding's lawyers is impermissible. This conclusion, however, depends on a number of factual assumptions that can be questioned.

EVALUATING EGOISM AS A MORAL THEORY

Now we are ready to evaluate egoism, using the four criteria established in Chapter 4. Keep in mind that some criticisms can be made of every moral theory; no theory is perfect. You should also note that a subjective element necessarily arises in evaluating moral theories. The following evaluations are my own, although they reflect widely held positions among moral philosophers. These evaluations are for your consideration rather than uncritical acceptance.

Criterion 1: Consistency

Many critics of egoism argue that it gives rise to incompatible moral judgments. Consider case 3, "Should a Lawyer Reveal the Truth?" Suppose the lawyer defined his interests in terms of success in getting the best decisions for his clients, and David's father defined his interests in terms of getting information about his son, assuming he became suspicious that Zimmerman was concealing information that was important to his son's health. The lawyer would conclude, "I should not reveal information about David's aneurism." The father would conclude, "The lawyer should reveal information about my son." Thus, the same moral philosophy directs the lawyer both to reveal and not to reveal the information. This kind of inconsistency is not found in most moral philosophies. From the utilitarian standpoint, for example, the lawyer either should or should not reveal the information, depending on which decision maximizes utility. Utilitarian moral philosophy does not yield two incompatible moral judgments about the same situation.

The egoist might attempt to answer this problem of inconsistency by reformulating the apparently incompatible moral judgments in terms of two differing viewpoints. The first moral judgment could be formulated as "From the standpoint of his interests, the lawyer should not reveal the information." The second moral judgment could be reformulated as "From the standpoint of his interests, the father should try to get the lawyer to reveal the information."

Unfortunately, this proposed solution does not eliminate the problem. It still seems to yield two incompatible moral claims, only this time the incompatibility is in the form of incompatible advice to two different people. It is correct to say both that "The lawyer has the right to try to keep the information secret" and "The father has the right to try to get the information he wants from the lawyer."

The egoist might respond that this incompatibility has been stated too harshly. The egoist could make a distinction between *judging* that others have certain rights and *advocating* that others act in accordance with those rights. As an impartial egoist, the lawyer might judge that the father has the right to try to get the information from him, but he still would not advocate that the father do this, because it would be against his own interests. Similarly, the father could judge that the lawyer has the right to conceal the information from him, but he would still not advocate that he do this.

This maneuver still does not solve the problem. The lawyer and the father are still unable to advocate that others pursue courses of action that they know they have a right to follow. We saw in the first chapter that the moral point of view requires impartiality, which implies that the egoist should be able to advocate that others follow the same course of action that he follows. The egoist is apparently unable to be impartial in this sense, however. I shall leave it to you to decide whether this point is a highly damaging "inconsistency" that makes egoism untenable or simply one of the characteristic features of egoism.

Criterion 2: Justification

The most common justification of the egoistic moral standard is an appeal to psychological egoism. *Psychological egoism* is the view that all human behavior is motivated by self-interest. After making the claim for psychological egoism, the egoist then points out that a person never has an obligation to do something he cannot do. We could never have a moral obligation to pick up 10,000 pounds of steel, because it is physically impossible to do so. She then advances the claim of psychological egoism—namely, that people do, in fact, act solely out of motives of self-interest and cannot do otherwise. The egoist then maintains that we do have moral obligations. Because our only legitimate moral obligations are ones we can fulfill, and because we are only able to act out of motivations of self-interest, the only moral obligations that we have are to act in our own interest.

One can attack the logic of the argument itself and try to show that the ethical egoist cannot fully support her case on the basis of psychological egoism, even if psychological egoism is true. For the fact that humans can only act out of motives of self-interest—even if it is true—does not prove that these motives are the morally correct ones. It might only show that human beings are not capable of acting morally. At any rate, there is nothing inconsistent about saying that we always act out of self-interest but that doing so is still wrong.

The second kind of attack on the argument from psychological egoism to ethical egoism questions the validity of the claim that we always act out of motives of self-interest. Most of us would probably say that the psychological egoist has a great deal of truth on her side. Many apparently altruistic acts really are done because of self-interest. But some human actions do appear to be motivated by considerations other than self-interest. Parents often make sacrifices for their children that are difficult to explain in terms of selfishness. Heroic actions on the battlefield and in civilian life also seem to involve more than considerations of one's own well-being.

Morally praiseworthy actions are not the only actions that have motivations other than self-interest. Malice and hatred are often no more selfish than actions we admire. People often attempt to harm their enemies at great cost to themselves. They may try to kill or injure the enemy even when doing so will cost them large sums of money, reputation and social status, or even their own lives.

Here the convinced psychological egoist will reply that whatever a person does he does because he gets satisfaction from it. If a mother sacrifices for her children, she does so because she gets more satisfaction from seeing them have a happy childhood or a good education than from anything else. If a person spends his life's savings to get revenge on his enemy, he does so because he finds more satisfaction in seeking revenge than in having his money.

Perhaps an example will show the limitations of this argument. A story (perhaps apocryphal) is told that Abraham Lincoln was once trying to convince a friend that all men were prompted by selfishness in doing good. As the coach in which they were riding crossed a bridge, they saw an old razor-backed sow on the bank making a terrible noise because her pigs had fallen into the water and were in danger of drowning. Lincoln asked the driver to stop, lifted the pigs out of the water, and placed them on the bank.

> When he returned, his companion remarked, "Now, Abe, where does self-ishness come in on this little episode?" "Why, bless your soul, Ed, that was the very essence of selfishness. I should have had no peace of mind all day had I gone on and left that suffering old sow worrying over those pigs. I did it to get peace of mind, don't you see?[16]

Lincoln's argument is based on a misconception. If he had not cared for the pigs' welfare, he could not have derived pleasure from helping them. Had he not had a prior desire for something other than his own happiness, he would not have experienced satisfaction from helping them. His own satisfaction was not the *object* of his action but rather the *consequence* of his preexisting desire for the animals' welfare. This example illustrates the fact that all actions cannot be egoistically motivated. If my welfare consists of the satisfaction of desires, some desires must exist before the desire for my own welfare.

---

[16] Quoted from the *Springfield* (Illinois) *Monitor*, in Joel Feinberg, "Psychological Egoism," in his *Reason and Responsibility*, 6th ed. (Belmont, CA: Wadsworth, 1985). Feinberg's chapter is a valuable discussion of psychological egoism, and the argument based on this example is derived from it.

Although most philosophers have found the thesis that *all* human behavior is motivated by self-interest implausible, they may still concede that a great deal of human behavior is so motivated. Hobbes scholar Gregory Kavka calls this position *predominant egoism*, which he defines as the view that "self-interested motives tend to take precedence over non-self-interested motives in determining human actions."[17] The claim that non self interested motives usually give way to self interested motives is much more plausible and may still provide a reasonably strong foundation for ethical egoism. The egoist could still claim that, because most actions are egoistically motivated, egoism is more compatible with the facts of human nature than any other moral philosophy. This point would still be a strong argument in its favor.

Criterion 3: Plausibility

A third way of evaluating a moral philosophy is to compare the moral judgments it produces with our most strongly held moral beliefs. Consider the following argument against egoism from the standpoint of the criterion of plausibility.

Most of us have certain things we would not be willing to do even to advance our own welfare. We probably would not be willing to kill, and many of us would not be willing to steal, even to advance our own interests against those of others. We also have strong loyalties that do not seem to be based on self-interest, such as loyalties to family members or other loved ones. We have seen that egoists can explain these obligations in their terms. They can explain our refusal to steal or kill in terms of reciprocity agreements with other egoists: they will not kill or steal from us if we will place similar restraints on our behavior. They can also explain loyalties to family and loved ones in terms of the relationship of their welfare to our own. Nevertheless, critics maintain that these are not the real reasons for our behavior and moral convictions in these areas. We do not kill or steal because we believe these actions are wrong, and we believe they are wrong because they violate the rights of others. Similarly, we are loyal to family and those we love because of our concern for their well-being *for their sake*, not because of what their welfare contributes to ours.

Egoism does seem incompatible with the reasons most of us would give for many of our actions. In itself, this conclusion does not constitute a refutation of egoism, but it does count as a mark against it.

Criterion 4: Usefulness

In our discussion of the criterion of consistency, we have already shown that egoism can give advice to different people that places them in conflict with each other. For example, the lawyer should try to keep information about David's aneurism secret, and the father should try to discover it. This means that egoism is often not useful in resolving moral conflicts when interests diverge.

---

[17] Kavka, *Hobbesian Moral and Political Theory*, p. 64.

Here is another example illustrating the same problem. When the Second World War was over, the British press published a story regarding two female counterspies. During the war, the Allies had finally broken the Nazi code, and the British War Office discovered that the Nazis knew the true loyalties of the two counterspies. The War Office also knew that, if the women returned to Nazi Europe, they would almost certainly be caught, tortured, and killed. Yet, if they did not return, the Nazis would probably infer that their code had been broken and would change it. The British and their Allies then would lose their major source of intelligence about Nazi war plans for at least two more years. As a result, the two counterspies were sent back to Europe without the knowledge that their identity was known by the Nazis. They were never heard from again.

What was the right thing to do? How does one resolve such a clear conflict of interests? The egoist can only advise each person in the dispute to follow his own self-interest. This approach means that the officials in the War Office should have ordered the counterspies back to Europe and should not have informed them of the danger. If they had been aware that their identity was known by the Nazis, the counterspies should have resisted this order in every possible way. If one believes that a primary function of morality is to resolve disputes arising from a conflict of interests, egoism seems particularly ill suited to accomplish this aim.

The conflicts between act and rule egoism that were illustrated in cases 1 and 3 reveal another problem egoism has in resolving moral disputes. Consider the issue of obeying the law raised in case 1. Bryan would probably prefer living in a society where everyone (including him) obeyed the law, as opposed to a society where nobody obeyed the law. But his first preference might be to live in a society where everyone obeys the law except him, assuming that he could escape punishment for disobeying the law. This situation would give him the protection of living in a law-abiding society, while affording him the advantages of breaking the law when it is in his interest to do so. Thus, he might agree with other egoists to obey the law (rule egoism) but secretly disobey it when it is in his interest to do so (act egoism).

This tendency of the egoist to move from rule egoism to act egoism also limits the usefulness of egoism in resolving moral disputes. It means that egoists' ability to agree on mutually acceptable rules for resolving moral conflicts is always in danger of being undermined by every egoist's desire to maximize her own interests.

CONCEPT SUMMARY

Egoistic moral theory faces a problem of internal coherence because it advises each person to follow his own interests. Thus, the same action can be right, because it promotes my interests, and wrong, because it is contrary to your interests. The justification of the egoistic moral standard by an appeal to psychological egoism is weakened by the fact that the claim that we always act from self-interest seems false. The fact that much human behavior is motivated by egoism, however, still lends support to ethical egoism. Egoism often gives reasons for moral judgments that are at odds with the reasons most of us would offer, generating problems of plausibility. It also encounters problems in attempting to resolve conflicts of interest, because it can only advocate that individuals follow their own self-interest. A further problem with egoism in resolving moral conflict is that an egoist is always tempted to disobey mutually agreed-on rules to accomplish her own ends, which limits the value of such rules in resolving moral conflict.

6

The Ethics of Natural Law

Cardinal Joseph Ratzinger, head of the Congregation of the Doctrine of the Faith of the Roman Catholic Church, criticized a statement of American Roman Catholic bishops that gave implicit permission to church hospitals and agencies to provide information on condoms as a potential safeguard against AIDS. This permission was later rescinded after criticism from Rome.

A document on this subject released in Rome under Cardinal Ratzinger's approval said, "The safe-sex approach to preventing HIV/AIDS, though frequently advocated, compromises human sexuality and can lead to promiscuous sexual behavior." The document continued by warning, "Not only is the use of prophylactics an attempt to halt the spread of HIV technically unreliable; promoting this approach means, in effect, promoting behavior which is morally unacceptable."

The Rev. Albert Ogle, an Episcopal priest who directs the All Saints AIDS Service Center in Pasadena, California, criticized the bishops' reversal on the question of condoms and AIDS for "not addressing what is really happening in their communities." "The reality," Ogle said, "is that young people in our parishes are being infected by the virus and will get sick and die and infect others because the church has painted itself into a corner over birth control."[1]

---

[1] Russell Chandler and John Dart, "Bishops' Panel Rejects Condoms in AIDS Battle," *Los Angeles Times*, October 13, 1989, p. A3.

This controversy reflects the continuing influence of the tradition of natural-law moral philosophy, which condemns both sexual promiscuity and the use of "artificial" forms of birth control such as condoms. This tradition is especially associated with the Roman Catholic Church, but its influence is not confined to that institution. Many people have a deep-seated feeling, especially with regard to sexual conduct, that if something is "unnatural," it is also immoral. Even the law sometimes makes reference to "unnatural acts" with the obvious intent of condemning them as wrong. The words *unnatural* and *immoral* are closely connected in popular thought. On the other hand, the connotation of the word *natural* is strongly positive. We tend to think that if something is "natural," it must also be right.

We shall see that much of this talk of what is and is not "natural" has little to do with the more sophisticated versions of natural law. Nevertheless, natural-law moralists do teach that human nature and the ethical life are connected. Our primary life goal should be to realize as fully as we can our potential as human beings. This statement resembles egoism but has an important difference. Whereas the egoist strives to realize his own individual preferences, whatever they may be, the natural-law theorist advocates realizing those goods specified by a nature that he has in common with his fellow human beings. Thus, the moral standard in natural law has an objective quality that egoism lacks.

We can easily see why the natural-law tradition provides an attractive approach to the problem of determining a moral standard. If ethics is supposed to regulate human conduct, the purpose of this regulation must surely be for the good of human beings themselves, and it is reasonable to believe that this good is determined by the requirements of human nature. What more reasonable foundation could any ethical system have than human nature itself?

Nevertheless, the appeal to human nature as a basis for making moral judgments encounters difficulties. Does this appeal imply that "doing whatever comes naturally" is right? Can a person who has a natural tendency to lie justify her lying behavior by an appeal to natural law? How do we determine the standards of conduct that our human nature presumably entails? In this chapter, we shall look at the tradition in moral philosophy that raises such difficult questions and yet continues to influence our moral thinking.

THE NATURAL-LAW MORAL STANDARD

What Is Natural Law?

The term *natural law* can be misleading. It implies that ethical laws are like "laws of nature" or scientific laws. An example of a scientific law is Boyle's law in physics, which states that the product of the pressure and the specific volume of a gas at constant temperature is constant. But scientific laws are *descriptive*; they state how phenomena in nature do in fact always behave. Ethical laws, on the other hand, are *prescriptive*; they stipulate how people *should* behave, whether or not they do so. Natural-law theorists assume that human beings have free will and that they can decide whether to act as they ought to act. This discussion implies that the word *law* has more in common with civil laws than with natural laws, because both civil and ethical laws can be disobeyed. Natural phenomena presumably always act according to the laws of nature, whereas people do not always behave either legally or morally.

But the analogy with civil laws can also be misleading, for the point of the term *natural* is to contrast ethical laws with the laws of governments. When the Roman jurists were looking for legal concepts that could apply throughout the Roman empire, they turned to the philosophy of natural law precisely because it proposed that certain ethical laws are "natural" rather than "conventional"; that is, they apply equally to all human beings, regardless of the conventions, customs, or beliefs of their particular society. These natural laws for all human behavior could thus serve as a basis for judging people's actions throughout the Roman empire. Therefore, we can say that *natural law* refers to ethical guidelines or rules that stipulate what people ought to do rather than what they in fact do and that they apply equally to all humanity, because they are rooted in human nature itself.

The term *natural law* can be misleading because it inevitably brings to mind some kind of ethical legalism—the belief that hard-and-fast guidelines cover every possible detail of conduct. This characterization, however, is unfair to the natural-law tradition. The greatest exponent of natural law, Thomas Aquinas (1224–1274), believed that the basic outlines of proper human behavior are relatively clear. But he also taught that, the closer we come to particular moral judgments, the more prone we are to error and the more room we must make for differences of opinion. Some contemporary natural-law theorists even believe that natural law has a historical dimension, so that what is right in one epoch may not be right in another. Whether or not the view is accepted, the lively discussions of ethical issues in the Roman Catholic Church, where natural-law thinking is especially prominent, show that natural-law theorists by no means believe that all ethical problems have already been solved. The word *law* merely refers to the prescriptive character of the rules that should govern human behavior.

The natural-law theorist does, however, believe in an objective standard for morality. Moral truth exists just as scientific truth exists. The natural-law theorist cannot be an ethical relativist or an ethical skeptic; rather, he is committed to some form of moral realism. He generally believes we know the basic outlines of this standard, but this belief does not mean we have interpreted the implications of this standard correctly in every case. In ethics, as in science, human beings continually search for truth. The belief in objective truth should be no more stifling of human freedom and creativity in ethics than it is in science.

Human Nature and Natural Inclinations

What is the standard of truth in natural-law ethics? As an approximation, we can say that the standard is human nature. People should do whatever promotes the fulfillment of human nature. How, then, do we determine what human nature is?

Let us consider some analogous situations that illustrate the difficulty in describing human nature. We often find it useful to describe something's nature in terms of its function, the purpose it serves. For example, we can describe the nature of a pencil in terms of its function of enabling humans to make marks on paper. A "good" pencil is one that performs this function well, without smudging, scratching, or breaking, for example. Similarly, if an automobile's function is to provide transportation, a good automobile is one that provides comfortable, reliable transportation. The function of a tomato plant is to produce tomatoes, and a good tomato plant is one that produces many high-quality tomatoes.

We can also determine the function of human beings if we confine a person to one particular social role. The function of a farmer is to grow food, and a good farmer produces food efficiently and with proper care for the animals and land for which he has responsibility. By similar reasoning, we can say that a good father is one who attends diligently to his children's welfare. But now let us take human beings out of their social roles and ask simply, "What is the function of a human being?" Here we see the problem faced by those who attempt to base ethics on human nature. Generally speaking, the more complex the animal, the more varied its behavior and presumably the less clearly defined its function. The freedom of action possessed by human beings makes it plausible to argue, as some philosophers have, that human beings are characterized precisely by the fact that they have no set nature or function. How can we make sense out of natural law in the face of these problems?

Fortunately, we can take another, more promising approach to discovering what human nature is like. One way to determine a thing's characteristics is to observe its behavior. In chemistry, we learn about the nature of iron by observing how it reacts with other elements. Perhaps we can find out what human nature is like by ascertaining those "natural inclinations," as Aquinas puts it, that human beings have in common. To phrase it another way, perhaps we can discover what human nature is by identifying those goals that human beings generally tend to seek. These values would presumably reflect the structure of our human nature, which natural law directs us to follow. Therefore, we shall propose the following statement as the moral standard of natural law:

> MS: Those actions are right that promote the values specified by the natural inclinations of human beings.

How do we find out what these natural inclinations are? We might first consult psychologists, sociologists, or anthropologists. Some contemporary natural-law theorists use studies from the social sciences to defend their conclusions. However, the natural-law tradition developed before the rise of the social sciences, and a more informal method of observation was used to discover the basic human inclinations. Most natural-law theorists would maintain that these observations are still valid. We can divide the values specified by natural human inclinations into two basic groups: (1) biological values, which are strongly linked with our bodies and which we share with other animals, and (2) characteristically human values, which are closely connected with our more specifically human aspects. (We will not call this second group uniquely human values because some of the inclinations that point to these values, such as the tendency to live in societies, are not unique to human beings.) We can summarize the values and the natural inclinations that point to them as follows:

1. Biological Values
    a. *Life*—From the natural inclinations that we and all other animals have to preserve our own existence, we can infer that life is good, that we have an obligation to promote our own health, and that we have the right of self-defense. Negatively, this inclination implies that murder and suicide are wrong.
    b. *Procreation*—From the natural inclination that we and all animals have to engage in sexual intercourse and rear offspring, we can infer that procreation is a value and that we have an obligation to produce and rear children. Negatively, this inclination implies that such practices as sterilization, homosexuality, and artificial contraception are wrong.
2. Characteristically Human Values
    a. *Knowledge*—From the natural tendency we have to know, including the tendency to seek knowledge of God, we can infer that knowledge is a value and that we have an obligation to pursue knowledge of the world and God. Negatively, this inclination implies that the stifling of intellectual curiosity and the pursuit of knowledge, including the pursuit of the knowledge of God, is wrong. It also implies that a lack of religion is wrong.
    b. *Sociability*—From the natural tendency we have to form bonds of affection and love with other human beings and to form groups or societies, we can infer that friendship and love are good and that the state is a natural institution and therefore good. We thus have an obligation to pursue close relationships with other human beings and to submit to the legitimate authority of the state. We can also infer that war can be justified under certain conditions if it is necessary to defend the state. Negatively, this inclination implies that activities that interfere with proper human relationships, such as spreading slander and lies, are wrong. Actions that destroy the state's power are also wrong, so natural law finds a basis for an argument against revolution and treason, except when the state is radically unjust.

These natural inclinations are reflections of human nature, and the pursuit of the goods they specify is the way to individual fulfillment. Aquinas himself makes it clear that his enumeration of basic values, which closely parallels our account, is incomplete; other natural-law theorists have expanded the list to include such things as play and aesthetic experience. However, the list given here has had the greatest historical influence, and we shall assume it is basically adequate.

The more important issue raised by this list is the potential for conflict between the various values. What should we do when our need to defend ourselves requires that we kill someone else? What should we do when sterilization is necessary to prevent a life-threatening pregnancy? What should be done when contraception seems necessary to limit family size so that families can properly educate the children they already have? In each of these examples, one aspect of natural law seems to conflict with another, and the question arises whether these values have a hierarchy on which a decision can be based. The answer to this question brings into focus one of the most important and controversial aspects of natural-law moral—namely, its moral absolutism.

MORAL ABSOLUTISM AND THE
QUALIFYING PRINCIPLES

Moral Absolutism

Suppose you are on a military convoy from the United States to England during World War II. Your ship is attacked and sunk. Your life raft is carrying twenty-four persons, although it was designed to carry only twenty. You have good reason to believe that the raft will sink unless four people are eliminated, and four people on board have been so seriously injured in the catastrophe that they are probably going to die anyhow. Because no one volunteers to jump overboard, you, as the ranking officer on the boat, decide to have them pushed overboard. Are you morally justified in doing so? Many of us would say that under the circumstances you were, but natural-law theorists would say that you were not justified, even if everyone on the raft would have died otherwise.

Consider another wartime example. Suppose you know that some prisoners have information that will save a large number of lives. The only way to obtain the information is to threaten to kill the prisoners, but you know that they will not reveal what they know unless your threat is absolutely serious. To show them how serious you are, you have another prisoner, who has done nothing to deserve death, shot before their eyes. As a result of your action, the information is revealed and many lives are saved. Is this action justified? Many people would say that under these extreme circumstances it is justified, but natural-law theorists would say that it is not.

These examples point out one of the most significant aspects of natural-law theory: its absolutism. *Moral absolutism* can refer either to the belief that some objective standard of moral truth exists independently of us (what we have referred to as moral realism) or to the view that certain actions are right or wrong regardless of their consequences. Natural law is an absolutist moral theory in both senses, but the second meaning of absolutism is highlighted by our wartime illustrations. Natural-law theorists believe that *none of the values specified by natural inclinations may be directly violated.* Innocent people may not be killed for any reason, even if other innocent people can thereby be saved. The procreative function that is a part of our biological nature may not be violated by such practices as contraception and sterilization, even if these practices are necessary to preserve other values, such as a child's education or even the mother's life. Similarly, homosexuality violates the value of procreation and is prohibited, even if it is the only kind of sex a person can enjoy.

Natural-law theorists believe that basic values specified by natural inclinations cannot be violated because *basic values cannot be measured or compared*; that is, basic values cannot be quantified or measured by some common unit, so they cannot be traded off against one another. For example, we cannot divide the good of knowledge into units of value and the good of procreation into units of value so that the two can be compared on a common scale. Nor can the good of a single life be compared with the good of several lives; thus, we cannot say that a single life may be sacrificed to preserve many other lives. This idea is sometimes called the "absolute value" or "infinite value" of a human life, suggesting that a human life cannot be weighed against anything else, including another human life. Natural-law theorists also make this point by saying that basic values are *incommensurable*. Because we cannot measure values, we cannot calculate which consequences of an action are more important. Therefore, consequences cannot be used to determine the moral status of actions.

Another characteristic of natural law is that it is nonconsequentialist in character, even though it may not rule out consideration of consequences. Natural-law theorists insist that *moral judgments must include an evaluation of the intentions of the person performing the action.* The intention of an action is what a person wants to accomplish or "has in mind," as we say, in performing the action. For example, a person can give money to charity because he wants a good reputation in the community. The consequences of the action are good, but the person's intention is not morally praiseworthy. Some moral philosophers distinguish between a moral evaluation of the action and a moral evaluation of the intention of the person performing the action. Using this distinction, we can say that the action of giving money to charity is praiseworthy, but the person giving the money is not to be commended, because his intention was not praiseworthy.

Qualifying Principles

Because values are incommensurable and may not ever be directly violated, we may find ourselves in a moral dilemma in which any action we could perform violates some value and hence is immoral. For example, self-defense may sometimes require that we override the natural inclination of another human being to self-preservation. If we do nothing, we allow ourselves to be killed; if we defend ourselves, we kill someone else. To avoid the paralysis of action that would result from such moral dilemmas, natural-law theorists have developed two principles that are crucial in making moral judgments: the principle of forfeiture and the principle of double effect.

The Principle of Forfeiture   According to the *principle of forfeiture*, a person who threatens the life of an innocent person forfeits his or her own right to life. (An *innocent* person is one who has not threatened anyone's life.) Suppose you are a pioneer tilling his land one morning when two men approach you and say they are going to kill you and your family in order to take your land. Is it morally permissible for you to defend yourself, even to the point of killing them? Natural-law theorists answer the question in the affirmative. Even though you might have to kill your would-be assailants, they have forfeited their innocence by unjustifiably threatening your life. Therefore, they have forfeited their claim to have their natural inclination to self-preservation respected. We can make this point by distinguishing between killing and murder. *Killing* is taking the life of a noninnocent person, whereas *murder* is taking the life of an innocent person. When you take the life of a person who is attempting to kill you, you are killing him but not committing murder.

The principle of forfeiture can be used to justify not only acts of individual self-defense but also war and capital punishment. A defensive war may be justified under certain conditions, even though it involves killing other people, because the aggressors have forfeited their right to life. Similarly, murderers may justly be put to death because they have forfeited their right to life by killing others.

The Principle of Double Effect   According to the *principle of double effect*, it is morally permissible to perform an action that has two effects, one good and the other bad, if the following criteria are met:

1. The act, considered in itself and apart from its consequences, is good, or at least morally permissible. An act of murder violates this criterion because murder is bad in itself and apart from its consequences.

2. The bad effect cannot be avoided if the good effect is to be achieved. The moral significance of this criterion lies in the belief that if an alternative method that does not produce the bad effect is available and not used, we

must assume that the bad effect was intended. This criterion illustrates the important place that consideration of intent has in natural law. An action with improper intent is morally unacceptable even if it does not otherwise violate natural law. Another test must be passed, however, before we can say that an action is unintended. It is embodied in the next criterion.

3. The bad effect is not the means of producing the good effect but only a side effect. If the bad effect is a necessary means of achieving the good effect, the bad effect must be intended along with the good effect for which it is a necessary means, so the action is morally impermissible. This criterion also illustrates the importance of intention in natural law.

4. The criterion of proportionality is satisfied, in that the good effect and the bad effect are more or less equally balanced in importance. If the bad effect of an action is far more significant than any good effect, the action should not be done, even if the other criteria are met.

If these four criteria are met, the violation of a fundamental value may be considered as indirect rather than direct. Although we may still be said to *bring about an evil*, we cannot be said to *do* an evil, according to natural law. The best way to explain the principle of double effect is by example, so let us consider several applications.

In the first example, a pregnant woman who has tuberculosis wants to take a drug that will cure her disease, but the drug also has the effect of aborting the fetus. Is taking the drug morally permissible? The principle of double effect justifies taking the drug in this case, because all four of its conditions are met.

First, the act of taking the drug to cure a disease is itself morally permissible. In fact, considered in itself and apart from its consequences, it is morally obligatory for the mother to take the drug, for she is obligated to do what she can to preserve her own life.

Second, if we assume that the drug is the only one that will cure the disease and that the mother cannot put off taking the drug until after the baby is born, then the bad effect is unavoidable. By this criterion, then, the death of the child is not intended. We must clarify here what natural-law theorists mean. The bad effect is certainly foreseen; the woman knows the drug will produce an abortion. But an effect may be foreseen without also being intended, that is, without being the goal of the action. If another drug were available that would cure her tuberculosis without causing the abortion, presumably the woman would take it. Otherwise, it would be difficult to argue that she did not intend to have an abortion.

Third, the bad effect is not the means of achieving the good effect. An abortion is not a necessary step in curing a person of tuberculosis; rather, it just happens that the only drug that will cure the woman also causes an abortion. The abortion is an unfortunate and unintended side effect, due to the particular nature of the drug.

Fourth, a proportionally serious reason exists for performing the abortion. The death of the fetus is at least balanced by the saving of the mother's life. If the bad effect were serious (as in this case), but the good effect were relatively insignificant, the action would not be justifiable by the principle of double effect, even if the other conditions were met.

The criterion of proportionality is an exception to the earlier statement that values are incommensurable and that human lives cannot be weighed against one another. We have seen that it may also be considered an exception to the claim that consequences are not considered in moral evaluation. Here, consequences do play a part in natural-law reasoning. But note that consequences can be considered *only* when the other three conditions have been met. A more accurate statement, therefore, is that in natural-law theory, the consideration of consequences occupies some place in moral evaluation, but they are of secondary importance.

Two other examples will further illustrate how the principle of double effect functions. Suppose I want to turn on a light so that I can read a book on ethics, but I know that throwing the switch on the wall that turns on the light will result in the electrocution of a workman on the floor below. Is it morally permissible to throw the switch?

First, turning on a light to read a book on ethics is in itself a permissible— even praiseworthy—action.

Second, the bad effect is unavoidable if the good effect is to be achieved. If another light could be turned on and I deliberately failed to use it, knowing the consequence is the death of the workman, then I could not argue that I did not intend to kill the workman.

Third, the bad effect (killing the workman) is not a means to reading philosophy but rather only an unfortunate and unintended side effect. Killing someone is not ordinarily a consequence of turning on a light.

But the fourth condition of the principle of double effect is not satisfied. The killing of a human being is not outweighed by the value of reading a book on ethics. Therefore, turning on the light is not justified by the principle of double effect.

Consider another example.[2] In the process of attempting to deliver a fetus, a physician discovers that the fetus is hydrocephalic. The fetus's large cranium makes normal vaginal delivery impossible; both the woman and the fetus would die in the attempt. Neither the mother nor the fetus would survive a cesarean section, so the only way to save the mother's life is to crush the skull of the fetus (craniotomy), thus rendering a vaginal delivery of the stillborn fetus possible. Would the craniotomy be justifiable by the principle of double effect?

First, the act of attempting to save the mother's life is morally permissible, even commendable.

---

[2] For a discussion of this case, see L. W. Sumner, *Abortion and Moral Theory* (Princeton, NJ: Princeton University Press, 1981), p. 116.

Second, there is no way to save the mother's life except by killing the fetus. The bad effect cannot be avoided if the good effect is to be achieved.

Third, the bad effect can only be seen as the means of producing the good effect. It makes no sense to talk about crushing the head of the fetus without also killing it. Because the death of the fetus must be considered the means of achieving the good effect, the third criterion is not satisfied. Each of the four criteria must be met for the action to be permissible, so we already know that the craniotomy is impermissible. However, for the sake of completeness, we shall consider the fourth criterion.

Fourth, both the fetus and the mother will die if the abortion is not performed; thus, the criterion of proportionality is satisfied. But because the third criterion is not met, the craniotomy may not be performed, and the fetus and mother must both die.

Natural-law theorists admit that this is a tragic case, and various attempts have been made to justify the craniotomy on other grounds. For example, some natural-law theorists argue that the principle of forfeiture can be invoked, because the fetus should be considered an aggressor on the life of the mother. Even though the fetus is innocent of any conscious motive to harm its mother, the actual effect of its growth is to threaten the mother's life. Natural-law theorists sometimes say that the fetus, having no malicious intent, is *subjectively innocent* but not *objectively innocent*, because it does threaten the mother's life. Whether this argument justifies an abortion will be left for you to decide.

CHECKLIST FOR APPLYING
NATURAL-LAW ETHICS

____ 1. Determine whether an action is in accord with the four fundamental values specified by human inclinations or whether there is some apparent violation of one or more of these values.

____ 2. If there is an apparent violation, determine whether the qualifying principle of forfeiture applies to the action.

____ 3. If there is an apparent violation, determine whether the qualifying principle of double effect applies to the action. For the principle of double effect to apply, all four of the following criteria must be met:

  a. The act itself must be good, or at least morally permissible.

  b. The bad effect of the action must be unavoidable if the good effect is to be achieved.

  c. The bad effect must not be the means of producing the good effect but only a side effect.

  d. The criterion of proportionality must be satisfied, in that the good effect must be at least as morally desirable as the bad effect is morally undesirable.

____ 4. Make a final decision on the morality of the action.

     a. If the action is in accord with the fundamental values, or if it is not in accord but is excused by one of the qualifying principles, the action is morally obligatory.

     b. If the alternative to the action is a violation of a fundamental value, the action is morally permissible.

     c. If the action is a violation of a fundamental value and the qualifying principles do not apply, the action is morally impermissible.

CONCEPT SUMMARY

The basic idea of natural law is that a person should promote those values that are the object of our fundamental human inclinations or tendencies. The realization of these values in a person's life will lead to a fulfillment of his human nature. As analyzed by natural-law theorists, these values include the biological values of life and procreation and the characteristically human values of knowledge and sociability.

Because natural law stipulates that no fundamental values may be directly violated, the question arises as to what action should be taken when situations seem to force a person to violate one of the values regardless of what is done. The qualifying principles of forfeiture and double effect are designed to remedy this problem. According to the principle of forfeiture, a person who threatens the life of an innocent person forfeits his own right to life. The principle of double effect provides four criteria that must be met for an action to be considered only an indirect violation of a fundamental value.

THE PERSONAL AND SOCIAL ETHICS OF NATURAL LAW

Duties to Self

In natural-law ethics, a person's primary duty to herself is to promote the realization in her life of the four fundamental values of life, procreation, knowledge, and sociability. The duties to oneself have positive and negative dimensions. I have a positive obligation to promote the values specified by natural law and a negative obligation not to act directly against those values.

Keep in mind that the negative obligations are more binding than the positive ones. Because of the absolutist orientation of natural law, we are never justified in directly violating a fundamental value, but we need not always actively promote these values. A certain amount of discretion is called for in determining when and how the fundamental values of natural law are to be promoted. For example, a person who decides not to marry and have a family so that she can devote herself to the service of God does not violate the requirements of natural-law morality. She may be failing to use her pro-creative powers, but she is not directly violating them. It is generally easier to determine when a person has violated a negative obligation than when she has violated a positive obligation. Not surprisingly, therefore, some of the best-known moral judgments of natural law are negative.

The moral duties to oneself arising from the biological values of life and procreation have received more attention than the moral duties derivable from the characteristically human values of knowledge and sociability. As we have already seen, self-defense is a positive duty, justified by the value of life. The value of life also requires us not to commit suicide, because suicide directly violates that value. Therefore, suicide has been condemned in the natural-law tradition.

However, some actions that appear to be suicide may not be, because the principle of double effect applies. When a soldier throws himself on a grenade to protect his comrades, he is acting directly to save the lives of his fellow soldiers, which itself is morally permissible. His own death is a tragic but unintended consequence of his actions. He may foresee his own death, but he does not directly intend it, for his death is neither a means to the good effect of saving other lives nor avoidable if his comrades are to be saved. Furthermore, the criterion of proportionality applies, because his death saves other people's lives.

The value of procreation leads to what is probably the most widely discussed conclusion of natural-law theory: the prohibition of "artificial" contraception. Because the use of contraceptive devices could be considered a violation of a duty to oneself, we can appropriately discuss it here. To show that contraception is intrinsically immoral, we need only point out that it violates the value of procreation, and this violation is not excused by either the principle of forfeiture or the principle of double effect.

We have seen that merely failing to use one's procreative powers to pursue another value, such as knowledge of God, is permissible. But, when a person chooses to have intercourse with his or her spouse and does something to prevent conception, he or she is directly acting against the value of pro-creation. Therefore, the action cannot be acceptable from the standpoint of natural law.

Attempts to avoid this conclusion by appealing to the principle of for-feiture and double effect are unsuccessful. The principle of forfeiture is inapplicable, because neither the parents nor the fetus may be considered noninnocent. In applying the principle of double effect, we might possibly argue that, when parents use contraceptive devices, their intention is to promote the value of knowledge by limiting their family size so that they can provide more effectively for their children's education. However, the prevention of conception is a direct means chosen by the parents to attain this end. Therefore, contraception must be considered a violation of natural law and hence immoral.

That sterilization is morally wrong is even more obvious from the natural-law standpoint. Although one might argue that the parents' intention is to provide more effectively for their children's education or to promote some other laudable end, the means to this end is the prevention of conception.

The situation is quite different if an action that produces sterility is taken for a reason that is legitimate in itself. Suppose a woman with uterine cancer has her uterus removed to save her life. The woman will no longer be able to bear children, but her action is still morally justifiable because sterility is not a necessary means to the end of saving the woman's life but merely an unintended side effect. Moreover, because life is a fundamental value, the woman must do what she can to save her life, as long as her action is not directly contrary to another basic value.

Natural-law theorists have not devoted as much attention to the negative and positive duties to self that might be derived from the values of knowledge and sociability, but these duties should be just as binding. An interesting exercise would be to consider the duties arising from these values. Obviously, a person has an obligation to develop her ability to pursue knowledge through education and to develop her capacities for relationships with other people. But what kinds of actions should be counted as a direct violation of these values? Do we directly violate the value of knowledge if we discontinue a promising education or if we stifle our scientific or philosophical curiosity?

Finally, it is not surprising that many people think that the pursuit of pleasure might be a duty to self. Many people seem to have a natural inclination to pursue pleasure, so why should it not be listed as a fundamental value? Natural-law theorists believe that, if we examine our motivations closely, we find that we do not pursue pleasure for its own sake. To understand this claim, consider the following possibility. Suppose you could be connected to an "experience machine" that would produce any sensations you desired.[3] You could have the pleasures of sex, the joy of eating, the euphoria experienced after jogging ten miles, or any number of other delightful experiences—all just by pressing various buttons on the machine. Suppose you could spend your entire lifetime connected to such a machine. Would you do it?

Most of us would probably choose to spend very little if any time connected to such a machine. The reason is that we want more than experiences. We want to *do* things, to *be* a certain kind of person, and to interact genuinely with other human beings in specific ways. Pleasure for its own sake is not a fundamental pursuit. You may be interested in considering whether you agree with this claim and whether you accept the natural-law theorist's claim that fame, power, and wealth are also not fundamental human pursuits.

---

[3] For a modified version of this idea (used for different purposes), see Robert Nozick, *Anarchy, State and Utopia* (New York: Basic Books, 1974), pp. 42–45.

Duties to Others

The biological and characteristically human values provide the basis for many negative duties to others. Besides the duty not to kill another person directly, including a human fetus, we also have a duty not to act directly against the values of knowledge and sociability. Deliberately discouraging a child's curiosity, for example, violates the value of knowledge. Lying is also an offense against another person's inclination to know the truth. Actions that destroy people's ability to relate to one another, such as slander and malicious gossip, violate the value of sociability. You can probably think of many other negative duties that follow from the biological and characteristically human values.

The extent of one's obligation to help others is controversial. Our obligation to help others is clearly limited by the requirement not to violate another basic value directly. I cannot donate my heart to save your life while I am still in good health, but some cases provide interesting problems for natural law. Consider the following case as an example.[4] In 1956, Leon and Leonard Madsen, two nineteen-year-old brothers, presented themselves to Peter Brent Brigham Hospital in Boston. Leon's only hope for life was a kidney transplant from Leonard. The hospital had performed the first successful kidney transplant in two adult identical twins in 1954. Is Leonard's donation of one of his kidneys morally permissible by natural law?

The question hinges on whether, in giving one of his kidneys to his brother, Leonard is acting directly against the value of his own life. The loss of a kidney is not a serious danger to life, but many natural-law theorists believe the donation nevertheless violates the integrity of the human body, because it is potentially life-shortening. The principle of double effect cannot justify the action because it is a means to the good effect. Natural-law theorists have generally taught that our obligation to help others falls short of this action. Could you set up any general guidelines for the limits of benevolence according to natural-law theory?

Social Ethics

Three principles characterize the natural-law approach to social ethics. First, the state has a right to defend itself against international and external enemies, as long as it is fundamentally just. Sociability is a natural human inclination, and humans cannot find fulfillment apart from association with other human beings. Consequently, the state is a natural institution for human beings, not an arbitrary, oppressive invention of tyrants. War is thus justifiable in certain circumstances if it is necessary to preserve the social order. But a war must be just, and natural-law theorists have developed a theory of the "just war" to define the legitimate conditions of war.

---

4 See Paul Ramsey, *The Patient as Person* (New Haven, CT: Yale University Press, 1970), pp. 165–197.

The first of these conditions is that a war must be declared by a lawful authority in the state and not by private individuals. Second, the war must have a just cause; that is, there must be a violation, attempted or accomplished, of the state's legitimate rights. Examples of just causes would include carrying off part of the population, seizing territory or resources or property, or casting a serious blow to the nation's honor that would weaken its authority. Third, the cause must be not only just but also known to be just by the rulers who declare the war. The rulers must have the right intention in starting the war. Fourth, the conduct of the war must include the right use of means. To seek a good through the direct violation of a basic value is morally wrong. The direct killing of innocents, for example, must be avoided.

A second principle of natural-law social ethics is that natural law is always more binding than the human laws of a particular state. As long as the laws of the state do not seriously violate the principles of natural law, citizens have an obligation to obey them. Nevertheless, when the moral wrongs perpetrated by the state are great, and when it can be reasonably predicted that a rebellion would succeed, revolution may be justified.

Outright rebellion is not, of course, the only way a citizen may act contrary to the laws of his country. In considering such actions as conscientious objection, for example, natural-law theorists often distinguish between the question of whether a citizen's action is *objectively correct* (in accordance with natural law) or *subjectively correct* (performed because of the right intentions). A conscientious objector's action in refusing military service may be objectively correct, because the war is actually unjust, but subjectively incorrect, because the objection is based not on moral grounds but perhaps on the fear of losing one's life. Or the objector's action can be objectively incorrect and subjectively correct, as when the war is just but the objector genuinely thinks it is not and so refuses to serve in the military. Of course, a citizen might believe a war is just when it is not, in which case military service would also be objectively incorrect but subjectively correct.

Natural-law theorists have always held that one's duty is to follow one's own conscience; that is, one's action should always be subjectively correct. At the same time, we also have an obligation to keep our consciences from being corrupted by factors like self-interest.

The third principle of natural-law social ethics is that the state should be organized for the common good. The state exists for the good of individuals; individuals do not exist for the state's benefit. Therefore, promoting the common good is nothing more than providing the conditions necessary to realize the four values of life, procreation, knowledge, and sociability. Natural-law theorists have insisted, for example, that citizens should be accorded a "just wage" that is sufficient both to allow them to enjoy an appropriate level of dignity and productiveness and to realize the moral values of natural law in their lives. Exploitation by private business or the government is wrong. Many natural-law theorists have been sympathetic with socialism and welfare-state policies as the most appropriate means for realizing these goals. Whether natural law is compatible with an enlightened form of capitalism is a question worth considering.

If the state is obliged to give citizens the opportunity to realize the values prescribed by natural law, does it follow that the state should force the values of natural law on its citizens? This conclusion has often been drawn by moral theologians, as the following passage by Bernard Häring illustrates:

> The state has a duty to assume an unequivocal position in relation to nat-
> ural and supernatural revelation. The Church was repeatedly forced to
> condemn the principle of the "liberal" state according to which every
> option, every doctrine, whether true or false, good or bad, has an equal
> right to be publicly expressed and defended through free speech and
> press. These so-called "liberal" principles, apart from dishonor to God,
> would ultimately lead the state to its own destruction. For its own
> survival, not to speak of progress, it must possess at least a minimum of
> certain and unassailable principles regarding truth and error, good and
> evil. Only through the unconditional possession of such principles can the
> state avoid the dilemma of anarchy which forbids nothing or legislation
> which is utterly arbitrary in its sheer legal positivism.
>
> To avoid very grave disunity in the public life of a nation, however, it
> is justifiable at times for the state to restrict its protection to the truths
> universally accepted by the major groups in its domain representing basic
> attitudes to life. And from a merely practical standpoint, it may go still
> further and grant the same freedom to any and every doctrine. However,
> such a situation is far from ideal.[5]

Häring's statement represents a completely different stand on the enforce-ment of morality from the egoist's libertarian position. What is the basis of this extreme position on the obligation of the state to enforce the principles of natural law? Häring argues that actions contrary to natural law dishonor God and eventually result in the destruction of the state. However, he also admits that the conclusions of natural-law morality might not be accepted by a given population. In this case, the generally accepted moral views should be allowed to prevail, even though the situation would be far from ideal, the ideal being the enforcement of moral precepts derived from natural law.

Häring believes that the conclusions of natural law are objectively right, that they are matters of reason rather than revelation. Its conclusions are available to all those willing and able to use their faculty of reason. Thus, in asking the state to enforce natural-law morality, Häring does not believe he is calling for the enforcement of an uniquely Catholic, or even Christian, moral

---

5 Bernard Häring, *The Law of Christ*, trans. Edwin G. Kaiser (Paramus, NJ: Newman, 1966), Vol. 3, pp. 120–121. Used with permission.

perspective. Like any natural-law moralist, Häring believes that he is advocating only what is in accord with human nature. From the standpoint of
natural law, therefore, by allowing the advocacy and practice of actions
contrary to true human inclinations, the state is not promoting human self-
realization but rather the distortion of human nature.

Nevertheless, Häring's statements shock most people who have been
raised in a democratic tradition. An interesting question is whether natural-
law theorists can work out a political philosophy more genuinely supportive
of individual freedom. Many sophisticated attempts have already been made in
this direction, and Häring himself provides one possible avenue. Recalling the
distinction between the objective and subjective morality of an action, we can
see what is behind Häring's observation that some people may genuinely not
be persuaded by the arguments of natural law. Because individuals should not
do what they think is wrong and should do what they think is right, regardless of the objective morality of the actions, the state must be careful in
forcing natural-law morality on its citizens. Even if natural-law moralists were
to allow more freedom in behavior than Häring does, however, they may still
believe the state is obliged to prevent immoral teachings and immoral
behavior from unduly influencing other people. In any case, the criterion of
the common good provides an instructive basis for a philosophy of the
obligations of government to its citizens.

CONCEPT SUMMARY

Duties to self are governed by the principle that a person has an obligation to
promote the realization in his life of the basic values specified by our natural
inclinations and not to do anything that directly obstructs the realization of
those values. Most of the duties to self discussed in traditional natural law have
concerned the biological values of life and procreation. An interesting
question to ask yourself is what positive and negative duties follow from the
characteristically human values of knowledge and sociability.

Duties to others include the duty not to kill another person directly or to
violate the values of knowledge (for example, by lying) or sociability (for
example, by slander). Many other duties follow from the four fundamental
values. The extent of one's positive obligations to others is limited by the duty
not to violate obligations to oneself. The question of donating vital organs
poses an interesting test case of the limits of others' duties.

Three principles characterize the natural-law approach to social ethics.
First, the state has a right to defend itself against internal and external
enemies, as long as the state is fundamentally just. Second, natural law takes
priority over human laws, and it may sometimes provide a justification for
civil disobedience or even revolution. Third, the state should be structured in
a way that promotes the realization of the four values of natural law in its
citizens' lives.

APPLYING THE ETHICS OF NATURAL LAW

We can now apply natural law to some cases involving moral decision, following the methodology outlined in the checklist.

Case 1: AIDS and Condoms

Let us consider the controversy over the use of condoms as a way to prevent AIDS, which was described at the beginning of this chapter.

Because of the different moral issues that arise in various instances of the use of condoms to prevent AIDS, it will be helpful to treat first the use of condoms to prevent AIDS in heterosexual vaginal intercourse between married couples and then consider all other uses of condoms to prevent AIDS. We shall refer to this first category of sexual relations as *procreative intercourse*, because married couples would have intercourse in a context in which procreation would be justified from the standpoint of natural law. Natural-law theorists hold that the natural mode for producing children for human beings is in the context of monogamous heterosexual marriage. Other sexual relationships would include nonvaginal intercourse between married partners, vaginal and nonvaginal intercourse between unmarried heterosexual partners, and oral and anal intercourse between homosexual partners. We shall refer to this second category of sexual relations as *nonprocreative intercourse*, because the mode of intercourse is incapable of producing children, or the partners would probably not wish to produce them. To sharpen the issue further, we shall focus on the morality of actually *using* condoms rather than the morality of *advocating* the use of condoms.

1. The use of condoms is an "artificial" mode of contraception and a violation of the natural tendency to procreation. Therefore, it is morally illegitimate unless the principles of forfeiture or double effect can be invoked.

2. The principle of forfeiture is inapplicable to either procreative or nonprocreative intercourse. A person with AIDS has done nothing worthy of death, so he has not forfeited his own right to life.

3. If the use of condoms to prevent AIDS is morally permissible, it must be because the principle of double effect is satisfied.

    Let us begin by considering procreative intercourse. To apply the principle of double effect, we must describe the action and its effects. In this case, the action is the use of condoms in marital vaginal intercourse. The good or morally desirable effect is the prevention of the transfer of the HIV virus. The bad effect is the prevention of conception.

    a. Married couples who have a long-standing monogamous relationship would not need to use condoms, but we can consider a newly married couple, where one or both of the partners had been sexually active before marriage. Here the use of condoms would be desirable to prevent the spread of the HIV virus, assuming the couple had not taken the test for its presence, or the test is not reliable, or some suspicion exists that the couple might still be sexually active outside the marriage. Although sexual activity outside the marriage cannot be justified by natural law, the use of condoms in marital intercourse is a different issue.

If it makes sense to consider the use of condoms apart from the consequence of preventing conception or the transmission of the HIV virus, then we should consider the action in itself morally permissible.

b. If one partner has the HIV virus, or there is a suspicion that he or she has, then the bad effect of using condoms can be avoided while achieving the good effect only by refraining from intercourse altogether. Because natural-law theorists usually consider intercourse an obligation of married partners, this alternative is not acceptable. Therefore, if there is reason to believe a partner might have the HIV virus, the use of condoms might be considered unavoidable.

c. The application of the third criterion is controversial. The prevention of conception is not, strictly speaking, the means of controlling the spread of AIDS. Condoms are used to prevent the entrance of the HIV virus into the other partner's body, not to prevent conception. From this perspective, the use of condoms might appear morally permissible. However, in attempting to control the spread of the HIV virus, the transmission of *all* bodily fluids from one sexual partner to the other must be stopped—including sperm, which can carry the virus. Hence, the prevention of the transmission of sperm (and therefore the prevention of conception) must be a part of the means employed. So the use of condoms in heterosexual vaginal intercourse by a married couple would seem to violate the third criterion.

d. If we consider the risk of loss of life through HIV infection a greater evil than the violation of moral principles involved in the use of condoms, then the principle of proportionality is satisfied.

Because criterion c is violated, procreative intercourse, using condoms to prevent AIDS, is morally impermissible.

Now let us consider nonprocreative intercourse in its various forms. To apply the principle of double effect, we must again describe the action and its effects. In this case, the action is the use of condoms in nonprocreative intercourse. The good or morally desirable effect is the prevention of the transfer of the HIV virus. The bad effect is the provision of a degree of safety that allows nonprocreative intercourse to occur more easily. That is, the bad effect is the encouragement of promiscuity.

a. The use of condoms, considered in itself and apart from its consequences, will again be considered morally permissible.

b. The transmission of the HIV virus can be prevented by refraining from nonprocreative intercourse, so the bad effect is not unavoidable in promoting the good effect.

   c. The provision of an environment in which intercourse that is impermissible from natural law's standpoint can more easily take place is a means of preventing the spread of the HIV virus. Therefore, the bad effect is a means to the good effect.

   d. If we consider the risk of loss of life through HIV infection a greater evil than the violation of moral principles involved in the use of condoms, then the principle of proportionality is satisfied.

      Because criteria b and c are violated, nonprocreative intercourse with condoms is also morally impermissible.

4. We can conclude that the use of condoms to prevent AIDS is morally impermissible in both procreative and nonprocreative intercourse.

Case 2: The Morality of Obliteration Bombing

During World War II, both the Germans and the Allied Forces bombed civilian residential areas, a practice called "obliteration bombing." Probably the two most famous examples of this practice, in which conventional explosives were used, were the German bombing of London and the Allied bombing of Dresden, Germany. Let us confine ourselves to the bombing of Dresden and ask whether this action was permissible by the principles of natural law.

1. The focus must be on the killing of civilians in Dresden. This feature of the action makes it an apparent violation of natural-law morality. Hence, we must ask whether the principles of forfeiture and double effect serve to make the bombing morally permissible.

2. The principle of forfeiture raises the conceptual problem of whether the civilians in Dresden should be considered innocent. If we assume that the criteria of just-war theory were met—that is, the Allied Forces were fighting a just war and the Germans were not fighting a just war—then the Germans in uniform were noninnocent, and attacking them was morally justified. But most civilians in large cities were connected with the war effort in a very indirect way. Unless civilians are employed in the production of military hardware, most natural-law theorists would probably count them as innocent. Many Germans may have had little knowledge of the reasons for the war; in a nondemocratic state, they certainly had no part in starting it. Therefore, the civilians in Dresden should be considered innocent, and the principle of forfeiture does not justify the bombing.

3. Some have argued that an appeal to the principle of double effect could justify the bombing. According to this argument, the direct and intended effect of the bombing was to destroy war industries, communications, and military installations, whereas the damage to civilian life was unintentional and indirect. But a careful analysis of the conditions of the bombing will not sustain this argument.

a. We shall consider the action under analysis to be the bombing of Dresden, the good effect to be the shortening of the war, and the bad effect to be the deaths of innocent civilians. Bombing an enemy city cannot be said to be intrinsically immoral. We have shown that war can be justified by natural law, and we shall assume that the Allied cause could be defended by just-war criteria. Therefore, the Allies had a right to attack German cities.

b. Let us assume that there was no other way to shorten the war except by bombing cities. If the desirable end is described as "shortening the war," bombing the cities would be unavoidable in achieving that end, so the second criterion of the principle of double effect is met.

c. The third criterion asks whether the bad effect—namely, killing innocent civilians—was a means to the good effect. Destroying German morale through terror was, on the testimony of military documents themselves, an object of the bombing. And the means of inducing terror and consequent demoralization was the deaths of innocent civilians. Therefore, the third condition of double effect is not met.

d. We can also question the allegation that the principle of proportionality was satisfied by the belief that obliteration bombing would shorten the war. That goal was speculative, futuristic, and problematic, whereas the evil effect was definite, immediate, and widespread. Thus, we shall conclude that this criterion is also not met and that the principle of double effect does not apply.

4. Because the Allied attack on Dresden involved the destruction of innocent human life, and because the principles of forfeiture and double effect do not excuse it, we must conclude that the action was morally impermissible by natural-law theory.

Case 3: The Suppression of Galileo

Galileo Galilei (1564–1642) has a strong claim to the title of founder of modern science. At first he accepted the Ptolemaic theory that the sun and planets revolved around the earth. But his invention of the telescope and the discovery of the satellites of Jupiter led him to confess his adherence to the Copernican system in 1610. In 1616, the Office of the Holy Inquisition took the important step of entering the works of Copernicus on the list of forbidden books and declaring his teaching heretical. In 1632, Galileo published his *Dialogue on the Two Principal Systems of the World*, in which he contrasted the Ptolemaic and Copernican systems of astronomy. He thought that, if he merely gave an "objective" account of the differences between the two systems, he would not offend the Inquisition and would thereby avoid persecution.

Galileo's sympathies with the Copernican system were all too evident, however, and the Inquisition banned his book and summoned him to Rome for a hearing. After being threatened with torture, Galileo was forced, on June 22, 1633, to go down on his knees and renounce the doctrine that the earth revolves around the sun and to swear that he would cease any further promotion of Copernican astronomy. He lived for several more years under conditions of virtual house arrest but was still able to produce his greatest scientific book. However, the spectacle of Galileo's persecution inhibited the advance of science. Can the silencing of Galileo be justified by the principles of natural law?

1. This issue raises the problem of how to properly promote the natural inclination to know. Natural law requires that we promote the natural inclination of humans to know, but the question is how best to accomplish this. The leaders of the Inquisition would no doubt have described their action of silencing Galileo as promoting the inclination to know, arguing that they were defending truth against error by defending the astronomical system that seems to be in agreement with Holy Scripture. From our perspective, their action should probably be described as obstructing the inclination to know by silencing free inquiry, which we regard as essential to the discovery of truth.

   What is implied by the natural-law requirement to promote knowledge, defending the truths of Holy Scripture or defending free inquiry? In Galileo's time, there were different conceptions of the authority of Scripture in science and the value of free inquiry, and it is not clear that contemporary views are an appropriate basis for evaluating actions that took place centuries ago. However, adopting the contemporary perspective is probably more instructive for us today, so I shall assume that the proper way to promote the natural inclination to know is to promote free inquiry. However, I shall also assume that from the natural-law viewpoint, protecting Holy Scripture has some value as well. Because suppressing free inquiry is, by this account, a violation of a natural inclination, the only way to avoid the conclusion that the Inquisition's action was morally impermissible is to find an excusing condition in one of the two qualifying principles.

2. Galileo had not threatened anyone's life; he had done nothing to forfeit his own right to life. This consideration is important, because Galileo was threatened with torture and possible death. Natural-law theorists might argue that a person can do other things to forfeit his status as an innocent person, such as teach heretical doctrines that endanger the souls of others. However, this point presupposes that Galileo was wrong, so I shall assume that the principle of forfeiture is not relevant.

3. To analyze the action of the leaders of the Inquisition from the standpoint of the principle of double effect, we must be able to distinguish an action, a good effect, and a bad effect. The action, as we have described it, was forcing Galileo to renounce his adherence to Copernican astronomy. The good effect was promoting Scripture's authority. The bad effect was

denying individual freedom to state one's views and seek truth. Can the action of the Inquisitors be justified by the principle of double effect?

a. Forcing Galileo to renounce his public adherence to a scientific view is an act that seems inherently contrary to the inclination to know, even if we consider the act apart from any future consequences regarding the inhibition of free inquiry. Therefore, I shall assume that the first criterion is not met. There is no need to continue the analysis, because the principle of double effect cannot be used here. But, in this case, it will be instructive to proceed with the rest of the analysis.

b. The Inquisitors would probably disagree with most people today on the question of whether denying freedom of expression was avoidable in promoting Scripture's authority. However, we shall assume that it was avoidable, so that the second criterion was not met. Denying individual freedom was probably unavoidable if the authority of Scripture was to be protected, so we shall assume that the second criterion is met.

c. The means used to achieve the end of protecting Scripture was the denial of freedom of inquiry. So this criterion is also not met.

d. The leaders of the Inquisition would probably have said that their action passed the test of proportionality, because the negative consequences of Galileo's suppression were outweighed by the fact that Scripture was defended. But this claim is questionable, because the suppression of opinion (even if it is false) is probably not the best way to defend Scripture. Besides, the test of proportionality is relevant only if the other tests are met. We may conclude that this criterion is also not passed.

4. Because the action of the leaders of the Inquisition violates the value of knowledge by suppressing the right to dissent, and because the two qualifying principles are inapplicable, we must conclude that the Inquisitors' action was morally impermissible.

This case illustrates the difference that factual assumptions and conceptual issues can make in the ethical analysis of a case. The Inquisitors had very different ideas from most of us about the place of free discussion and the authority of Scripture in the pursuit of truth. I shall leave it to you to determine whether, using the ideas prevalent in their time, the Inquisitors could have justified their action from the standpoint of natural law.

EVALUATING NATURAL LAW
AS A MORAL THEORY

We are now ready to evaluate natural law, using the four criteria set up in Chapter 4. I will give you my own evaluations and try to defend them.

Criterion 1: Consistency

Natural-law ethics is, for the most part, internally consistent, but some theorists have found a problem in the use of the principle of forfeiture to justify the direct taking of life. Traditional natural-law theorists take an absolutist position regarding the values of life, procreation, sociability, and knowledge, and they maintain that these values can never be directly violated for any reason. But the principle of forfeiture has seemed, even to some natural-law moralists, to be a violation of the absolute value of life, for it allows the direct taking of life. Killing in war and self-defense can be justified by the principle of double effect, because we can argue (although perhaps implausibly) that the direct intent of these actions is to protect the country or one's life. However, the principle of double effect cannot justify capital punishment, because it can only be counted as a direct taking of life. Here the principle of forfeiture is required if the taking of life by capital punishment is to be justified. Because capital punishment has been considered morally permissible by traditional natural-law moralists, the principle of forfeiture has been essential. It is interesting to consider whether the principle of forfeiture is a legitimate part of natural-law morality or whether its use in natural law arguments is inconsistent with the theory.

We have also pointed out that the criterion of proportionality seems like an exception to the claim that values are incommensurable and cannot be weighed against one another. It also seems to be an exception to the view that consideration of consequences plays no part in natural-law ethical analysis. The response of the natural-law moralist to this objection is that weighing values and considering consequences is permissible only within the confines of the principle of double effect and even then only after the other criteria have been considered. Perhaps we would be correct in saying that weighing values and considering consequences is only a secondary method of ethical analysis and not a primary method as it is in consequentialist theories.

Criterion 2: Justification

Natural-law morality has been associated with religion since the advent of Christianity, so we might suppose that its advocates would attempt to justify the moral standard of natural law by an appeal to the will of God or divine revelation. But natural-law theorists have held that ethical truth is available to all human beings through the natural use of their reason, whether or not they accept a particular religious revelation. Certain religious injunctions, such as observing the Sabbath in Judaism or partaking of the Lord's Supper in Christianity, are derived exclusively from revelation. But, apart from such special commands, revelation is not necessary for us to know how we ought to live. What, then, is the basis of our knowledge of ethical truth that is equally available to all people? We have seen that it is human nature or, more specifically, the natural inclinations of human beings; but we still have not explained how these natural inclinations are known or how they establish ethical truth. Let us consider one account of the foundations of natural law.[6]

We can begin by considering some of the principles or norms that underlie our thinking in areas not necessarily related to ethics. For example, in science we assume that all occurrences in nature have an adequate reason, even if we do not know what this reason is. In ordinary experience, we assume that the things we see are real unless we have reason to believe we are experiencing an illusion. Such principles cannot be proven, for they would be presupposed in any possible proof. But, although they cannot be proven, they are obviously valid to anyone who has any experience with scientific inquiry or even practical living. To deny them is to disqualify oneself from the pursuit of knowledge. In this sense, these principles are self-evident.

Some natural-law theorists believe that certain ethical theses underlie our action in the same way. In particular, we assume in our action that value exists in life, procreation and child rearing, sociability, and knowledge. One way to see the self-evident nature of these values is to observe that anyone who denies them finds that he has refuted himself. We can illustrate this claim by showing self-refutation in the skeptical assertion that knowledge is not a good. One natural-law theorist states the contradiction in the skeptic's assertion in this manner:

> One who makes such an assertion, intending it as a serious contribution
> to rational discussion, is implicitly committed to the proposition that he
> believes his assertion is worth making, and worth making *qua* true; he thus
> is committed to the proposition that he believes that truth is a good
> worth pursuing or knowing. But the sense of his original assertion was
> precisely that truth is not a good worth pursing or knowing. Thus he is
> implicitly committed to contradictory beliefs.[7]

Some natural-law theorists believe that similar demonstrations can be given for the other basic values, although the arguments have not been worked out in detail.

An important point is that, according to this version of natural-law theory, something is not good because we have a natural inclination to pursue it. Rather, we have a natural inclination to pursue it because it is good. Natural inclinations are indicators of those goods that we tend to pursue. Yet it is also true that, if our human nature or the general human condition were different, we might pursue different goods.

Even if we accept the argument that knowledge is a good, similar arguments for the other three values of natural-law morality are not readily available. Nor does this argument establish that these values can never be violated—that, for example, the good of procreation could not be violated to care better for the

---

[6] See John Finnis, *Natural Law and Natural Rights* (Oxford: Clarendon, 1980), pp. 59–75.

[7] Ibid., pp. 74–75.

children we already have. In other words, the natural-law theorist finds it difficult to establish the absolutism that characterizes her position, in both of the
senses in which this term is used. She encounters difficulties in identifying natural inclinations and establishing that the values specified by these inclinations
are objectively valid. She also faces difficulties in establishing that the values of
natural law can never be violated. Thus, the claim of the natural-law theorist
that the values of natural law are clear and objectively valid for all people has
not been demonstrated.

Criterion 3: Plausibility

As we have seen, a moral theory can be evaluated in part by comparing the
moral judgments it produces with our own prior moral beliefs about these
issues. Natural law produces a number of moral judgments that many of us find
difficult to accept. Although our objection is inconclusive, because our moral
judgments may be incorrect, the comparison is important. These seemingly
implausible judgments produced by natural law fall into two primary categories.

First, in situations of "life against life," in which human life will be lost
regardless of what decision is made, natural law teaches that innocent people
must never be directly killed, even if the result is greater loss of life in the long
run. For example, natural-law moralists hold that, when a choice must be
made between pushing a person off a life raft or letting everyone drown, we
must choose the second option. When the choice is between bombing civilians and shortening a war, thereby saving many lives, or not bombing civilians,
thereby producing greater overall loss of life, we must again choose the second
option. Finally, even when both the mother and the fetus will die if an abortion is not performed, natural law teaches that an abortion is immoral, unless
the principle of double effect is applicable. These conclusions seem implausible, even cruel, to many people, yet they follow from the absolutist character
of natural-law ethics—the view that a fundamental value must never be
directly violated.

Second, natural law often seems to place excessive emphasis on the physical
or biological values, giving them importance equal to or greater than the characteristically human values. The most widely known example of this tendency
is the stress on procreation in marriage. Traditional natural law holds that the
primary function of marriage is procreation and that the secondary function is
companionship; that is, primary emphasis is placed on the biological function
of reproduction, a function that human beings have in common with other
animals. Characteristically human qualities, such as the capacity for love and
commitment, are given secondary status. This view seems inconsistent with the
form of natural law we have advocated, according to which the biological and
characteristically human values are of equal importance. However, our proposed concept of natural law prohibits the use of contraception, because it is a
direct violation of the value of procreation. Most people probably feel that the
value of procreation should be violated to allow a couple more fully to enjoy a

love relationship or more adequately to care for the children they already have. Why should procreation be a value that can never be violated?

Many contemporary natural-law theorists have agreed that the character-istically human values should be given priority over the biological values. They criticize traditional natural-law theory for being too "physicalistic" or exhibiting the trait of *physicalism*, which is the understanding of human acts in terms of their physical or biological function.[8] Some natural-law theorists would regard as excessively physicalistic any version of natural-law theory that gives greater or even equal importance to the physical or biological values of life and procreation. For example, they might argue that, in marriage, love (sociability) and the proper education of children (knowledge) should have priority over any obligation to produce more children. Similarly, a concern for the quality of life as exhibited in the capacity for meaningful relationships (sociability) might justify euthanasia in situations in which a person is dying of cancer. By the same kind of reasoning, the traditional natural-law prohibi-tions of sterilization, homosexuality, masturbation, and many other practices could also be reversed. Do you believe this restructuring is compatible with natural-law morality?

Criterion 4: Usefulness

To help people think clearly about moral issues and reach conclusions in diffi-cult cases, a moral theory must provide a clear, plausible method for resolving moral controversies. Natural law has been reasonably successful in this regard. Natural-law moralists generally agree on many important ethical issues. However, the determination of whether a fundamental value has been violated is sometimes difficult, which impairs the usefulness of natural-law moral theory. Recall that a basic value may never be directly violated, but it may be indirectly violated when the principles of double effect and forfeiture apply. The application of these principles is often difficult, impairing the usefulness of the theory.

CONCEPT SUMMARY

Some natural-law theorists believe that traditional natural-law theory is inconsistent in using the principle of forfeiture to justify the direct taking of life, as in capital punishment. The use of the criterion of proportionality also raises problems of consistency with regard to the natural law claim that basic values must never be weighed against one another and that consequences are not crucial in ethical analysis. Natural-law moralists also have difficulty justify-ing their fundamental values. They sometimes attempt to justify the basic

---

[8] See Charles E. Curran, "Natural Law and Contemporary Moral Theology," in his *Contemporary Problems in Moral Theology* (Notre Dame, IN: Fides, 1970), pp. 97–158.

values of natural-law morality by arguing that the values are necessarily assumed in all human activity; however, this demonstration has not been completely worked out. Furthermore, the arguments do not show that basic values may never be violated.

Natural-law theory also does not agree with our prior moral beliefs in several important respects. First, it does not agree with our previous moral beliefs in its claims that life can never be taken. Most of us would probably agree, for example, that a mother should have an abortion when both she and the fetus will otherwise die. Second, natural law also disagrees with most people's moral convictions in its insistence that the biological values have an importance equal to or greater than the characteristically human values. This tendency to understand human action in terms of its biological or physical function is called *physicalism*.

The usefulness of natural-law ethics is limited by the fact that we sometimes have difficulty determining when a fundamental value has been directly violated.

7

The Ethics of
Utilitarianism

In 1958 and 1959, the *New England Journal of Medicine* reported a series of experiments performed on patients in the Willowbrook State School, a home for retarded children in Staten Island, New York.[1] The experiments were designed to confirm the usefulness of gamma globulin as an immunization against hepatitis, improve the serum, and learn more about hepatitis. The school was already experiencing a low-grade hepatitis epidemic. Researchers obtained the consent of the parents, because the children were both underage and retarded. The children were divided into experimental groups and control groups that received hepatitis virus at various levels of infectiousness and gamma globulin inoculations at various strengths. Some of the gamma globulin was given below the strength known to be effective. Children who contracted the disease suffered the usual symptoms (enlargement of the liver, vomiting, anorexia), but all of them recovered.

When these experiments became public knowledge, they produced a storm of controversy. Many people objected that the children had been "used" in a morally unacceptable way. But the experimenters pointed out that the children would have been exposed to the virus anyhow, none of them had died, and

---

[1] Robert Ward, Saul Krugman, Joan P. Giles, A. Milton Jacobs, and Oscar Bodansky, "Infectious Hepatitis: Studies of Its Natural History and Prevention," *New England Journal of Medicine* 258, No. 9 (February 27, 1958), pp. 407–416; Saul Krugman, Robert Ward, Joan P. Giles, Oscar Bodansky, and A. Milton Jacobs, "Infectious Hepatitis: Detection of the Virus during the Incubation Period and Clinically Inapparent Infection," *New England Journal of Medicine* 261, No. 15 (October 8, 1959), pp. 729–734.

valuable medical knowledge was gained from the experiments. Judged in terms of overall human well-being, the experiments do seem to be justified.

If the argument of the experimenters appeals to you, you may be a utilitarian. The basic question a utilitarian asks in determining the moral status of an action is "Will this action produce greater overall human well-being?" For the utilitarian, human well-being is the only good, although some utilitarians also include the well-being of animals. Utilitarians also consider everyone's well-being to be of equal value. Utilitarianism is thus midway between egoism and altruism. The egoist is concerned only with her own happiness, and the altruist is concerned only with the happiness of others. For the utilitarian, her own well-being is neither more nor less important than the well-being of anyone else.

Utilitarianism has its roots in eighteenth-century England, but it flowered in nineteenth-century England, particularly in the writings of Jeremy Bentham and John Stuart Mill. It greatly influenced liberal legislation in England and the United States in the twentieth century and is probably the basic moral philosophy of most nonreligious humanists today.

Utilitarianism is one of the most powerful and persuasive traditions of moral thought in our culture. In fact, many moral controversies, such as the debate over euthanasia, can best be understood as a conflict between utilitarianism and traditional Hebrew-Christian morality. Jewish and Christian theorists generally condemn active euthanasia (for example, taking an injection of poison), even though passive euthanasia (for example, termination of lifesaving medication) may sometimes be allowed. Their reasoning is usually based on the belief that God created human life, and only He has the prerogative of directly ending it.

But what if one does not believe in God? What if one believes that human life is solely the product of nonconscious forces and that the only source of value in the universe is human existence? Then one might conclude that the only possible good is the well-being of humanity. If an individual who is dying of incurable cancer sees only suffering for himself and those he loves, with no discernible good to come out of that suffering, why should he not take his life? If this course of action will produce the most overall human good or well-being, what better way of determining the right thing to do?

Even someone who takes a religious perspective might well find utilitarianism attractive. Would a loving God not be concerned primarily with human welfare? Some religious utilitarians maintain that the utilitarian perspective is compatible with religious values. Thus, for both religious and nonreligious people, utilitarianism is an attractive moral position.

THE UTILITARIAN MORAL STANDARD

Before we formulate a utilitarian standard, we must mention the concept of "audience." In deciding what is morally right, I must take into account all those affected by my action. We shall refer to those affected by a course of action as the audience of the action. Thus, from the utilitarian standpoint, the *audience* of an action includes all of those whose well-being could be either increased or decreased by one's action.

The well-being of each member of the audience should count equally. Each person should count for one and none for no more than one. But because the utility (welfare) of various members of the audience is sometimes incompatible, the best I can do is to seek the greatest total utility. Also, many (probably most) utilitarians now believe that the evaluation of particular actions should be based on the utility of the general moral rules underlying these actions, not on the actions themselves. Taking both of these considerations into account, we can formulate the utilitarian moral standard in the following way:

> MS: Those actions (or moral rules) are right that produce the most utility, or at least as much utility as any other actions (or rules).

Now we are in a position to discuss several aspects of this moral standard in more detail.

The Definition of Utility

How shall we define *utility*? Some utilitarians have maintained that *utility* is synonymous with *happiness* or even *pleasure*. But, unfortunately, these terms are defined differently by different people. And if we specify a particular definition of happiness or pleasure, we seem to be forcing our own values on others.

For example, John Stuart Mill, an important nineteenth-century utilitarian, argues that human beings have capacities that animals do not have and that, when we are aware of those capacities, we cannot regard anything as happiness unless it includes them. In particular, we must give "pleasures of the intellect, of the feeling and imagination, and of the moral sentiments a much higher value as pleasures than those of mere sensation."[2] Mill believes we can confirm the judgment that these pleasures have a higher value than the pleasures of food and sex, for example, simply by asking those who have experienced both kinds of pleasure which they prefer. Would you really want to exchange places with a person who has had all of his physical desires satisfied but who has no close personal relationships, no intellectual or artistic interests, and no goals other than pleasure? Most of us would conclude, Mill believes, that it is better to be a dissatisfied Socrates than a satisfied fool.

However, not everyone who has experienced both the pleasures of the intellect and the pleasures of sex will always choose the former over the latter. The novelist D. H. Lawrence believes that we relate most meaningfully to other human beings and obtain our deepest communication with the nature of things through sexual acts. So, as Mill himself acknowledges, the most we can

---

[2] John Stuart Mill, *Utilitarianism* (New York: Liberal Arts Press, 1957), p. 10.

say is that a majority of people who have experienced the various kinds of pleasure usually prefer the pleasures of the intellect, feelings, and imagination. But even so, have we established that the majority is right? It seems that the utilitarian cannot really define utility in terms of the "higher" pleasures without being arbitrary.

Perhaps it would be better to define *utility* as the satisfaction of any preferences or desires a person might have. But this definition seems too broad and permissive. Jack the Ripper satisfied his preferences by killing people. Must the utilitarian advocate that Jack satisfy his preferences even though they conflict with the desire of his victims to live?

There may be a way out of this dilemma. For the utilitarian, the satisfaction of any preference must be considered a "good" in some sense, but it need not be a good toward which the utilitarian aims. The utilitarian's goal is the greatest total amount of satisfaction of preferences or desires. Some desires, such as the desire to become a cancer researcher, contribute at least potentially to the satisfaction of others' desires as well, such as those who have cancer. Most of our desires are relatively neutral with respect to the desire satisfaction of others. Thus, my desire to buy an ice cream cone after class neither contributes to nor detracts from your desire to go back to your apartment. Still other desires, like those of Jack the Ripper, decrease the ability of others to satisfy their desires. These categories of preferences or desires can be classified according to their claim to satisfaction, beginning with those that have the highest claim:

1. Preferences whose satisfaction contributes to the preference satisfaction of others
2. Preferences whose satisfaction is neutral with respect to the preference satisfaction of others
3. Preferences whose satisfaction decreases the preference satisfaction of others

When we arrange the categories of preference satisfaction into such a hierarchy, we can see that the utilitarian should aim at the satisfaction of preferences in the top two categories if he wishes to achieve the greatest total amount of preference satisfaction. Although this solution to the problem of defining *utility* is not without its difficulties, it does seem to avoid the problem of arbitrariness inherent in the first attempt. We can therefore be content with our definition of *utility* as preference or desire satisfaction.

Distribution versus Quantity of Utility

This solution assumes that the utilitarian wants to do what produces the *greatest total amount* of utility or preference satisfaction. This means that, when we have a choice between an action that produces the greatest total amount of utility and one that produces the greatest distribution of utility, we must choose the former. Consider a situation represented by the following table:

Action	*Number of People Affected*	*Units of Utility per Person*	*Total*
Act 1	2	100	200
Act 2	50	2	100

Note that act 1 affects only two people, but it gives each of them a hundred units of utility and gives no one any disutility, so that the total quantity of utility is two hundred units. The alternative act affects fifty people, but it produces only two units of utility each, for a total of a hundred units. The act producing the greatest quantity of utility would not provide for its widest distribution, and the act producing the widest distribution would not produce the greatest quantity. Which action should be performed?

In accordance with the guideline set out in the previous section, a utilitarian must choose act 1. If a utilitarian chooses act 2, he can justify his choice only by adding another criterion, having to do with the distribution of utility, to the utilitarian moral standard. For example, the moral standard might say that those actions (or moral rules) are right that produce the most utility, or at least as much utility as any other actions (or rules), *provided the utility is equally distributed.* This addition not only severely restricts the ability of the utilitarian to maximize utility, but one has to ask, "What is its basis?" It seems to have a basis in a concern for justice (equal distribution) rather than anything connected with the utilitarian standard.

Most utilitarians have therefore concluded that this addition would introduce serious inconsistencies into the utilitarian position and so must be avoided. Nevertheless, eliminating any direct consideration of the distribution of utility raises questions about the compatibility of utilitarianism with ordinary standards of justice. We shall return to this issue later.

The Place of Animals

The third and final question concerns the types of beings whose preferences are to be considered. Should the audience over which utility is maximized be confined to human beings? If utilitarianism takes the satisfaction of preferences as the only thing that is good in and of itself, why should only the preferences of human beings be considered? Do not all animals have preferences or, at least, wants or needs? Mill seems to admit the force of this observation when he says that happiness should be secured not only to human beings but, "so far as the nature of things admits, to the whole of sentient creation."[3] Even though we use the concept of preference satisfaction rather than happiness, the point is the same.

One of the most eloquent and moving pleas for the consideration of animals is made by Jeremy Bentham, the founder of modern utilitarianism. In

---

[3] Ibid., p. 16.

a passage written when black slaves in parts of the British Empire were treated the way we treat animals today, Bentham says:

> The day may come when the rest of the animal creation may acquire those rights which never could have been withholden from them but by the hand of tyranny. The French have already discovered that the blackness of the skin is no reason why a human being should be abandoned without redress to the caprice of a tormentor. It may one day come to be recognized that the number of legs, the villosity of the skin or termination of the *os saccum*, are reasons equally insufficient for abandoning a sensitive being to the same fate. What else is it that should trace the insuperable line? Is it the faculty of reason, or perhaps the faculty of disclosure? But a full-grown horse or dog is beyond comparison more rational, as well as a more conversable animal, than an infant of a day, a week, or even a month old. But suppose it were otherwise, what would it avail? The question is not, Can they reason? nor Can they talk? but, Can they suffer?[4]

Here Bentham makes the capacity to suffer (and, of course, he would include the capacity to enjoy) the characteristic that entitles a being to consideration from a utilitarian standpoint. The capacity for suffering and enjoyment is not just another characteristic like the capacity for language or higher mathematics. It is a prerequisite for having any claim to ethical consideration at all. A stone does not have any such claim precisely because it cannot suffer or enjoy. Animals have such claims because they can suffer and enjoy. Therefore, we have little justification for considering only human beings in our utilitarian calculations.

The human-centered ethical orientation of much Western ethics has been called "speciesism" by Peter Singer, a utilitarian advocate of the rights of animals.[5] Just as the white racist fails to regard the interests of blacks as having the same importance as the interests of whites, so the speciesist excludes animals from having a claim to our consideration. Humans may suffer more intensely than animals, because of their greater self-consciousness and ability to anticipate the future. Therefore, human interests can often outweigh animals' interests. Nevertheless, equal suffering should count equally, according to the advocates of animal rights. So, in a utilitarian calculation, animal suffering or enjoyment should count equally to that of human beings in considering the morality of actions or rules, insofar as it is of the same degree or intensity. This position has some interesting implications for issues such as eating animal flesh, using animals in experimentation, wearing animal skins, hunting of all types, and keeping animals as pets and as circus and zoo exhibits.

---

[4] Jeremy Bentham, *Introduction to the Principles of Morals and Legislation*, Chap. 17, Sect. 1, note; quoted in Peter Singer, *Practical Ethics* (Cambridge, MA: Cambridge University Press, 1979), pp. 49–50.

[5] Singer, *Practical Ethics*, Chap. 3.

ACT UTILITARIANISM AND
RULE UTILITARIANISM

One of the most frequently discussed issues in utilitarian theory is the distinction between act utilitarianism and rule utilitarianism. Because the difference in applying these two versions of utilitarianism can be difficult to understand, let us begin our discussion with an example.

John finds himself with a final average in a philosophy course that is ten points below passing. Without a passing grade, he cannot graduate and take the coaching job he has been offered. He approaches his professor with the following argument:

> If you give me the ten points on my final average, I will not tell anyone. I know the information would hurt both of us. I'm married and have a small son. I will be out of school soon, and my job is in another state. If I do not graduate, I will lose the job offer, and my family and I will endure considerable hardship. In fact, I may have to drop out of school, because I am out of money. I studied as much as I could, but I find philosophy hard to understand and work forty hours a week. This has been a tough semester for me.

Suppose you are the professor and you know that John's story is true. Your concern is not simply to protect your own interests; rather, you want to do whatever produces the greatest total utility for those affected. What should you do?

The answer to this question depends in part on whether you are an act utilitarian or a rule utilitarian. Here is a summary of the difference between these two forms of utilitarianism:

> *Act utilitarianism* judges the morality of an action by whether the action itself produces the most utility, or at least as much utility as any other action.

> *Rule utilitarianism* judges the morality of an action by whether the moral rule presupposed by the action, if generally followed, would produce the most utility, or at least as much utility as any other rule.

What conclusions will these two versions of utilitarianism lead to in this particular case? Applying act utilitarianism, you would determine whether to give John the ten points on his final average by deciding which of the two alternative actions (giving or not giving the ten points) would produce more utility in this particular situation. To make this determination, you must consider how everyone in the audience would be affected by the two alternatives.

A good argument can be made that, according to act utilitarianism, you should give John the ten points on his final average. Assuming the arrangement is kept secret, you would suffer no negative consequences, except perhaps a general feeling of uneasiness or guilt. If you are a confirmed act utilitarian, you may not feel any remorse, because by your own moral standard your action is justifiable.

The other people who are directly affected by the action are John, his family, and the other students in the class. If John gets the ten points, his own desires will be met; he will graduate and get the job he has been promised. His family will then enjoy the benefits of a father and husband with a stable income. He may suffer some loss of pride, knowing that he has not fully earned his degree, but very likely this loss will be offset by the fact that he has a good job and can care for his family. He can also justify his action by remembering that he probably did the best he could under the circumstances.

The welfare of the other students will not be adversely affected to any significant degree. Assuming that you do not allow the one higher grade to influence the grades you give to other students, their standing in the class will not be affected, so you will conclude that greater total utility will be produced by giving John the ten points than by refusing his request.

Rule utilitarianism probably leads to a different conclusion. To see the difference, you must compare the utilities of the two alternative rules involved in this case. If you give John the ten points, the rule underlying your action could be formulated as:

Professors should assign grades according to the needs of students, not their merit.

If you decide not to give the ten points, the rule underlying your action could be formulated as:

Professors should assign grades according to merit, not the needs of students.

As a rule utilitarian, you will ask, "Which of the two general rules will produce the greater overall utility?" You will not be comparing the utility of two specific actions but that of two different policies. Would more utility be produced if professors generally graded according to need or if they graded according to merit?

Let us consider first the consequences of a general policy of grading according to need rather than merit. If this policy became widespread, grades would become relatively meaningless. Other teachers and prospective employers could not make any inference from grades to a student's true academic merit. They would have to spend a great deal of time talking to professors and asking questions such as, "I know John received an A in your course, but was he really an A student?" Grades would no longer have the prestige they once had, which might reduce many students' incentive to do well in school. Students could more easily deceive parents, teachers, fellow students, and prospective employers about their academic achievement.

Requiring that professors assign grades on the basis of merit seems not to have the same disadvantages. Although the present system of determining grades by merit is not without fault, it seems to produce more overall utility than the alternative system. Therefore, if the second rule is more justified by the utilitarian moral standard, it must be applied to John. He must be judged by merit rather than need, and his request must be denied.

As this example suggests, rule utilitarianism often leads to different, more plausible conclusions than act utilitarianism. Rule utilitarianism also does more justice to our belief that morality should be a matter of following rules; that is, it agrees with a widespread belief that a morally acceptable action is one we would willingly have others follow. Not surprisingly, then, many philosophers have favored rule utilitarianism over act utilitarianism. Following this tradition, we will use *utilitarianism* to mean rule utilitarianism. When we discuss act utilitarianism, we will specify so.

Act utilitarianism is an important adjunct to rule utilitarianism. It can be used, for example, when a rule and its most reasonable alternative produce approximately equal amounts of utility, in which case rule utilitarianism provides no basis for making a decision. If you cannot decide which of two alternatives is morally right by evaluating the utility of the rules underlying the two alternatives, look directly at the utility of the two actions themselves. If neither has appreciably greater utility, then either action is permissible by the utilitarian moral standard.

Keep in mind that for the utilitarian, nothing but utility is good in itself, and nothing but disutility is bad in itself. Particular actions and general rules must be evaluated by their consequences. Murder, rape, fraud, and theft are not somehow wrong in themselves; they are wrong only because they do not produce as much utility as alternative behaviors. If two or more actions or rules have the same utility, they are of equal moral worth.

FURTHER CONSIDERATIONS IN APPLYING RULE UTILITARIANISM

The basic idea of utilitarianism is simple: Rules or actions are right insofar as they promote utility and wrong insofar as they promote disutility. We have already seen some complications in applying this simple idea. Two additional issues, which we will encounter when we begin to apply utilitarianism, are (1) whether others will obey the rules that utilitarians find most desirable and (2) how we should go about formulating the rule presupposed by a particular action.

Will Others Obey the Rules?

In the example of the student who asked for a higher grade, we assumed that professors could realistically be expected to follow either of the two rules we formulated. Our assumption was most likely valid; college teachers would probably be able to adopt either rule. But, in some cases, the rule that produces the most overall utility is unlikely to be generally adopted under any circumstances we can reasonably imagine. Is a rule utilitarian still morally obligated to follow the ideal rule?

Let us first consider a trivial example to illustrate the point and then proceed to a more serious example to show how important this issue can be. Suppose you are walking to your class, and the most direct route is across the grass along a path that is well worn by frequent use. A sign posted nearby reads, "Please do not walk on the grass," but most people disregard it. Should you disregard the sign too? From a rule-utilitarian perspective, the rule that "Everyone should walk on the sidewalks rather than on the grass" will probably produce more utility than the rule "One may walk wherever one wishes." If everyone follows the first rule, we experience only minor inconvenience, the campus will have a neater appearance, and the maintenance crews will avoid the unnecessary expenses of filling the ruts and planting new grass, which will then be destroyed again.

But suppose you have good reason to believe that few people will follow this first rule. Moreover, from an act utilitarian standpoint, you should probably take the path across the grass like everyone else. You will avoid a minor inconvenience, and the grass will not be any worse because one more student takes the easier way. Many utilitarians would say that you are not obligated to obey the sign "Please do not walk on the grass" until you have reason to believe that it will be generally followed, even though a rule requiring obedience to the sign would actually produce greater utility if generally followed.

Now let us consider a more serious example. Suppose you are a manager for a foreign operation of a multinational corporation. Your plant is in South Africa, where racial discrimination is still widely practiced. Ideally, you would like to provide housing for your employees without regard to race or ethnic origin, but you know that such a policy would cause serious problems for your business. The plant might even be forced to close, and your employees would lose their jobs. You feel confident that, if everyone were to adopt it, the rule that "Business should provide housing for employees without regard to race or ethnic origin" would produce greater utility in the long run than the alternative rule of following discriminatory policies. You are just as confident, however, that few companies would freely adopt the ideal rule.

So the rule that could actually produce more utility, because it has a greater chance of being adopted, is "Business should adopt a policy of racially discriminatory housing in areas where this policy is the only practical one that can be followed." By following this rule, your business will at least be allowed to remain open and provide needed jobs. However, you do have to consider the example you are setting in following the traditional racist policies. If you have reason to think your example will cause others to rethink their practices, you should probably break precedent.

A general guideline for such circumstances might be as follows: When you have reason to believe that the ideal utilitarian rule will not be generally followed and that a less desirable rule, because it more likely would be generally adopted, would produce more utility, you should follow the less desirable rule.

How Should the Rule Be Formulated?

So far we have discussed rule utilitarianism as if only one rule and one clear alternative can be presupposed by a course of action. However, many actions can be described by more than one rule. It is important to use a rule that (1) describes all of the features of the action that are relevant from a utilitarian standpoint, (2) does not describe features that are morally irrelevant, and (3) is as general as possible. Let us consider each of these three guidelines.

First, the rule should describe all relevant features of the action from a utilitarian standpoint. Suppose you are driving along a highway and see an orchard full of ripe apples. You are hungry and wonder whether it would be morally acceptable to stop and pick several apples. The rule presupposed by the action might be stated as follows:

> A person should pick and eat fruit when he is hungry.

However, this rule does not adequately describe the situation and is therefore not an appropriate rule on which to base a moral decision. Its most obvious deficiency is its failure to mention at least one morally relevant fact: the apples belong to someone else, and they would be taken without the owner's permission. Because this fact is relevant to the utility that would be produced by the general adoption of the rule, you should restate the rule to include it:

> A person should pick and eat apples that do not belong to him when he is hungry.

This rule is a better description of the circumstances of the case and superior to the first rule for this reason. This is not to say that the utilitarian would find this rule justifiable from the utilitarian standpoint, but it is a more appropriate rule to test for its utility *because* it is a more adequate account of the morally relevant factors.

This rule still might not fully describe the situation under which you took the apples, however. Suppose you are experiencing severe dehydration and the apples are the only available source of water. You might formulate the rule to take this need into account:

> A person should pick and eat apples that do not belong to him if the apples are the only means of avoiding serious dehydration.

This rule would apply only to a small number of people, and its general adoption would probably produce more utility than the alternative rule requiring that the apples not be picked even under these extreme circumstances.

Second, the rules should not describe features that are morally irrelevant. If your name is Susan Brown and you are driving home after your first year in college, you might formulate the moral rule underlying your action as follows:

Everyone whose name is Susan Brown and who is returning from her first year in college should pick and eat apples that do not belong to her if the apples are the only means of avoiding serious dehydration.

This rule incorporates morally irrelevant features. It violates a criterion discussed in Chapter 1—namely, that moral statements have an impersonal character. Thus, names, dates, and places should not be included in moral rules.

Third, the rules should be as broad as possible, without being too broad. The rule must strike a balance between being too broad and too narrow. The first two guidelines indicate some of the factors that can make a rule too broad or too narrow. When relevant moral factors (such as the apples' belonging to someone else) are ignored, the rule is too broad. When irrelevant factors (such as Susan Brown's name) are included, the rule is too narrow. But rules can be too broad or too narrow in other ways. For example, as a utilitarian, you might well conclude that a rule covering many other types of actions would be acceptable. Rather than limit the rule to the circumstance having to do with picking apples and the possible harm of dehydration, it would be better to say:

Everyone should engage in petty theft if it is necessary to avoid serious harm.

Remember that the rules you are evaluating are supposed to be ones that could be adopted in a society. This rule is more likely to be a part of a moral code of a society than a rule limited to the particular case of eating apples. For this reason, it is probably a more adequate rule to test than any of the others.

Because moral rules are part of a larger system of moral rules, some utilitarians argue that the standard of utility should not be applied to particular rules, one at a time, but to a whole set of rules, even an entire moral code. We must ask of a moral code whether its general acceptance by most people in a given society would produce more or less utility than the general acceptance of an alternative moral code. We have not used this version of rule utilitarianism because it is difficult to apply. Evaluating the utility of an entire moral code is no easy task, and it would take us far afield from our consideration of particular moral issues. Furthermore, it is still possible to modify a particular rule within a moral code by testing the rules much as we have been doing. So our method of testing particular rules would seem to be a part of any more elaborate version of rule utilitarianism.

The following two checklists cover rule and act utilitarianism. The first checklist covers rule utilitarianism, the form favored by many utilitarians. However, we must appeal to act utilitarianism in situations in which two rules produce equal utility or in which rule utilitarianism just does not seem to be appropriate. Also, it is often important to see the different conclusions reached by act and rule utilitarianism on the same issue.

CHECKLIST FOR APPLYING RULE UTILITARIANISM

____ 1. State the rule that is presupposed by the action you are evaluating. The rule should be specific enough to describe those features of the situation that would produce positive or negative utility but not so specific or impractical that it could not realistically be adopted by a society.

____ 2. State the most reasonable alternative rule or rules, keeping in mind the precautions stated in step 1.

____ 3. Determine the proper audience for the rule—that is, the people or animals that would be affected by the rules.

____ 4. Identify the rule that would produce the greatest total utility, assuming that it could realistically be followed.

    a. The rule that produces the greatest utility or whose alternative produces the least utility is morally obligatory.

    b. Rules that produce less utility overall are morally impermissible.

    c. If two rules produce equal utility, or if for any reason a rule cannot be formulated, it is permissible to resort to act utilitarianism to decide the issue.

____ 5. Apply the obligatory or permissible rule to the particular action. If no rule is justified, move to act utilitarianism.

CHECKLIST FOR APPLYING ACT UTILITARIANISM

____ 1. Describe the action and the most reasonable alternatives to the action.

____ 2. Determine the proper audience for the act—that is, the people or animals that would be affected by the action.

____ 3. Identify the action that would produce the greatest total amount of utility, assuming it could realistically be followed.

    a. The action that produces the greatest total amount of utility is morally obligatory.

    b. Actions that produce less overall utility are morally impermissible.

    c. If two or more actions produce equal utility, they are equally morally permissible.

CONCEPT SUMMARY

Utilitarianism is a highly influential moral philosophy in contemporary society. One of the most widely accepted forms of utilitarianism defines *utility* as preference or desire satisfaction. The most consistent form of utilitarianism is one that disregards the distribution of utility (that is, whose preferences are satisfied) and aims simply for the greatest total utility or preference satisfaction. A consistent utilitarianism must take account of the preferences of animals as well as humans, especially the natural tendency of all animals to avoid suffering. However, because humans have a higher degree of self-consciousness and the ability to anticipate the future, they have greater capacity to suffer and enjoy. This capacity justifies giving human preferences special consideration.

Act utilitarianism focuses on the utility produced by a particular action, whereas rule utilitarianism focuses on the utility produced by the general acceptance of the rule presupposed by an action. These two forms of utilitarianism can sometimes lead to different moral conclusions, and many utilitarians favor rule utilitarianism as the more adequate version of utilitarian theory. However, act utilitarianism is still useful in determining what to do when two rules seem equally acceptable from a utilitarian standpoint.

In applying rule utilitarianism, it is important to ask yourself whether the rule that would produce the greatest utility is one that others would be likely to follow. If others are not likely to follow it, the best procedure is to adopt a rule that does have a chance of being generally accepted. Several guidelines for selecting the rule to test in rule utilitarianism are available: (1) the rule should describe all of the features of the action that are relevant from a utilitarian standpoint; (2) the rule should not include features that are morally irrelevant; (3) the rule should be as broad and inclusive as possible, without leaving out morally relevant features.

UTILITARIAN PERSONAL AND SOCIAL ETHICS

In applying utilitarianism thus far, we have resolved moral problems by referring to the utilitarian moral standard; that is, we have analyzed the rule presupposed by an action and then tested the action by the standard of utility. But analysis is aided by knowing generally what the implications of utilitarianism are—that is, what kind of personal and social ethics the utilitarian moral standard supports. This section is devoted to clarifying these issues.

We must first, though, enter a cautionary note. Utilitarianism, like egoism, judges the morality of actions by their consequences. In both moral theories, knowledge of the consequences of actions (or rules, in the case of rule utilitarianism) is of central importance. The egoist cannot know which form of economic organization is justified by egoism unless he knows which one produces consequences that are most compatible with his own self-interest. Similarly, the utilitarian cannot know what character traits or types of behavior or forms of social organization are justified by the utilitarian moral standard unless she knows what consequences they produce and which consequences are most conducive to utility.

This point means that any discussion of the general implications of utilitarian theory must presuppose the truth of certain factual assumptions. If these assumptions are questioned, the implications drawn from them must also be questioned. It is important, therefore, for you to identify the factual assumptions made in the following discussion and decide whether you agree with them.

Duties to Self

In the personal ethics of utilitarianism, a person's actions must be governed by those rules that in general lead to the greatest total utility. But this statement does not mean that I will make my maximum contribution to the well-being of others if I am doing something that I am unsuited for or that I detest. If I find my greatest satisfaction in being an engineer or a gardener, a physician or a plumber, I should follow that occupation. I will probably make my greatest contribution to the general well-being by doing what gives me the greatest satisfaction.

This observation shows that self-realization has a legitimate place in utilitarian ethics, although it must always be the means to the promotion of utility. Of course, if my greatest talent is robbing banks, I should not realize this talent, because it will not contribute to the general welfare. Nevertheless, utilitarianism clearly takes account of the psychological egoist's observation that all of us are powerfully motivated by considerations of self-interest. The utilitarian can argue that, in large measure, utilizing these motivations for utilitarian ends is possible.

In some important areas of duties to self, utilitarianism leads to different conclusions than traditional Hebrew-Christian morality. We have seen that natural-law ethics condemns suicide and euthanasia as violations of the sanctity of human life. A moment's consideration of this issue shows that the utilitarian will take a very different stance from a natural-law theorist. Just as we must count a desire to go on living as a reason against killing, so we must count a desire to die as a reason for killing. One can have a preference for dying as well as a preference for living.

Utilitarianism can even justify "active" as well as "passive" euthanasia. The Hebrew-Christian tradition has placed great emphasis on the distinction between acts and omissions. But utilitarians judge the morality of an action by its consequences—in particular, those consequences that affect the satisfaction of preferences. If two actions, one a commission and the other an omission, both have the same consequences in terms of preference satisfaction (or, as some might say, the same "bottom line" in terms of utility), they should not have different moral evaluations from the utilitarian standpoint.

Suppose a terminal cancer patient is receiving life-sustaining medication. The patient asks the physician to help him end his life. In one version of the story, the physician administers a lethal injection; in the other, she omits administering the life-sustaining medication. If the death is equally swift and painless in both cases, the utilitarian would have to evaluate the two acts as morally equivalent. In this situation, the physician would probably omit the life-sustaining medication; but if the lethal injection produced a faster and less painful death, the utilitarian would find this "active" method to be the more morally desirable. In any event, the active-passive distinction would not be the deciding factor.

One qualification should be made in the claim that it is only the "bottom line" with which the utilitarian must be concerned. Although this claim is true, *all* of the consequences of a general practice (in the case of rule utilitarianism) or all of the consequences of a particular act (in the case of act utilitarianism) must be considered. For example, suppose it could be shown that the widespread practice of active euthanasia resulted in a diminished regard for human life that is contrary to utility. This consideration must be considered as one effect of euthanasia, and it might be sufficient to overbalance any positive effects of the practice.

You can probably think of other issues within the category of duties to oneself for which the utilitarian would reach conclusions different from traditional Hebrew-Christian beliefs, especially the beliefs of natural-law theorists. What would utilitarians say about the morality of sterilization, masturbation, or the self-giving of vital organs, for example? A measure of the influence of utilitarianism is that the moral beliefs of many people already appear to be undergoing a change in the direction of the utilitarian approach to these issues.

Duties to Others

Utilitarianism can easily justify many of he common rules of morality relating to other people. Prohibitions against murder, theft, and fraud follow from the observations that such activities, if generally practiced, would not promote the general welfare. A more interesting case to consider from the utilitarian standpoint is the controversial case of abortion.[6] The utilitarian believes that human beings do not deserve special consideration simply because they supposedly have a soul. Rather, consideration must be based on possession of traits that allow a being to have interests or preferences, such as rationality and self-consciousness, and the ability to experience pain or enjoyment. Killing is wrong when it conflicts with the interest of living beings in staying alive, and the degree of interest a being can have depends on the extent to which it possesses these traits. The fertilized egg immediately after conception cannot possibly feel pain or be aware of anything. It cannot, therefore, have interests that deserve to be considered in a utilitarian calculus. As the fetus grows, it develops the capacity to feel pain and perhaps even to experience a degree of consciousness, but a calf, pig, or chicken has more developed interests than a

---

6 See pages 5, 24, and 33 for earlier discussion of this topic.

fetus. By the utilitarian moral standard, we should accord the life of a fetus no greater value than the life of a nonhuman animal at a similar stage of self-consciousness and capacity to feel pain.

Antiabortion advocates might argue that even before the fetus is sufficiently developed to have interests, it is at least *potentially* a being that can have interests. Does this potentiality not deserve respect? From a utilitarian standpoint, potential interests might seem to merit little if any consideration in comparison to the actual interests of more developed fetuses and human beings. But utilitarians do consider the potential interests of human beings who will live in the future. If these interests are considered, why should the interests of early fetuses not also be considered?

One important difference is that future generations will actually exist at some point in the future, but fetuses may never exist if a decision is made to have an abortion. Another difference is that utilitarians consider the interests of future generations *in general*, not the interests of particular individuals who may exist in the future. Thus, there are important differences between the interests of individual fetuses, especially at very early stages, and the interests of future generations. Whether these differences are important enough to justify disregarding the interests of early fetuses is a matter of controversy.

If we disregard the interests of early fetuses, what specific conclusions should we arrive at regarding the morality of abortion from the utilitarian standpoint? Peter Singer has proposed that fetuses of less than eighteen weeks are very unlikely to be capable of feeling anything at all, because their nervous systems are insufficiently developed. Therefore, we cannot say they have any interests to protect. Abortions during this period, Singer believes, should pose no moral problems. Between eighteen weeks and birth, when the fetus certainly has a capacity to feel and may even be conscious, abortion should not be taken lightly. But even here the serious interests of the mother would ordinarily override the rudimentary interests of the fetus.

These same arguments apply to a newborn baby. A week-old baby is not a rational and self-conscious being. In fact, by the standards we have developed, the life of a newborn baby is of less value than the life of an adult pig, dog, or chimpanzee. Utilitarians might argue that killing newborn babies has some other antiutilitarian consequences, such as promoting a lower regard for human life that could increase the incidence of killing adults. But unless such arguments can be made, the utilitarian must conclude that infanticide can be justified, at least on some occasions. Again, these views contrast sharply with Hebrew-Christian morality. But the utilitarian argues that we should modify our views to bring them into line with what he believes to be the more plausible utilitarian standard.

Social Ethics

The general principle governing utilitarian social ethics is that equal consideration should be given to the preferences of everyone affected by social policies, with a view to achieving the greatest total satisfaction of those preferences. Three implications of this guideline are especially interesting.

First, most utilitarians have argued for democratic government as a means of achieving the utilitarian ideal of maximizing the satisfaction of preferences. The best way to ensure that the maximum number of preferences is satisfied is for each individual to exercise control over the government by means of the vote. Democracy also tends to encourage the development of an active, responsible character. Some utilitarians have found still another reason for preferring democracy to other forms of government. When citizens have the responsibility of deciding governmental policies, however indirectly, they tend to develop capacities of self-determination that are more conducive to self-realization than the more docile and passive character traits fostered by nondemocratic political orders.

Second, utilitarians have favored the maximum degree of individual freedom, especially in the realm of ideas. In his important essay *On Liberty*, John Stuart Mill observes that one can easily assume that, when democratic government has been established, the battle for individual liberty has been won. However, Mill argues, the majority may still be inclined to restrict the rights of dissenting minorities, especially when the ideas of minorities are highly unpopular. Mill believes that this is a mistake and that the rights of dissenting minorities can be defended on utilitarian grounds. He maintains that allowing individuals to pursue their own ideas and beliefs leads to the discovery of truth. In what some have called the "free marketplace of ideas," the best ideas will survive in the competition with other ideas. For example, science requires intellectual freedom so that ideas may be openly advanced and criticized to discover the truth. The same freedom is required in other areas, such as politics. The best way to conduct a society can be discovered only by allowing citizens the freedom to advance ideas and then allowing other citizens to expose their flaws.

Mill assumes that the discovery of truth leads to utility. Although he does not make any extended argument for this claim, we may assume his argument to be that knowledge of the consequences of actions provides the basis for a more effective pursuit of the utilitarian ideal. Thus, a utilitarian will support individual freedom, because individual freedom leads to the discovery of truth, and the discovery of truth promotes the greatest satisfaction of people's preferences.

Third, twentieth-century utilitarians have often argued for extensive welfare measures and at least a partial redistribution of wealth. Democracy and freedom for individual dissent are not enough to ensure maximum preference satisfaction. Equal opportunity does not compensate for the deleterious effects of a destructive family life. Perhaps even more important, it neglects the importance of genetic endowment. We know that early training has a great deal to do with emotional stability and how much effort individuals will expend to achieve their goals. We also know that IQ, physical health, and stamina, and probably many other traits, are primarily genetic. Therefore, even if equal opportunity is provided, those with more fortunate family and social backgrounds and more desirable genetic endowments will be in a better position to satisfy their interests. They will be able to pursue more interesting and lucrative careers, achieve greater social prestige, and otherwise enjoy a more comfortable and rewarding life. This restriction of these advantages to the fortunate few will probably not produce the greatest total satisfaction of interests.

Some utilitarians, including Peter Singer, have proposed that the utilitarian ideal would be realized more completely if society could adopt the famous Marxist slogan "From each according to his ability, to each according to his needs."[7] But Singer and most other utilitarians realize the practical difficulties in fully implementing this ideal. In this situation, the ideal utilitarian rule will not, in fact, produce the greatest utility, because it has little chance of being generally adopted owing to the natural selfishness of most human beings. If we do not pay a person more for being a computer programmer than for cleaning offices, she may not make the effort to get the advanced training needed for computer programming. And will not the failure to use the talents of many of the most gifted people fully result in less total preference satisfaction? Most of the advances in society are produced by the more talented members. If they have no incentive to use their talents, we might all be worse off.

These considerations have convinced many utilitarians that social policy must reward individuals for using their inherited abilities rather than strictly according to their needs. Therefore, we should, within certain limits, reward the more talented members of society for their special achievements. This recommendation illustrates the earlier guideline that a practice should not be implemented if it has little chance of success, regardless of how desirable it may be from a utilitarian standpoint. A less desirable rule that would actually be followed will produce more utility. Nevertheless, many utilitarians still feel that providing the basic necessities for all citizens, as the welfare state attempts to do, is required by their philosophy.

APPLYING UTILITARIAN THEORIES

We can now apply utilitarianism to some problems that require moral decision, using the methodology developed in the checklist.

Case 1: The Willowbrook School

Let us begin by considering the case presented at the beginning of this chapter.
1. The rule followed by the administrators of the Willowbrook School is not easy to formulate. Should we consider subjecting the population in

---

[7] Ibid., p. 36.

general to a degree of pressure to participate in medical experiments, or should we confine the rule to inmates in public institutions? Should the rule mention that the children are retarded or that the risk is minimal and the chance of yielding valuable knowledge is great? The general guideline is that the morally relevant features must be included in the rule. From the utilitarian standpoint, the moral relevance is determined in part by whether the fact might affect the overall utility. But there are also other factors. As we have seen, the rule should be as general as possible and not include morally irrelevant factors.

Considering these factors, I have decided not to include the fact that the children are retarded, because the decision would be made by the parents in either case. I have decided to include the fact that the children are in a public institution, because the children are receiving benefits from the public. The state may thus have a right to expect something in return. The fact that the risk is minimal and that valuable knowledge may come from the experiments is important from a utilitarian standpoint because it is one indication that the benefit to others is likely to outweigh the potential harm to the children. The rule might be stated in the following way:

It is morally permissible to use mild coercion in getting inmates in public institutions to submit to medical experiments when the experiments promise substantial benefit to the general population (and perhaps the inmates themselves) and when risk is minimal.

2. The alternative rule should be the negation of this rule:

It is not morally permissible to use mild coercion in getting inmates in public institutions to submit to medical experiments when the experiments promise substantial benefit to the general population (and perhaps the inmates themselves) and when risk is minimal.

3. The audience of this rule would be the inmates of public institutions, the parents of the inmates (if the inmates are children), the administrators of the public institutions, the members of the medical profession who conduct such experiments, and anyone afflicted with the diseases that are the subject of the experiments. The general public is also affected, although to a lesser extent, in various ways that will be enumerated later.

4. The rule utilitarian approach requires that we distance ourselves from the particulars of the case at hand (except as illustrations) and consider the harms and benefits of a *general policy* represented by the two rules. The primary benefit of the policy described in the first rule is, of course, the valuable medical information that can be gained. The Willowbrook case illustrates the kind of knowledge that can result: confirmation of the value of gamma globulin, improvement of that serum, and increased knowledge of how the disease is transmitted. The information might benefit the inmates themselves (as it no doubt would in the Willowbrook case), and, if

useful information is gained, it will certainly benefit the many people who would be afflicted in the future with the disease being investigated.

In a more indirect way, the information will benefit the general public, for they will have the assurance that more effective treatment would be available if they should get the disease. The members of the medical profession would benefit by the policy outlined in the first rule, for they would enjoy the satisfaction and professional advancement that results from being able to conduct medical experiments.

The effect on the administrators and the parents of the inmates (if the inmates are children) is more difficult to determine. However, they would have the satisfaction of knowing that their children, or the inmates of their institution, are participating in medical experiments that have the potential of conferring a benefit on humanity.

Finally, the inmates themselves might have some satisfaction in knowing that they are participating in experiments that have the potential of benefiting large numbers of people. (In the Willowbrook case, the retarded children would probably have little satisfaction from this knowledge.)

The inmates would experience most of the negative effects. They would be subject to the risks and possible pain and discomfort associated with the experiments. The parents and administrators would have to endure the anxiety associated with the knowledge that the experiments might result in harm or even death to their charges. They would also have to endure the bad publicity that would result from harm to the inmates. The general public would also be negatively affected if they believed injustice had been done, perhaps wondering whether they might be subjected to a similar injustice if they were in a public institution. Finally, the medical profession might suffer a loss of prestige if the experiments were generally considered to be exploitative or otherwise immoral, even if these judgments had no utilitarian justification. The general public could also suffer harm as a result of diminished confidence in the medical profession.

5. Although some of the harms or potential harms (especially to the inmates) are real, the benefits of such policies would seem to outweigh those harms. The increase in scientific knowledge would benefit many future generations. This outcome would far overshadow the risk to the inmates, especially if the risk were controlled and relatively small. Therefore, the first rule has more in its favor from a utilitarian standpoint than the second rule and is morally obligatory.

6. Applying the first rule to the Willowbrook State School case, I shall conclude that the medical experiments were justified and in fact obligatory.

Case 2: The Morality of Whaling

Whales are mammals. Whale calves are fed and cared for by their mothers, and the bond between mother and child appears to persist beyond the period of lactation. Their nervous systems and the parts of the brain relating to the perception of pain are essentially similar to our own. Although some authorities say that the killing of a whale takes only five minutes, others say that it often takes much longer.

Whales are also social animals; they live in groups and relate to each other as individuals. Some species are monogamous, and, when one member of the family has been harpooned, other family members have been observed to wait offshore for days or even weeks for its return. Good scientific evidence backs up the ascription of a sophisticated emotional life to whales.

However, whalers in Japan and the Soviet Union (the two primary whaling countries) and other countries where whaling is permitted depend on whaling for their livelihood. Some whale products are quite useful to people. Whale oil is used to make soap and margarine, and whale meat is consumed by humans, livestock, and pets. Whales are also used for various commercial products, especially cosmetics.

So the question for the utilitarian is, If whaling can be controlled, to remove the threat of extinction, is it morally wrong to kill whales on a commercial basis?

1. The rule presupposed by the decision to kill whales on a commercial basis might be stated as follows:

    Whales should be killed for commercial use, as long as they are not threatened by extinction.

2. The rule presupposed by the decision not to kill whales on a commercial basis might be stated in the following way:

    Whales should not be killed for commercial use, regardless of whether they are threatened by extinction.

3. The relevant audience in this case includes the three groups affected by the possible decisions: those engaged in the whaling industry, those who use whaling products, and whales. If the second rule is generally followed, people in the whaling industry will lose their jobs. In Japan and the Soviet Union, this unemployment might involve a considerable hardship for a time, but the government could easily retain the affected workers, so their loss is not permanent. Because those who use whaling products can find substitutes, they stand to suffer no significant loss. Even if the price of certain products increases somewhat, monetary loss is relatively trivial in comparison with the whales' loss of life. The whales, of course, stand to suffer the more serious harm if the first rule is followed. Although humans probably outnumber whales, only the human beings affected by these two rules need to be considered. Furthermore, even whales who do not lose their lives may suffer the pain of separation from family members who have been harpooned.

4. It seems that a rule utilitarian analysis must conclude that the second rule would produce the greatest total utility, so it is morally obligatory. We have

no reason to believe that such a rule could not realistically be followed, because a number of nations have already discontinued whaling with no serious adverse consequences.

5. In this case, the rule is applied not to a particular situation but to a general practice. As the rule itself indicates, the conclusion must be that whales should not be killed for commercial use, even if they are not threatened by extinction.

Case 3: Reverse Discrimination

Allen Bakke, a white male, applied to the medical school at the University of California at Davis in both 1973 and 1974.[8] In both years Bakke's application was considered by the general admissions program, and he received an interview. His 1973 interview was with Dr. Theodore H. West, who described Bakke as "a very desirable applicant to [the] medical school." Despite a strong composite evaluation score of 468 out of 500, Bakke was rejected. His application had come late in the year, and no applicants with scores below 470 were accepted in the general admissions process after Bakke's application was completed. After his 1973 rejection, Bakke wrote to Dr. George H. Lowrey, associate dean and chairman of the admissions committee, protesting that the special admissions program operated as a racial and ethnic quota.

At the time Bakke was rejected, four slots were unfilled in the special admissions program for economically and educationally disadvantaged students. A total of sixteen slots in the freshman class of one hundred were reserved for students in the special admissions program. The students in the special admissions program did not have to meet the minimum 2.5 grade point average applied to regular students, and different standards were used in their general evaluation.

Bakke's 1974 application was completed early in the year. His composite score was 549 out of 600. Again Bakke's application was rejected. This year, as in the year before, applicants were admitted under the special admissions program with significantly lower composite evaluation scores as well as lower grade point averages and lower Medical College Admission Test scores. After the second rejection, Bakke filed a suit in the Superior Court of California.

The case eventually reached the U.S. Supreme Court, which rendered its decision on June 28, 1978. The justices were divided 4–4 on the principal issues in the case, with Justice Powell deciding with one group on one issue and with the other group on the second issue. On the one hand, the Court found that the special admissions program under which Allen Bakke was denied admission was unlawful and directed that Bakke be admitted. On the other hand, it found that institutions of higher learning could consider race as one factor in the admissions process.

---

[8] 483 U.S. 265; reprinted in James Sterba, *Morality in Practice* (Belmont, CA: Wadsworth, 1984), pp. 229–238.

From the standpoint of utilitarianism, are admissions policies like that of the University of California at Davis morally permissible, morally obligatory, or morally impermissible?

1. Any formulation of the rule under which the University of California at Davis was operating when it reserved sixteen slots for disadvantaged students will be controversial, because the concept of a *quota* produces legal and moral problems. However, we shall formulate the rule as follows:

    A medical school may reserve a small percentage (less than 20 percent) of its openings for disadvantaged students.

2. The alternative rule would be this:

    A medical school may not reserve even a small percentage (less than 20 percent) of its openings for disadvantaged students.

3. The audience consists of the four groups affected by the rule and its alternative: the disadvantaged students who are candidates for the special admissions program; the students who are applying through the regular admissions program; the minority population in the country, consisting primarily of African Americans, Latinos, Asians, and Native Americans; and the general population.

    The disadvantaged students stand to benefit the most from the first rule, which gives them a greater chance of being admitted to medical schools. Not only are the admissions standards lower, but the students are competing for one slot out of a hundred, whereas the regular students are competing for one slot out of eighty-four. The first rule has some negative effect on their interests, because their fellow students may regard them as inferiors who could not make it under normal competitive conditions. Their future patients might also have less confidence in them than in physicians who were admitted in the regular admissions program.

    The regular students would suffer the most direct harm to their interests, because they would have less chance of admission to medical school. They would also find it more difficult to predict whether they would be admitted, because factors other than merit would be considered. This uncertainty could affect their ability to plan their lives. However, regular students would perhaps receive some benefit from a more diverse student population, composed in part of disadvantaged students.

    The minority population would benefit if the disadvantaged students decided to serve in their communities. However, this outcome is not guaranteed. A more effective means of supplying physicians to serve in minority communities would be to select students who had demonstrated a prior commitment to this kind of work, regardless of their social or ethnic background. If the disadvantaged students did decide to serve in their own communities, the minority youth would benefit from the role models the physicians would provide.

It is difficult to determine how the interests of the general public would be affected by either the first or second rule. The general public might benefit from the decreased social unrest if minorities became convinced that the effects of past discrimination were being vigorously attacked. But this effect could well be counterbalanced by the feeling among the general population that many applicants were being unfairly treated.

4. We have extreme difficulty totaling up the harms and benefits to various interests and reaching a conclusion about which rule produces the greatest total utility. However, if the effects of past discrimination could be more quickly eliminated by policies of reverse discrimination, a good case can be made that the first rule is superior from a utilitarian standpoint. The bad effects of reverse discrimination would be temporary, and the good effects of eliminating the legacy of discrimination would be permanent.

Keep in mind that, in making the utilitarian calculation, no abstract considerations of justice can be brought into the picture. Justice is important for the utilitarian only insofar as policies that are perceived to be just or unjust affect the interests of individuals.

5. Assuming that the first rule does produce greater total utility, we shall apply it to the Bakke case. We could then include that, from the utilitarian standpoint, the preferential admissions policy is obligatory.

EVALUATING UTILITARIANISM AS A MORAL THEORY

Now we are ready to evaluate utilitarianism according to our four criteria. Remember that every moral theory has points of vulnerability; no perfect moral theory exists. This lack of a perfect theory is a major reason that several influential moral philosophies have evolved rather than one. As with the other theories, the following evaluations are my own, although they reflect the opinions of many moral philosophers.

Criterion 1: Consistency

The form of utilitarianism we have described does not suffer from obvious inconsistencies. If the utilitarian is willing to define right actions as those that produce the greatest total utility or interest satisfaction, without arguing that some interests are inherently better than others, he cannot be charged with inconsistency. The temptation to be inconsistent arises when the utilitarian moral standard generates conclusions about conduct that conflict with our ordinary moral ideas.

Criterion 2: Justification

For a moral philosophy to be acceptable, it must give some reason to believe the moral standard is correct. We have also seen that a moral standard is not susceptible to strict proof, because a moral standard cannot be derived from a higher moral standard, nor can it be derived in any direct or conclusive way from factual observation. What kind of justification, then, can be offered for the principle of utility? In a famous passage from Chapter 4 of *Utilitarianism*, John Stuart Mill presents some considerations that he hopes will convince his readers to accept the utilitarian doctrine. He starts by drawing an analogy between visibility and desirability, arguing that, just as the only proof that an object is visible is that people see it, so the only proof that anything is desirable is that people actually desire it. Then he points out that people do in fact desire happiness, so happiness must be desirable or good. Because each person's happiness is good for that person, the general happiness is a good to the aggregate of people.

If Mill intended his argument to be a "proof" of the utilitarian moral standard, he was certainly mistaken. Saying that something is "desirable" in the sense that it *is desired* by people has an entirely different meaning than saying that something is "desirable" in the sense that it *should be desired*; people may certainly desire what they should not desire. Another problem with Mill's argument, when taken as a proof, is that the fact that each person's happiness is a good for that person does not lead to the conclusion that promoting the general happiness is a moral obligation. People might be content to pursue their own happiness rather than the well-being of the majority. But these criticisms apply only if Mill was attempting to construct a strict proof, and his writings indicate that he was aware that the moral standard cannot be proven.

The most we can do, Mill may have believed, is show that the moral standard is a plausible one and that it commends itself to a rational person. Interpreted in this way, Mill's argument might be the following: People do desire their own happiness. This desire does not make happiness the right moral goal, but it does show that a morality based on happiness is solidly grounded in human nature. Such a morality is thus at least a possible candidate for a moral standard. If we combine this observation with the belief that a moral person has some obligation to others rather than merely to himself, we have some evidence to conclude that the happiness (or interest satisfaction) of others is a legitimate moral goal. Mill also believes that further evidence for the plausibility of the principle of utility can be derived from the fact that most of the moral beliefs we hold can be justified by the principle of utility.

Although these observations contain claims that can be questioned and certainly do not constitute a proof, they do lend plausibility to the standard of utility. If we believe that the institution of morality must be related to the human good, what more intrinsically plausible standard could we propose?

Criterion 3: Plausibility

One of the major problems with utilitarianism is that it appears to generate moral judgments that differ from our ordinary moral beliefs. We have already seen several moral issues in which this discrepancy arises. Another area in which these counterintuitive conclusions are generated is supererogatory acts—that is, acts that are "above and beyond the call of duty." We ordinarily distinguish between obligatory and supererogatory actions, but this distinction is difficult to make from the utilitarian standpoint, because any action that produces more total utility than an alternative action is obligatory. Actions that we ordinarily consider supererogatory often produce more utility than any alternative, so the utilitarian is forced to reclassify them as obligatory.

Consider the following example.[9] Suppose your foolish neighbor confides that he is mortgaging everything he can to make a speculative investment that you are convinced will be disastrous for him and his family. If you expend enough time and effort, you believe, you can dissuade him from making the investment, whereas no one else can do so. The disaster you anticipate for him would be far greater than any inconvenience and embarrassment you would suffer in dissuading him. A utilitarian would argue that, on the whole, greater preference satisfaction would result if we adopt the rule that "Everyone who has adequate reason to believe that the course of action a neighbor proposes will be disastrous to that neighbor has the duty to dissuade that neighbor if he can do so without grave inconvenience or embarrassment." But are you morally obligated to follow such a rule? The question is not simply whether you ought to express your opinion to him; you should surely do so. But is it your duty to embark on a lengthy attempt to change his mind? The rule utilitarian must answer yes, but most of us would not.

Our moral intuitions may also seem to conflict with utilitarianism in the area of justice. When Jesus of Nazareth was killed, Caiphas, the Jewish high priest, justified the killing with the claim that Jesus' crucifixion, however unjust, would avert a greater disaster—possibly a rebellion against the Jewish authorities or a Roman persecution of the Jewish people. Consider the rule "Judges may not depart from the law, except if, by doing so, they can avert a major calamity to their nation or to the world." A rule utilitarian might object that such a rule would so discredit the judiciary that public life would be gravely injured, but such might not be the case. Some might even sleep better knowing that their judges would not be overscrupulous in applying the law during a national emergency. Thus, a rule utilitarian might be forced to admit that a miscarriage of justice is morally justified.

In the face of such objections, the utilitarian has two options: to reject ordinary beliefs as invalid because they conflict with utilitarian theory or to

---

[9] For this example and a discussion of utilitarianism and its problems with supererogation and justice, see Alan Donagan, "Is There a Credible Utilitarianism?" in *Contemporary Utilitarianism*, ed. Michael D. Bayles (New York: Doubleday, 1968), pp. 194–198.

argue that utilitarian moral theory does not really conflict with ordinary beliefs. Most utilitarians have attempted to show that utilitarianism can account for our ordinary moral beliefs, especially those relating to supererogation and justice. Let us consider how the utilitarian might do this.

If she wants to argue that utilitarian theory can make a place for supererogatory actions, she might make the following argument. Praising those who perform supererogatory acts is in accordance with utility, but condemning those who fail to do so is not. The distinction between obligatory and supererogatory acts could be based on the differing abilities of people to perform unusual acts of bravery and self-sacrifice. The interest of morality is not served by requiring people to perform actions that are simply too far beyond their abilities, because this overtaxing would only inspire contempt for morality in general. Moreover, people who attempt risky acts are likely to fail, thus creating negative utility. On the other hand, when supererogatory actions are performed, they should receive praise, because they do contribute to the well-being of others. Whether this response is adequate is left for you to decide.

The problem of justice requires more sophisticated treatment. The utilitarian can certainly argue that, in general, rules requiring justice have greater utility; they inspire confidence in the judicial system and a sense of safety and well-being among the citizenry. However, if a serious conflict arises between two rules, a different approach may be necessary. For example, the utilitarian might argue that a conflict exists between the rule "Administer justice fairly" and the rule "Do what is necessary to save the nation from disaster." In such a case, the utilitarian would maintain, doing what leads to the greatest overall interest satisfaction in the particular situation is justifiable, so that in the case of Jesus, Caiphas was right to imply that one man's dying for the people was expedient. We must appeal, in other words, to act utilitarianism to resolve a conflict between two rules, when both are justified by utility. As before, you are left to decide whether this reply is adequate.

Criterion 4: Usefulness

A moral theory must provide a clear, workable method for resolving moral disputes, including disputes about which moral rule to adopt. The utilitarian decides on moral rules by determining their consequences for utility. But do we have the knowledge to trace the consequences of even a single action, much less the consequences of a general rule? Consider how a utilitarian would investigate the morality of premarital sexual relations. She would use the best available scientific data to determine the extent of possible negative consequences of the widespread practice of premarital sex, such as an increase in the number of pregnancies outside of marriage, a rise in the incidence of venereal disease, greater psychological disturbances, and the long-range effect on the stability of marriage. She would also have to investigate the advantages from a utilitarian standpoint of the widespread acceptance of the practice, such as the increased enjoyment of sex and a decrease in sexual frustration during the years when the sex drive is especially strong. She would also investigate the possibility that people would have a healthier, more relaxed attitude toward sex and that sexual adjustment in marriage might be improved.

How adequately can we determine these consequences, especially the long-range consequences, such as the effect on sexual adjustment and the stability of marriage? Without knowing these effects, the utilitarian cannot pass judgment on the morality of premarital sexual relationships from the utilitarian standpoint. She must either recommend that present practices be continued or that we experiment in new directions without fully knowing whether the results will be good or bad. Neither alternative is wholly satisfactory from the utilitarian standpoint. You will encounter problems like this one when you evaluate many practices from the utilitarian perspective.

In dealing with the problem of consequences, some utilitarians have admitted that they must assume what has been called the "ripples–in–the–pond postulate"; that is, they must assume that the important consequences of an action occur in relative proximity in time and place to the action itself. Just as the ripples produced by dropping a pebble in a pond are strongest near the point of impact, so the consequences of an action must be assumed to be most significant relatively near the action. But what if an action, such as adding minute amounts of a pollutant to the atmosphere, produces insignificant effects for centuries and then suddenly results in a catastrophe? Perhaps many other practices would have few negative consequences for a while but, after a few generations, would produce highly negative ones. What reason do we have for believing that the ripples–in–the–pond postulate is valid? And even if it is, can we calculate even the near-at-hand consequences of an action or rule?

The utilitarian's response is that we can at least have a rational opinion about the general consequences of many actions, and, if we have no opinion, perhaps we should hold to traditional moral rules. The standard of utility at least provides a method for evaluating some moral rules. The utilitarian may also argue that, if we do not know the consequences of adopting a given rule, we *should not* be able to pronounce on its morality. Furthermore, the problem of knowledge of consequences emphasizes again the importance of the social and physical sciences in utilitarian morality. Lack of knowledge about consequences is not so much a fault of utilitarian theory as it is a problem of the human condition, the utilitarian argues. Do you think this response is adequate?

CONCEPT SUMMARY

Because the utilitarian judges a rule by its consequences, any rules derived from the utilitarian moral standard must make assumptions about the consequences that will result from following the rules. If these assumptions are not accepted, different rules may be justified. Utilitarian personal ethics should be governed by the principle that the most effective way to contribute to the general welfare is usually to develop one's own abilities. Although utilitarianism may condone traditional moral views in some areas of personal ethics, it does not support the traditional prohibitions against suicide and euthanasia. Utilitarianism can also justify many of the common duties to others, such as the duties not to commit murder, theft, or fraud, but it does not support the prohibition of abortion.

In the area of social ethics, utilitarianism has been taken by its classical advocates to justify democracy and individual liberty. More recent exponents of utilitarianism have sometimes argued that greater utility will be produced if the state attempts to provide for the basic needs of all citizens, regardless of their financial resources. Special rewards, however, must still be given to the more talented members of society to induce them to make the maximum contribution.

Utilitarianism is an internally consistent moral philosophy. Mill's "proof" of utilitarianism fails as a proof, but it does give reason to believe that utilitarianism is a plausible moral philosophy. Utilitarianism leads to some counterintuitive moral judgments, especially regarding supererogation and justice. The utilitarian's ability to resolve moral problems is sometimes limited by our ignorance of the full consequences of the actions and general moral rules.

8

The Ethics of
Respect for Persons

On April 3, 1990, a baby girl was born to a couple that conceived the child to serve as a bone marrow donor for their daughter, Anissa, who was dying of leukemia. Abe and Mary Agola, who live in the Los Angeles suburb of Walnut, named the baby Marissa Eve. Fetal tests showed that the baby's marrow was compatible with Anissa's, and doctors said the transplant could occur in six months. There was a 70 to 80 percent chance that the transplant would cure Anissa.

Mr. Agola had to undergo a reversal of his vasectomy, and Mrs. Agola, who is in her mid-forties, had only a 73 percent chance of conception and a 23 percent chance of conceiving a child who would be a compatible donor.

Medical ethicists voiced qualms about creating one child to save another. The baby, they said, was not conceived "as an end in itself, but for a utilitarian purpose." The Agolas said they were hurt by such talk and that they would love the baby even if it proved to be an incompatible bone marrow donor for their stricken daughter.

Patricia Konrad, the couple's physician, said the bone marrow transplant would pose little risk for the baby. The procedure requires the infant to be put under general anesthesia to block pain while a needle is inserted into the hip bone to remove the marrow. Leukemia, a cancer of white blood cells, is typically treated by killing blood-producing cells with chemotherapy radiation and then transplanting compatible bone marrow into the patient. After waiting almost two years, the couple had failed to find a suitable living donor for Anissa. The odds of doing so are about 1 in 20,000. Mr. Agola told a reporter, "We just can't stand idly by and do nothing about it and wait for Anissa to die."[1]

Although we naturally sympathize with Mr. Agola, we may be troubled by the conditions under which Marissa was conceived. Was she merely being "used" by her parents and her sister as a source of bone marrow? Was Marissa's dignity as a human being in her own right being disregarded in her conception? Would we want such a practice to become widespread?

Most of us consider these questions fundamental to the nature of morality; they certainly have been central to the Western ethical tradition. According to the Talmud, the whole law can be summarized in the statement "Do not do to your fellow what you hate to have done to you."[2] And in Matthew 7:12, Jesus says that the whole law and the prophets can be summarized in the saying "In everything do to others as you would have them do to you." The Greek and Roman Stoic philosophers also believed that all humans possess a divine "spark" that gives them a fundamental human dignity and equality.

Sometimes we express a closely related moral insight by distinguishing between things and persons: persons should not be treated as mere things or manipulated in a way that disregards their states as moral beings. Slavery is wrong, for example, because it treats people as commodities, regardless of the purposes they might have set for themselves. A slave owner can treat a human being like an object. Slavery fails to give proper respect to the personhood of the slave, and it is certainly not a condition we would want for ourselves.

We shall refer to this ethical tradition, whose central theme is that equal respect must be paid to the personhood of all human beings, as *the ethics of respect for persons*. It is an attempt to give a philosophical formulation to the basic ethical insights of the Hebrew-Christian and Stoic moral traditions. The ethics of respect for persons has been closely connected with Immanuel Kant (1724–1804), the greatest thinker of the German Enlightenment and one of the most important modern moral philosophers. Kant's terminology is too forbidding and his arguments often too obscure to allow any straightforward exposition of his moral philosophy here. We shall use his philosophy in this text only as a general guide. Readers who are familiar with Kant will recognize his influence in many places, but keep in mind that this chapter is a discussion of the ethics of respect for persons, not Kant's moral philosophy.

We shall use two of Kant's formulations of the moral standard as the basis for our discussion, even though our interpretation of these standards will often differ from his. Kant himself believes that the two standards are equivalent, that they will always lead to the same conclusion regarding what is right or wrong. We have reasons to doubt this claim, so we shall stipulate that, for

---

1 "Conceived to Save Her Sister, a Child Is Born," *New York Times*, April 7, 1990, p. 8.

2 Rabbi Dr. I. Epstein, ed., *The Babylonian Talmud* (London: Soncino, 1948–52), p. 31a; quoted in Alan Donagan, *The Theory of Morality* (Chicago: University of Chicago Press, 1977), p. 57.

an action to be morally permissible by the ethics of respect for persons, it must pass both versions of the moral standard.

The version of the moral standard we will look at first is the universalization principle. We shall discuss a test for its proper application, which we shall call the self-defeating test. The second version of the moral standard is the means-ends principle. We shall consider two tests for its proper application: the negative test and the positive test. Let us examine these principles and tests in turn.

THE UNIVERSALIZATION PRINCIPLE AS A VERSION OF THE MORAL STANDARD

The idea that equal respect is due to all human beings is the basis for the universalization principle. We can formulate this principle as a moral standard of the ethics of respect for most persons in the following way:

> MS 1: An action is right if you can consent to everyone's adopting the moral rule presupposed by the action.

Like rule utilitarianism, this standard focuses on the evaluation of rules rather than individual actions. If we look only at actions, how can we determine whether our action is the same as the one we are willing to have others follow? Let us propose that we are willing to have others perform the same action if we are willing to have them adopt the moral rule that underlies our own action. This proposal assumes that every action involving moral choice does, in fact, presuppose a moral rule.[3]

To apply the universalization principle, we must first determine the moral rule presupposed by the action being evaluated. Suppose we are considering the possibility of obtaining some money by making a false promise to repay it. The rule presupposed by our action might be something like this:

> Everyone should obtain money by falsely promising to repay it.

Our second task is to decide whether we can consent to others' following the universalized rule. To do so, let us apply the self-defeating test.

The Self-Defeating Test

The question posed by the self-defeating test is this:

> Can I consent to others' acting simultaneously according to the same rule I use without undermining my own ability to act in accordance with it?

---

[3] My account of rules is in some ways like Kant's discussion of what he calls "maxims." But, again, I am not giving an exposition of Kant.

To determine whether I can consistently consent to others' acting according to the same rule I use, we must attempt to imagine realistically the conditions necessary for everyone to use this rule and the consequences that would normally follow if everyone did so simultaneously.[4] In the case of our current rule, the predictable result of everyone's performing the action in question would be that no one would lend money based on a promise to repay, because everyone would assume (correctly) that such promises were lies. This result would undermine my ability to borrow money on the basis of a (false) promise to repay. Only if we postulated that people do not learn from experience could we consistently intend that others live by the same rule we adopted. So the rule is self-defeating.

Keep in mind that the self-defeating test assumes that we ask what would happen if I and others follow the rule simultaneously. Obviously, if I adopt my policy of dishonesty now and others do not adopt the policy until a year from now, I could get away with a lot of false promises in the meantime. The case would be different if others adopt my policy at the same time I do, and the policy would be self-defeating.

This conclusion about the morality of making false promises is not surprising; the self-defeating test would not be a very convincing test for morally permissible actions if it could not rule out false promising as immoral. Nevertheless, other examples seem to cause more trouble. Some people argue that the universalization principle runs into difficulties with respect to an occupation such as farming, because it is no more desirable that everyone grow food than that no one grow food. Consider the following abbreviated but acceptable formulation of the rule:

Everyone should grow food.

I can certainly consistently intend that I and everyone else will grow food without fear of defeating my own rule. This state of affairs was once almost universal, and it still prevails in some parts of the world. But now consider the alternative rule:

Everyone should not grow food.

I can certainly intend that I and all others will not grow food. This rule would lead to starvation, but starving people can refuse to do things as well as the best fed. So the rule is not self-defeating.

What shall we say, then, about the morality of growing food, because both the rule and its alternative can be universally followed? One scholar has proposed that, when both a rule and its alternative can be consistently universally adopted,

---

4 See Onora Nell, *Acting on Principle: An Essay in Kantian Ethics* (New York: Columbia University Press, 1975), pp. 63–81. My version of the self defeating test owes much to Nell's book, even though important differences exist. For an account of Kant's use of this same example that is probably closer to his intentions than either mine or Nell's, see Robert Paul Wolff, *The Autonomy of Reason: A Commentary on Kant's Groundwork of the Metaphysic of Morals* (New York: Harper & Row, 1973), pp. 165–169.

acts in agreement with the rule or its alternative will both be classified as morally permissible; that is, they are neither required nor forbidden. In this case, we are neither required to grow food nor forbidden to grow food. Either action can be seen as morally acceptable behavior. This solution reflects the way we tend to think about such an issue and is generally consistent with the universalization principle.[5]

Another example illustrates an important aspect of the self-defeating test—namely, that a rule can be self-defeating if the *point* or *purpose* one has in mind is defeated with the action's universalization. We can illustrate this with an example having to do with whether we have an obligation to obey the civil authorities. First, consider the following rule:

Everyone should obey the civil authorities.

It seems clear that we can consistently and simultaneously consent to the universal adoption of this rule. We can without any problem accept the conditions required to carry out the intention, such as the general knowledge of and respect for law and authority. We can also accept the predictable results of successfully carrying out the rule, such as a safe, peaceful, and orderly society. This rule is not self-defeating. On the other hand, consider the alternative rule:

No one should obey the civil authorities.

We can argue that we cannot consistently and simultaneously consent to this rule, for the results would be general chaos; pursuit of any goal with reasonable prospect of security and success would be impossible. Although, in a narrow sense, continuing to disobey the civil authorities under these chaotic conditions might be possible, the *purpose* a person most likely has in mind by this disobedience (namely, gaining an advantage over her law-abiding fellows) would, no doubt, be undermined. Thus, the rule is self-defeating.

Many examples demonstrate how universalizing a rule covering a given action undermines the point of the action. Suppose you are considering cheating on your next quiz. You believe that everyone else could cheat as well as you, so your action could be universalized. This may be true, but the universalization of your action would undermine or at least seriously weaken the *purpose* you have in mind in cheating—namely, to make a better grade than your classmates. This example shows the importance of considering the fullest consequences of the general acceptance of a rule. It also demonstrates that we have no completely mechanical way to determine whether a rule can be consistently and simultaneously adopted. Applying the universalization principle requires imagination and may sometimes be controversial. In the next section, we shall consider some of the problems in applying the universalization principle.

---

[5] See Nell, *Acting on Principle*, p. 79.

Guidelines for Applying the Universalization Principle

One problem in applying the self-defeating test has to do with how broad or narrow to make the rule to which you apply the self-defeating test. We know that more than one rule can be used to describe a given action, and the particular rule we see as underlying an action can make an enormous difference in our evaluation of the action.

Suppose I am scheduled for an important job interview and know that I would have a better chance at the job if I tell the interviewer that I intend to stay with the company for many years if I am hired. Actually, I have my eye on another position that is not available now, but I would take the more desirable position if it were offered. To get my first job, however, I lie about my intentions to stay with the company. Now, I might be able to universalize this action in the sense that others could lie too, but my point in lying would be undermined if every other interviewee lied too. However, I could still get around this problem by tailoring the rule to my own circumstances, as this rule illustrates:

> If my name is John Brown and I am interviewing for a job with ABC Chemical, and I really want to work for XYZ Chemical, I may lie about my intentions to stay with ABC Chemical if this is necessary to get the job.

This rule can satisfy the self-defeating test only because it applies to only one person. We can easily see in this case that the rule is inappropriate, but precise guidelines for how specific a rule can be without being too specific cannot be given. We can only say that the rules should not be too specific or too broad. A rule is too specific if it contains references to particular places, times, or persons.

A rule that allows for no exceptions, however, is often too broad. Few of us would be willing to accept the consequences of a rule that says "Never lie." If an obviously crazed man comes into the room with a bloody knife in his hand and asks you for John Jones, I would probably think it morally justifiable to tell him a lie. We are much more likely to accept the consequences of a rule that allows lying in certain situations, such as "I can lie when it is necessary to save an innocent life." In other words, a rule must be specific enough to take into account the morally relevant facts.

Aside from these general guidelines, a person is alone in formulating the rule that seems most adequately to describe his or her own action or the action of another person. Because we know more about our own motivations and the circumstances of our own lives than about the motives and circumstances of another person, we are in a better position to formulate descriptions of our own actions than the actions of others. So we must always be cautious in evaluating others' actions.

Another interesting class of examples is one in which neither the rules nor their alternatives can be consistently universalized. Consider the following rule:

Everyone should buy shoes but not sell them.

Here, I clearly cannot consent to the universal adoption of this rule, because all purchases require simultaneous sales. But a similar conclusion follows when we consider the alternative rule:

No one should buy shoes, but everyone should sell them.

If both a rule and its alternative are self-defeating, actions in accordance with the rule or its alternative would appear to be morally impermissible. Therefore, we shall assume that in such situations either a new rule must be formulated or the universalization principle gives no direction, and we should consider only the means–ends principle.

THE MEANS-END PRINCIPLE AS A VERSION OF THE MORAL STANDARD

A hypothetical person called John Whiteman is a racist of the old school: he believes that all blacks should be slaves. He would even be willing to be enslaved himself if he were found to have "black blood." Most of us would consider his view to be the very model of immorality, so we are more than a little disturbed to realize that Whiteman's position passes the test of the universalization principle. His viewpoint is not self-defeating, because everyone's holding this position and acting in accordance with it would not prohibit Whiteman from holding his views.

The fact that such a patently immoral action can pass the test of the universalization principle points out the inadequacy of this principle as a complete guide to morality. Relatively few actions are self-defeating, although the test is useful when it does apply. The universalization principle emphasizes the equality of all human beings, which is an important part of the ethics of respect for persons. It provides a minimal condition for morally acceptable rules. But the condition is not sufficient for a morally acceptable action, as this example shows. For this reason, we must consider another version of the moral standard of the ethics of respect for persons—the means–ends principle. The principle can be stated as follows:

MS 2: Those actions are right that treat human beings, whether you or another person, as an end and not simply as a means.

What does it mean to treat someone as an end rather than a means? The answer to this question goes to the heart of the distinction between things and persons. Persons or moral agents have a capacity to formulate and carry out their own goals, whereas things have their purposes determined from the outside. A pencil sharpener, for example, was manufactured to perform a specific function, as was a coffee mug. Human beings, on the other hand, can determine their own purposes. This capacity of persons or moral agents to determine their own purposes is the basis of the means–ends principle. We shall say that "treating a person as an end" means respecting the conditions necessary for his or her effective functioning as a moral agent.

Before examining the conditions for the effective exercise of one's moral agency, however, we should ask what is meant by the reference to treating someone "simply as a means." This phrase implies that in some sense treating a person as a means is legitimate. In relating to other people in our day-to-day lives, we often do treat them as a means in the sense of being relatively unconcerned with their status as persons. When I go to the post office, I have no special interest in the aspirations of the postal worker who sells me stamps, other than a general positive attitude toward her. In one sense, I do treat her as a means to my end of obtaining stamps. But I do not treat her simply or merely as a means, because I do nothing to negate her status as a moral being.

Many social relationships involve the element of treating others as a means, but not solely as a means. I may treat my doctor as a means to recover from my illness, but I do not treat him simply as a means, because I do not deny him his status as a person. Students treat their professors as a means to gaining knowledge and getting a degree, but they do not treat them simply as a means, because they do not obstruct the professors' humanity. Social relationships would be impossible if treating a person as a means were not permissible in this limited way.

Preliminary Concepts

The basic idea of the means–ends principle is simple, but its application is often difficult. To help you apply the principle, we shall discuss three issues: (1) the conditions of moral agency, (2) the principle of forfeiture, and (3) the principle of equality.[6]

The Conditions of Moral Agency Two fundamental conditions are necessary for a person to act as a moral agent. The first is freedom or voluntariness, whereby a person controls or initiates his behavior by his unforced choices. The second condition is purposiveness or well-being, whereby a person sets goals for herself and has the abilities necessary for achieving them. Let us consider both of these conditions.

The condition of freedom or voluntariness naturally brings to mind the right to protection from violence and coercion. In acts of violence, such as robbery or rape, a person's freedom is diminished. He is acted on with direct physical or psychological compulsion and has no opportunity for consent. In acts of coercion, such as forced prostitution, a person gives his consent but has no real free choice in doing so. Deception also limits the freedom of others; in

---

6 The following discussion relies heavily on Alan Gewirth, *Reason and Morality* (Chicago: University of Chicago Press, 1978), especially pp. 199–271, 338–354.

deception the person gives unforced consent, but only as a result of falsehoods or misrepresentations intentionally presented to him.

A person's freedom may be interfered with in other ways as well. Physical or mental illness, willful ignorance or self-deception, and obsessive submission to some dominating passion like drugs or alcohol can limit a person's voluntary action. Lack of knowledge is also a major impediment to free decisions.

The other condition necessary for moral agency is what we have called well-being—namely, the goods necessary for carrying out one's freely chosen purposes. If a person can choose goals but has no ability to carry them out, his moral agency is worth very little.

Several categories of goods are necessary for effective moral agency. Alan Gewirth has divided these goods into three categories. *Basic goods*—such as life, food, clothing, shelter, physical health, and emotional stability—are prerequisites of our purposive action. *Nonsubtractive goods* are abilities or conditions needed for maintaining undiminished one's level of purpose fulfillment. These goods include not being lied to, cheated, defamed, or insulted and not having one's promises broken or one's privacy invaded. We have already seen that breaking promises not only violates the self-defeating test but also tends to lower a person's capacity for action. Finally, *additive goods* are abilities and conditions needed for raising the level of purpose fulfillment. These goods include owning property, having a sense of well-being and self-respect, and being treated in a nondiscriminatory way. Additive goods also include the virtues of character—such as courage, temperance, and prudence—that enable people to pursue their goals more effectively. Other aspects of freedom and well-being also are important for one's being able to act as a moral agent. It is impossible to enumerate all aspects, but they will often be important in making moral decisions.

The Principle of Forfeiture   The means–ends principle requires that I treat everyone, myself and others alike, as ends and not mere means. The universalization principle also implies that everyone should live according to the same rules, which means that a person loses the right to be treated as an end if he does not treat others this way. Therefore, the ethics of respect for persons requires a principle of forfeiture, much as in natural law. The principle of forfeiture says that, if I treat others as mere means, I forfeit my rights to freedom and well-being. I do not necessarily forfeit all my rights, but in general my rights are forfeited in proportion to the rights of others that I trespass.

When the state punishes a criminal by putting him in prison or taking his life, he is deprived of some of the aspects of freedom and well-being necessary for his full functioning as a moral agent. Nevertheless, many believe that the punishment is justified, because the criminal by his action has treated someone else as a mere means. Whether he has committed theft, fraud, rape, murder, or some other crime, he has done something to deprive others of their freedom or well-being. Punishment is a legitimate response to this action and does not violate the means–ends principle.

Criminal action is not the only way in which a person may forfeit some of his rights to be treated as an end and never as a mere means. If I slander or insult you, it might be appropriate for you to hit me or in some other way limit my freedom or well-being. When a businessperson or professional, through negligence, endangers the safety of her client or the general public, it may be appropriate to reprimand her or deprive her of her job, even if nothing worthy of legal action has been done.

Application of the principle of forfeiture is appropriate when a person either voluntarily or by implication enters into certain kinds of relationships. If you and I own two different stores that are competing for the same business and I eventually run you out of business, I am certainly harming your freedom and well-being. Still, I may be justified in running you out of business, because one implicitly consents to this possibility when entering the competitive business environment.

The Principle of Equality Another issue that you will frequently encounter in applying the means–ends principle is the problem of conflicting obligations. Recall the story of the two female counterspies who were in Britain during World War II. While they were there, the Allies learned that the Nazis knew their identity. If they were sent back, they would almost certainly be apprehended, tortured, and killed. What should have been done from the standpoint of the ethics of respect for persons?

The problem is that someone's freedom or well-being will be harmed regardless of which alternative is taken. If the counterspies are returned to the continent, they will suffer loss of freedom, physical violence, and death. If they are not returned, the Allied cause will lose a considerable advantage in the war, and probably many additional lives will be lost. Someone's freedom and well-being will be harmed with either alternative.

The idea of equal treatment implicit in the two moral standards again provides the fundamental guideline. The principle of equality says that, when someone's freedom or well-being must be violated, people should be treated equally unless reasons exist for them to be treated otherwise. Some additional criteria will be helpful in carrying out this principle: In treating everyone equally as an end, we must consider (1) how important the aspects of freedom and well-being are that are being threatened, (2) how severely these aspects will be limited, and (3) whether the aspects of freedom and well-being involved would be directly or indirectly violated.

If we applied these criteria to the case of the counterspies, we would probably come to the following conclusions: (1) The aspects of freedom and well-being involved are of the highest importance: ability to make a free decision and physical life itself. (2) The values of the women are seriously threatened; that is, they would suffer not simply harm to their freedom or well-being but loss of life and freedom altogether. Those who would be killed or injured because of the prolongation of the war would also suffer loss of life and freedom. (3) The threat to the women is obviously more direct and immediate than the threat to the Allied soldiers and civilians who would be harmed by the loss of access to the Nazi code.

Applying the principle of equality, we would probably conclude that returning the counterspies to the continent was morally wrong according to the ethics of respect for persons, primarily because their rights are more directly and severely violated. They were being used as mere means. If we are to justify returning them to Germany, we must use utilitarian considerations rather than arguments derived from the ethics of respect for persons.

Consider another example. Suppose a physician is asked by one of her patients to perform a sterilization. The physician believes sterilizations are morally impermissible, but no other physician practices in the rural area who could perform the procedure. In this case, someone's moral agency will be violated no matter what decision the physician makes: either the patient will have to go elsewhere to obtain the sterilization, or the physician will have to violate her conscience. How would one resolve the conflict problem by the principle of equality?

Using the three considerations suggested by the principle of equality, we can make the following observations: (1) Violation of conscience is a more serious violation of one's moral agency than going to another physician for the sterilization. (2) The physician's conscience will be directly violated, whereas the patient will presumably be able to obtain the sterilization elsewhere. (3) The threat to the physician's moral agency is more direct and immediate than the threat to the patient's moral agency. Therefore, the physician should not perform the sterilization.

We can use two tests to determine whether we are treating a person as an end and not as a mere means. The negative test asks whether a person's freedom or well-being is threatened by our actions. (Have we treated the person as a mere means?) The positive test asks whether we have assisted others in achieving their freedom and well-being. (Have we treated them as an end?) We shall see that the negative test is always applicable, whereas the positive test is only sometimes applicable. Therefore, we shall begin with the negative test.

The Negative Test

Our first inclination might be to argue that we should never override the rights of others, but the preceding considerations have shown us that sometimes we must. In situations involving criminal activity or a conflict of obligations, someone's freedom or well-being must be overridden. Keeping this point in mind, we shall formulate the question that constitutes the negative test of the means–ends principle:

Does the action override my own or others' freedom or well-being?

As discussed in the previous section, this test is not always easy to apply. Let us consider several guidelines that will be useful in applying it.

First, the principle of forfeiture may be relevant. If John has violated another person's freedom or well-being, his freedom or well-being can justifiably be violated. When we imprison criminals, we violate their freedom and well-being, but we do so legitimately because the criminals have violated the freedom and well-being of others. This same consideration applies to corporate entities. When a corporation pollutes the environment in a way that violates the law, fines and other types of punishment imposed by the state violate the freedom and well-being of the corporation and its stockholders. But this violation is justified because the corporation has forfeited some of its rights by illegal conduct.

Second, sometimes it is impossible to avoid a situation where someone's freedom and well-being will be diminished. In such cases, we have a conflict problem that must be resolved by using the principle of equality to determine where the most serious violations of moral agency occur. For example, suppose Jane is a young engineer who finds that a certain pollutant that her plant is emitting poses a minor health risk to inhabitants of the surrounding area. The pollutant is not restricted by the government, and she wonders whether she should advise her superior to try to eliminate the pollutant. Remedying the problem will be expensive and probably make the plant less profitable, thereby forcing management to lay off some employees. What should she do?

It is not clear that the principle of forfeiture applies to the company and its stockholders, for the threat to health is not serious. But it certainly does not apply to the employees who will lose their jobs if the necessary anti-pollution devices are installed. Yet either the inhabitants in the surrounding area will suffer an impairment of their health, or some employees will lose their jobs. In such situations, a "balancing act" must be performed, just as in a utilitarian estimation of positive and negative utilities, except that we are balancing the violations of rights rather than positive and negative utilities. We must balance the infringements on the freedom and well-being of stockholders and employees against the infringements on the freedom and well-being of those who are adversely affected by the pollutants.

The Positive Test

The positive test of the means–ends principle requires that we do more than simply refrain from interfering with our rights to freedom and well-being and those of others. We also must positively contribute to others' status as moral agents, as well as our own. However, this obligation does not require that we devote our lives slavishly to helping others achieve a fuller state of self-realization. We would then be treating ourselves as a mere means to the good of others, which is forbidden by the means–ends principle itself. Therefore, each individual must determine when, where, and how this moral obligation is to be fulfilled with respect to others. So we will state the question posed by the positive test as follows:

Does the action assist oneself (or others, in certain circumstances) in achieving one's own (or others') freedom and well-being?

To see how this test might be applied, let us begin with an example.

Thirteen-year-old Jason Simmons has been diagnosed as having a ruptured appendix. His physician says he needs immediate surgery; however, Jason has been attending Christian Science services and has come to believe in healing through prayer. He does not want surgery, even though his parents do. Disregarding legal questions for the moment, should the physician defend the boy's right not to have surgery, or should she go along with his parents' request?

Applying the ethics of respect for persons, the rule presupposed by the position Jason has taken might be formulated as follows:

People should be allowed to follow their own convictions, even if the result is their death.

The self-defeating test is not violated by this rule, because Jason could pursue his course of action even if the rule presupposed by his action is universalized. His action would pass the negative test of the means–ends principle, because he is not interfering in an illegitimate way with others' freedom or well-being. Although he would be interfering with his parents' desires to keep him alive, his action does not deny them an equal freedom to determine their own lives. Must we conclude, then, that it is morally impermissible for the physician to oppose Jason's request?

This case involves paternalism, which we may define as using coercion to get another person to do or refrain from doing something for his or her own good. In the usual version of paternalism, which we shall call *strong paternalism*, another person determines what is for my own good. Strong paternalism is clearly incompatible with the means–ends principle, because it allows the freedom of other people to be overridden. Another kind of paternalism, called *weak paternalism*, says that paternalistic coercion can be used, but only to the extent necessary to preserve a person's freedom. Several circumstances—such as ignorance, intellectual immaturity, emotional disturbance, and social pressures—can decrease a person's ability to make a free, informed decision under these circumstances or to enable someone else to make a decision for that person. The use of paternalistic coercion, the weak paternalistic argues, actually protects the individual's long-term freedom.

Does the positive test of the means–ends principle apply in any way to weak paternalism? I believe it does. We have already seen that the central idea in the means–ends principle is the preservation of people's ability to act as moral agents. The basic thrust of the positive test, then, must be that in certain situations we have an obligation to actively promote the status of others as moral agents. Weak paternalism is simply the use of coercion to preserve that status when it is threatened. Therefore, weak paternalism can be justified by the positive test of the means–ends principle.

The key issue in this example for the ethics of respect for persons is whether Jason is making a genuinely free and informed decision. If he is, then living by the principles of Christian Science, even at the risk of losing his own life, represents his true goal. However, if Jason's decision is not genuinely free and informed, that choice does not represent his true goal. Several factors might prevent him from making a free and informed decision. For example, a thirteen-year-old boy may not be intellectually mature enough to evaluate the religious teachings on which he is basing his decision. Or he might be under undue emotional pressure from his peers or Christian Scientists whom he has come to respect. Or he may be rebelling against his parents in his decision.

To justify disregarding Jason's wishes, the physician must believe that she is actually assisting him in achieving greater long-range freedom. She must also feel that her special relationship as the boy's physician provides the proper occasion for the application of the means-ends principle. Because we can plausibly argue that a boy of Jason's age is not in a position to make a free and informed decision about such a serious issue and that the special patient-physician relationship does justify the obligation to help Jason realize his true goals, paternalistic action by the physician seems permissible.

There are at least two types of situations in which the positive test seems clearly applicable and one in which its application is more controversial.

First, the positive test should be applied when a special relationship of moral obligation exists between the people involved. The story about Jason illustrates two of the most important such relationships—namely, professional relationships and family relationships. Both parents and professionals have a special obligation to help others realize their goals. By voluntarily assuming a parental role, parents incur an obligation to help their children grow into autonomous moral agents. Similarly, by voluntarily assuming her role as a professional, a physician incurs an obligation to help her patients return to health, and a lawyer incurs an obligation to help her clients achieve justice in the legal system. The same obligation applies to other professionals and anyone who has assumed a relationship of special obligation to another person.

Second, the positive test should be applied when one person can help another in a significant way with relatively little sacrifice to himself. Being in a position to help another person in dire need produces an obligation in accordance with the positive test of the means-ends principle. Suppose John is fishing in his boat and suddenly becomes aware that someone is struggling in the water several hundred feet away. The person is shouting for help and obviously is in immediate danger of drowning. John could easily rescue him but does not do so, and the person drowns.

Most people would agree that John ought to have tried to rescue the drowning man. But why? John's behavior passes the self-defeating test, so if John's action is immoral by the ethics of respect for persons, it is because it violates the means-ends principle. It does not violate the negative test, but it does violate the positive test. John is in a position to help a person in extreme danger with relatively little cost to himself. John's relationship to the person (his being in a position to help) therefore imposes an obligation to aid the person in distress.

It is interesting to apply this same kind of reasoning to the question of famine relief. Does this same principle that we are obligated to help others in significant need when we can do so at relatively little cost to ourselves apply to people in other countries? Does distance or the fact that the starving people of Ethiopia live in another society negate our obligation to help them? Is any help we give to them superogatory or obligatory?

Finally, some people believe that the very fact that people live in the same society justifies taxing the relatively wealthy to help the relatively less well off to have a more comfortable and satisfying life. Even if we have no special relationship to the needy (other than living in the same society with them), and if their need is not extreme, the obligation is valid, according to some advocates of the ethics of respect for persons. Whether this obligation exists and how far it extends are matters of considerable controversy. However, if this obligation exists, it must have limits; otherwise, the more gifted would be used as mere means to help the less fortunate. But we must keep in mind that the principle of equality requires that everyone be treated equally as an end, insofar as is possible. We shall return to this idea in discussing the social ethics of the morality of respect for persons.

We are now ready to summarize the steps in applying the ethics of respect for persons in a checklist. However, one further problem should be mentioned. If both the action and its alternative fail one or more of the tests, either action will ordinarily be considered morally permissible unless one of the actions violates the tests more flagrantly than the other. To settle this issue, do not use utilitarian considerations, but determine which action constitutes the least serious violation of the moral agency of others. The principles of forfeiture and equality will often be useful.

CHECKLIST FOR APPLYING THE ETHICS OF RESPECT FOR PERSONS

____ 1. Determine the most appropriate rule presupposed by the action whose morality you are evaluating.

____ 2. Apply the self-defeating test of the universalization principle, which asks whether others could act by the rule without undermining the possibility of your acting according to the rule and the conditions necessary to act according to the rule. Remember also that the rule must be universalized at the same time as the action being tested.

____ 3. Apply the negative test of the means-ends principle, which asks whether the action overrides the freedom or well-being of oneself or others.

____ 4. If relevant, apply the positive test of the means-ends principle, which asks whether the action assists oneself (or others, in certain circumstances) in achieving one's own (or others') freedom and well-being.

____ 5. Make a final decision on the morality of the action.

    a. If it passes the test of the universalization principle and the negative test of the means-ends principle (and the positive test where applicable), it is morally permissible.

    b. If it is morally permissible and its alternative violates the universalization principle or the negative test of the means-ends principle (or the positive test where applicable), it is morally obligatory.

    c. If it fails either the universalization principle or the negative test of the means-ends principle (or the positive test where applicable), it is morally impermissible.

    d. If both the original action and its alternative fail one or more of the tests, either action will ordinarily be considered morally permissible. Sometimes one alternative should be chosen because it does not violate the three tests as seriously as the other alternative.

CONCEPT SUMMARY

The ethics of respect for persons takes as its central theme the equal dignity of all human beings. Our formulation of it is expressed in terms of two moral principles.

The first principle, the universalization principle, states that an action is right if you can consent to everyone's adopting the moral rule presupposed by the action. The test for this principle involves asking whether the universalization of the rule would undermine the possibility of acting in accordance with the rule (the self-defeating test).

The means-ends principle says that an action is right that treats human beings, whether you or someone else, as ends and not simply as means. Two tests for the satisfaction of this principle are the negative test and the positive test. The negative test requires that an action not override people's freedom or well-being. The positive test requires that I promote my own freedom and well-being and help others, under certain conditions, to achieve theirs. The positive test is applicable in a special relationship, such as the relationship of a professional to her client or of parents to their children. It is also applicable when others are in dire need or perhaps when people are a part of a common social order.

In applying the means-ends principle, we must remember these two points: First, a person may forfeit some of her freedom or well-being by violating the freedom or well-being of others or by voluntarily entering into relationships that subject the person to such a possible forfeiture. Second, where everyone's freedom and well-being cannot be satisfied, all persons should be respected equally, insofar as possible.

THE PERSONAL AND SOCIAL ETHICS OF THE ETHICS OF RESPECT FOR PERSONS

We are now ready to look at the implications for personal and social ethics of the ethics of respect for persons. You will usually find that the means–ends principle provides the most helpful guidance, but both principles are sometimes useful.

Duties to Self

The most useful guideline here is the means–ends principle. You may be inclined to ask, "How can I treat myself as a mere means? Isn't the idea self-contradictory?" Yet a moment's reflection will show that we can indeed act in a way that diminishes or destroys the conditions we need to exist as effective goal-creating, goal-pursuing beings. A review of these conditions will suggest some of the duties we owe to ourselves according to the ethics of respect for persons.

The first condition is physical life itself. I have a duty under normal conditions not to destroy or impair my health or the physical integrity of my body. The question of suicide, however, is an especially interesting issue in the category of duties to self. It might seem that I have a duty never to kill myself, because my death would destroy an essential condition for all further action. But perhaps my goals and values dictate that my life should end, in which case a conflict arises between my pursuit of my goals now and the conditions necessary for their pursuit in the future. Suppose I am dying of cancer, that for a few months I will be enduring great pain, and that in this condition I will lose my personal dignity. I will no longer be able to pursue, let alone realize, my goals. Under such circumstances, my freedom can take priority over my well-being. My wish to die should have priority over the fact that my death will nullify all possibilities of achieving any future goals.

This same obligation to preserve the condition of physical life also justifies self-defense in most circumstances. If someone threatens my life, I have the right and even the obligation to defend myself against this threat. The principle of forfeiture shows that I am not illegitimately overriding the goals of the one who attacks me.

The second condition is physical and mental well-being. I also have a duty under normal conditions to promote my physical and mental health. The positive test of the means–ends principle applies to duties to self, because I have a special obligation to my own freedom and well-being. In most instances, increasing my general knowledge and education will also promote my abilities to pursue my goals. An interesting exercise might be for you to decide which virtues or traits of character would enhance your abilities to act as a purposive agent.

Duties to Others

Ordinary moral prohibitions against harming others—through such acts as murder, rape, theft, and physical assault—are easy to justify by the ethics of respect for persons. These acts directly override the freedom and well-being of others, so they violate the means-ends principle.

Our obligation to help others, especially when help can be given with relatively little cost to us, follows from the means-ends principle. We have already seen that failure to help others in distress violates the positive test of the means-ends principle, as long as giving the aid does not seriously jeopardize our own status as ends.

The means-ends principle provides especially useful and insightful tests in the area of sexual morality. Even our language about sexual relationships often sounds as though it was derived from the means-ends principle. Treating someone as a "mere sex object" is treating the individual as a thing rather than a person. If we treat someone as a mere means in a sexual relationship, we are not treating that person as a goal-creating, goal-pursuing agent. In rape, for example, a person uses violence or coercion to override the freedom of another to choose her own sexual partner.

However, by far the most common way of treating another person as a mere means in a sexual relationship is by some form of deception. The boy who tells his girlfriend "I love you" or "We'll get married if you get pregnant" without meaning it is depriving her of the ability to make an informed decision about a sexual relationship and is thereby treating her as a mere means. Seducing someone into a demeaning sexual relationship is also using that person as a mere means, because it diminishes his self-esteem and reduces his ability to act effectively as a goal-pursuing agent.

Not all nonmarital sexual relationships are based on deception, nor are they all degrading. Suppose, for example, that two college students establish a sexual relationship based on mutual affection and pleasure, but neither is sure it is love. Each person knows the other's intentions, so no deception is present and the relationship is not demanding. They take proper precautions against pregnancy but have agreed that, if a pregnancy results, they will get married or at least will properly care for the child. What can we say about the morality of this relationship? The universalization principle does not pose a problem, because the rule underlying the relationship can be universalized without being self-defeating. What, then, about the means-ends principle? Neither person is overriding the freedom of the other or diminishing the ability of the other to be an effective goal-pursuing agent. However, some would want to point out the likelihood of mutual self-deception when sexual passion is involved. Whatever we conclude about the morality of such relationships, clearly the ethics of respect for persons provides the basis for a positive, insightful approach to sexual morality.

Social Ethics

The principle that governs the social ethics of respect for persons is that social institutions should respect the freedom and well-being of others by following rules that are universally applied; that is, the state should treat all individuals equally as ends and not mere means. How is this task accomplished? We have seen that the means-ends principle has both a positive and a negative test. Both of those tests have important implications.

Let us first consider the negative aspect of the state's responsibility to its citizens. This function is what libertarians call the minimal state. It involves the state's protection of citizens' rights not to have their rights to freedom and well-being overridden by other citizens or the state itself. This protection is needed in several areas. First, the state must protect citizens against murder, theft, fraud, and physical violence. Without these protections, individuals do not have the conditions necessary to realize their purposes. Second, the liberty of individual conduct should extend to the economic sphere. Economic goals are central in many people's lives, and the right to pursue these goals should be protected as long as the rights of others are not seriously impaired. Third, the individual should have as much freedom as possible in the area of beliefs and lifestyle, including freedoms of speech, the press, religion, and assembly. Laws regulating controversial activities like polygamy or homosexuality can be justified only when the activity regulated poses a clear threat to the liberty of others.

The state also has positive obligations to its citizens. This function is what we shall call the *supportive state*.[7] The relationship of the state to its citizens and of citizens to one another requires that the positive test of the means–ends principle be applied, which in turn requires the state to promote its citizens' freedom and well-being. The state could not claim political authority without a commitment to the welfare of its citizens, and citizens have some obligation to one another by virtue of their living in the same society. Thus, the state should make some provision for the health, education, and general welfare of its citizens and give special support for those who, through no fault of their own, are not able to provide for themselves.

The question inevitably arises whether the positive obligation of the state can be fulfilled without violating the goals of other citizens. In taxing productive citizens to provide for the disadvantaged, is the state not using productive citizens as mere means? Is the state not limiting the moral agency of the advantaged to provide for the disadvantaged? The answer is that we must adopt our usual policy of dealing with conflicts produced by the application of the means-end principle. We must remember that the final obligation is to

---

[7] See ibid., pp. 312–327.

treat everyone equally as ends insofar as possible; we must try to produce a situation in which the least serious violations of the principle are produced. Thus, the advantaged must be taxed to provide benefits for other members of society, but the gifted should be allowed to keep most of the wealth they have earned. This requirement is made not to preserve incentive to productivity, as in utilitarian social ethics, but to avoid violating the status of the gifted as ends and not mere means to the good of others. You must determine just how these guidelines should be followed in practice.

CONCEPT SUMMARY

We can act in ways that destroy the conditions necessary for our existence as effective moral agents. Therefore, we have a duty to preserve our life and health, pursue an education, and develop whatever abilities and character traits are important for advancing our status as individuals.

The negative duties to others that are a part of most moral philosophies—such as the duties not to commit murder, theft, or fraud—are justified by the universalization and means-ends principles. A duty to help others in distress is mandated by both principles, if carrying out this duty does not require us to treat ourselves as mere means to the ends of others. Respect for persons also provides many useful insights into sexual morality.

The principle that governs the social ethics of respect for persons states that social institutions should be designed to help citizens function as effective goal-pursuing agents. Thus, the state has an obligation to protect citizens from one another and to help the disadvantaged achieve their freedom and well-being.

APPLYING THE ETHICS OF RESPECT FOR PERSONS

Now let us apply the ethics of respect for persons to some problems that require moral decision, using the methodology outlined in the checklist.

Case 1: The Case of Baby Marissa

We shall begin by considering the case presented in the introduction to this chapter.

1. The rule presupposed by the Agolas in conceiving Marissa might be formulated in the following way:

   Parents may conceive children whose tissue is to be used in an attempt to save the life of another person, as long as the child is not harmed by the use of the tissue.

2. The self-defeating test asks whether the Agolas could conceive Marissa with the purpose of using her tissue in an attempt to save Anissa's life if other people felt free to do the same sort of thing when the occasion arose. The answer to this question is that the widespread acceptance of the practice would make it easier for the Agolas to do what they did. No doubt one of the most difficult aspects of the Agolas' experience was having to endure the widespread criticism of their action. Therefore, we can conclude that if the rule were generally adopted, the Agolas would find it easier, not more difficult or impossible, to act in accordance with the rule themselves.

3. The negative test of the means-ends principle asks whether the action of the Agolas overrides their own freedom or well-being or the freedom and well-being of anyone else. It certainly does not override their freedom and well-being. They undertook the action out of their desire to save their daughter's life. The only other person whose freedom and well-being is threatened is Marissa herself. There is little question that Marissa would not have been conceived if the Agolas had not wanted to save Anissa. The fact that Mr. Agola had to undergo a reverse vasectomy indicates that the couple did not intend to have any more children. So in a sense it is clear that Marissa's conception came about primarily because the couple wanted to save Anissa's life. In this sense, Marissa was "used" to save the life of Anissa.

But at this point the distinction between being used as a means and being used as a mere means is significant. It is difficult to see how Marissa will be used as a mere means, because otherwise she would not have been conceived at all, and (more importantly) she will not be permanently harmed by the medical procedure. According to the Agolas' physician, she will not be harmed physically. The pain, if any, will be temporary. Presumably she will also not be harmed emotionally.

The only sense in which Marissa's life prospects might be damaged is by the knowledge, which she will inevitably acquire, that she was conceived in an attempt to save her sister's life. But if Marissa is shown the same love and care that Anissa has evidently been given—and the Agolas assure us that she will—there is no reason to believe that this will be a serious problem.

Critics of the Agolas' action might argue that if everyone adopted this rule, human life might be regarded with less respect. Perhaps our society might descend a "slippery slope" to a state in which children could be conceived for medical uses in circumstances where the child's life prospects would be seriously damaged by the medical procedures necessary to make use of their tissue. Or perhaps children could even be killed to be used for tissue and organ transplants.

The issue of how much weight this consideration should be given is not easy to decide. Certainly it is relevant in considering the long-term effects of the action. If the Agolas' action did contribute to other children being treated as mere means, this would be a relevant consideration. Here we have a factual issue that vitally affects our moral assessment of the Agolas' action. But this issue is difficult to settle, and in a liberal society, we have no good reason to believe that the Agolas' action would have such deleterious consequences. Therefore, we shall conclude that the negative test is not violated.

It may also be worthwhile to mention that children are often conceived by their parents with certain goals in mind other than simply producing another human being. Parents want heirs and descendants to carry on the family name or to obtain the social status that comes with having a family. Or they may want someone to support and care for them in old age. Peasants had children to help them tend the fields. Kings and queens conceived children to be heirs to the throne and ensure peace in the kingdom. If we do not believe these are examples of using children as mere means, we must ask whether any morally relevant difference exists that is significant enough to warrant placing the Agolas' action in a different category altogether.

4. The positive test of the means–ends principle is relevant because the Agolas are the parents of Marissa and Anissa and therefore have an obligation to promote their freedom and well-being. The question is whether the decision of the Agolas to conceive Marissa assists both Marissa and Anissa in achieving their freedom and well-being. Clearly the action is an attempt to assist Anissa, so the only question has to do with Marissa. Again, it should be recalled that she would never have been born apart from her parents' desire to help her sister, and there is every indication that she will be raised in an environment in which her moral agency will be fully respected. Therefore, we have no clear reason to believe that the positive test has been violated.

5. The rule passes both the universalization principle and the negative and positive tests of the means–ends principle. Therefore, the Agolas' action is permissible by the ethics of respect for persons. The alternative rule could be stated in the following way:

> Parents may not conceive children whose tissue is to be used in an attempt to save the life of another person, even when the child is not harmed by the use of the tissue.

This rule also passes the self-defeating test. If everyone adopted this rule, it would make it easier for the Agolas not to have attempted what they did. In fact, one of the most difficult aspects of their experience was the public disapproval.

The rule would not require the violation of Marissa's freedom and well-being, because following the rule would mean that she would never exist. Nor would it directly violate Anissa's freedom and well-being. The only question is whether it would violate the positive test. The Agolas' argument was that Marissa's conception was an attempt to save Anissa's life. "We just can't stand idly by and do nothing about it and wait for Anissa to die," Mr. Agola told reporters. Their argument, in fact, was that failure to conceive Marissa would have violated the positive test. However, there are questions as to how far one need go in fulfilling the positive test. A certain amount of discretion is permitted, and the unusual nature of the Agolas' action suggests that they might have refrained from doing it without violating the positive test. Therefore, we shall conclude that the positive test would not have been violated by this rule either.

Because both the first rule and its alternative are permissible, we shall assume that the Agolas' action was permissible but not obligatory by the ethics of respect for persons.

Case 2: Deceptive Psychological Testing

Dillard Johnson is a psychologist employed by the personnel department of a large corporation. One day his superior comes to him with a proposal: "Dillard, the company is worried about the possibility that some of our employees may try to form a union in the next year or two. We have always had good relationships with our employees, but we believe a union would change that. I want you to research the literature in your area and find out whether you can furnish us with a test for employees that will measure union sympathy. You should disguise the purpose of the test. Make it look like a test for new employment opportunities or something like that. Can you do this for us?"

Dillard knows he has a good chance to impress his boss with his value as a psychologist in the personnel department, but he has questions about the ethical propriety of complying with the assignment. What should he do?

1. The issue raised by Dillard's boss is one of obtaining information from people that may be used against them and in a manner that does not involve their knowledge or consent, but the moral issues raised would be somewhat different in other apparently similar cases. For example, if the test were for sexual orientation or political persuasion, it would be even more questionable because information about these aspects of an employee would not ordinarily be job related. An employer would have even less right to this information than information about an employee's union sympathy. However, there is even a question whether the employer has a right to know about the union sympathies of his employers.

   Because the issues raised may have to do with the type of information sought as well as the means of getting it, we shall formulate the rule so that it applies to this particular action. The fact that Dillard is a psychologist is also morally relevant because deceptive practices of this sort might be permissible when done by other people even if not permissible when done by a psychologist. Therefore, we shall include this feature in the rule as well. A rule that takes into account these morally relevant factors can be formulated as follows:

Employers may ask psychologists to devise tests that measure the union sympathies of employees under conditions that deceive the employees as to what is being measured.

2. The self-defeating test asks whether a given employer (for example, Dillard's employer) could act in accordance with the rule if the rule described were a general practice. If it were generally known that psychological tests were deceptive, there might be much greater reluctance to take the tests. People who take psychological tests, knowing that they might serve a covert purpose, would probably attempt to determine what the real purpose of the test was. Even if the tests are well devised, their true purpose might become generally known after the tests are given a number of times. In addition, much more general distrust of psychologists might develop if it were widely known that they participated in this kind of deception.

   On the other hand, many people probably already believe that psychological tests often have a hidden purpose. And if a given test were used only a few times or in different areas, it is doubtful that its true purpose would be found out, so the rule might not be self-defeating if it were universalized. Therefore, we shall conclude that the rule could be universalized without being self-defeating.

3. The negative test of the means-ends principle asks whether directing psychologists to create such tests overrides the freedom or well-being of either the psychologists who are assigned the task of devising the test or the employees who take them. With respect to Dillard, the question is whether his professional integrity is compromised by the assignment to come up with the test. Many psychologists would believe that it is. But probably the clearest argument can be made from the employees' standpoint.

   Whether employees are required to take the tests or merely encouraged to do so under the (illusory) expectation of job advancement, both their freedom and well-being are diminished. By being subjected to deception, they suffer an infringement on their freedom. By unknowingly divulging knowledge that could lead to their dismissal or job reassignment, they suffer an infringement on their well-being.

   Dillard's boss might argue that Dillard and the employees implicitly consented to the kind of information gathering he is proposing when they became employees: Dillard to use his professional expertise to benefit the company and the employees to follow their superiors' instruction. Besides, it might be argued, the attempt to get the information that the company wants is legitimate from the standpoint of good management. However, it is doubtful that the doctrine of implicit consent can be extended to such deceptive activities, and knowledge of union sympathies, insofar as it is necessary at all, can be gained in less clandestine ways. Therefore, we shall conclude that the rule probably violates the negative test from Dillard's standpoint and certainly violates it from the employees' standpoint.

4. The question whether the positive test of the means–ends principle applies to the relationship of employers to employees is an interesting one. Certainly employers have an obligation not to violate the moral agency of their employees, but the extent of their positive obligation is more questionable. If the obligation does apply, the employer certainly violates it in this case. However, we shall give the employer the benefit of the doubt and hold that the positive test does not apply.

5. Because the negative test has been violated, we can conclude that the request of Dillard's boss is impermissible from the standpoint of the means–ends principle.

Now let us consider the alternative rule:

Employers may not ask psychologists to devise tests that measure the union sympathies of employees under conditions that deceive the employees as to what is being measured.

This test passes the universalization principle: refraining from using such tests would not undermine others' ability to do the same thing. The only people whose freedom and well-being would be infringed by the alternative rules are the managers and stockholders of companies. They would be somewhat restricted in what they could ask their professional employees to do and might be restricted in the information they could obtain, or at least in the way they could get it. But in any case, applying the principle of equality seems to show that the infringement of the freedom and well-being of the psychologists and employees is more serious than the infringement of the freedom and well-being of managers and stockholders. Managers and stockholders might be deprived of some useful information, but employees would suffer invasion of their privacy and possible loss of jobs, and psychologists would suffer violation of their professional integrity. We shall assume that the positive test is not relevant, but, if it is, the alternative rule would pass the test.

We shall conclude that the alternative rule is morally acceptable. Because the first rule is unacceptable, action in accordance with the alternative rule is morally obligatory.

Case 3: Surrogate Mothers

In a 7–0 opinion, the New Jersey Supreme Court recently ruled that commercial surrogate motherhood contracts are illegal. It nevertheless allowed custody of Melissa Elizabeth Stern, the child at the center of the Baby M case, to remain with her father, William Stern, and his wife, Elizabeth. In March 1987, almost a year before the decision of the New Jersey Supreme Court, Judge Harvey R. Sorkow of the State Superior Court of New Jersey had ruled in favor of Mrs. Stern, allowing her to adopt the baby, and against the baby's biological mother, Mary Beth Whitehead-Gould.

"We thus restore the surrogate as the mother of the child," the justices of the New Jersey Supreme Court said. "She is not only the natural mother, but also the legal mother, and is not to be penalized one iota because of the surrogate contract." The Court did allow the Sterns to retain temporary custody of the child, perhaps reflecting their concern over testimony revealing that Gould-Whitehead's home life was not the best. Gould-Whitehead had divorced her husband of thirteen years and had married a sixteen-year-old accountant who was the father of the child she was pregnant with at the time.

In a ninety-five-page opinion, the court found the contract between the Sterns and Whitehead-Gould violated the state's adoption laws because it involved a payment for the child. A $10,000 fee was specified in the 1985 contract between the Sterns and Whitehead-Gould. "This is the sale of a child, or at the very least, the sale of a mother's right to her child, the only mitigating factor being that one of the purchasers is the father," the court said. "The surrogacy contract creates, it is based upon, principles that are directly contrary to the objectives of our laws," Chief Justice Wilentz wrote. "It guarantees the separation of a child from the mother; it looks to adoption regardless of suitability; it totally ignores the child; it takes a child from the mother regardless of her wishes and her maternal fitness, and it does all of this, it accomplishes all of its goals, through use of money."

The New Jersey Supreme Court did not prohibit women from freely becoming surrogates as volunteers, as long as no money was exchanged, and the surrogate mother had the right to revoke her decision.[8]

Is surrogate motherhood for money a violation of the ethics of respect for persons?

1. The rule presupposed by the contract between the Sterns and Whitehead-Gould might read as follows:

   People may make an irrevocable contract involving the payment of a fee, whereby a woman agrees to conceive a child by the sperm or a married male, as long as the contract is made without coercion and with full access to the relevant information, and the male and his legal wife can provide an adequate home for the child.

2. The rule would seem to pass the self-defeating test. No doubt a number of women, like Whitehead-Gould, would reverse themselves after making a contract to be a surrogate mother and decide they wanted to keep their child. Perhaps their anguish at having to comply with the contract would

---

[8] Robert Hanley, "Surrogate Deals for Mothers Held Illegal in New Jersey," *New York Times*, February 4, 1988, p. A1.

deter many women from making such a contract in the first place. If all women were to be deterred for this reason, then the universalization of the rule would indeed be self-defeating. It is highly doubtful, however, that this situation would arise, so the rule does not seem to be self-defeating.

3. The negative test of the means-ends principle requires that the freedom and well-being of anyone affected by the rule should not be overridden; in this case, the freedom and well-being of the surrogate mother and the fetus are most at peril, but the freedom and well-being of the Sterns must also be considered.

    Whitehead-Gould reversed herself on whether she wanted to keep her child, but the fact that a person is prohibited from reversing herself on a decision that was freely made does not seem to be a violation of the means-ends principle. As long as there is one free and informed decision, a person's moral agency has been preserved. Information is not sufficient to determine whether Whitehead-Gould's decision was not fully free and informed, but we have no reason to believe it was not.

    Chief Justice Wilentz argued that a surrogate mother contract bypasses the usual requirement that the adopting parents should have to prove themselves qualified to raise the child in a competent manner. However, the court itself did not consistently follow this argument, because it allowed surrogate mother contracts as long as no money was involved.

    A more interesting fact is that parents who conceive their children in the normal way are already exempt from these requirements, so the question raised is whether surrogate motherhood is more like adoption or normal parenthood. The truth is, of course, that it has analogies and disanalogies with each. Like normal parenthood, the conception involves the father's sperm; like adoption, the conception involves the egg of the mother who gives up the baby. The fact that there is an exchange of homes for the baby and that the biological mother does not raise the child is also analogous to adoption. Perhaps the analogies with adoption are more extensive, so that the failure to provide safeguards for the child is a problem, but even here laws could be enacted to ensure that the parents who are to raise the child should pass the same criteria as adopting parents. The court itself seemed to recognize this possibility when, according to the *New York Times* report, it virtually invited the New Jersey legislature to enact new laws governing surrogate motherhood.

    One might argue that in some sense the baby is being "used" as a means to promoting the wealth of the surrogate mother and the happiness of the new parents, but the child is not being used as a mere means unless its freedom and well-being are overridden. If the baby is properly raised, there is no reason to believe the child is being used as a mere means in this sense.

4. The positive test of the means-ends principle is relevant, because parents do have an obligation to promote the well-being of their children. This obligation would apply to both the Sterns and Whitehead-Gould. It is

difficult to see that the surrogate mother is promoting the freedom or well-being of the fetus in any special way. On the other hand, she is not overriding its freedom and well-being as long as the child is placed in an adequate home. The parents who receive the child would promote the child's freedom and well-being by properly raising it. Therefore, the positive test is passed, or at least not violated.

5. The alternative rule can be stated as follows:

    People may not make an irrevocable contract involving the payment of a fee, whereby a woman agrees to conceive a child by the sperm of a married male, even if the contract is made without coercion and with full access to relevant information, and the male and his legal wife can provide an adequate home for the child.

    This rule also passes the self-defeating test, because everyone could consistently follow it. It does not pass the negative test of the means-ends principle, because it denies the freedom of parents like the Sterns and potential surrogate mothers like Whitehead-Gould to enter into such contracts. It might be thought of as promoting the freedom and well-being of the fetus, because it does not allow conception for the purpose of supplying other people with children. But we have already seen that there is no reason to believe the freedom and well-being of the child need protection, as long as parents who receive the child are capable of providing an adequate home for it.

Because the first rule passes all of the tests and the second rule does not, we must conclude that giving legal permission to engage in contracts for surrogate motherhood is morally obligatory.

Case 4: Buying and Selling Blood

Plasma International had a problem. Headquartered in Tampa, Florida, it had profited from the world's need for whole blood and plasma by buying blood in the southeastern United States and selling it at a reasonable price. Most of its donors, however, were people who used the money to buy wine. When several cases of hepatitis were reported in the users of Plasma International's blood, the company began looking for a new source.

Using a team of medical consultants, Plasma International found the ideal donors in the West African nation of Burami. The company negotiated agreements with several tribal chieftains and was able to buy blood for beads and trinkets. The cost of buying the blood amounted to about 15 cents a pint, but the same pint was sold for about $25.

When the story of Plasma International became public, it provoked a storm of criticism. How can Plasma International justify exploiting the ignorant tribespeople? How can it buy blood so cheap and then sell it to people who are sick or injured and must have the blood at any price?

Sol Levin, a former stockbroker in Tampa and one of the founders of the company, failed to see what was wrong, and we might imagine his argument. He was providing a needed service: supplying uncontaminated plasma and whole blood at market prices. He was giving the African tribespeople what they wanted for their blood. Otherwise, they would not have had the opportunity to exchange their blood for anything. Furthermore, there was no indication that substandard procedures were used to collect the blood or that the tribespeople were harmed medically by the donation. Finally, the blood recipients were paying reasonable prices by market standards.[9]

This example raises several moral questions, but one such question focuses on the relationship of Plasma International to the African donors. Was the purchase of the blood at these low prices justifiable by the morality of respect for persons?

1. The methods used to extract the blood were evidently safe, which should be made a part of the rule. Otherwise another set of morally relevant considerations would be introduced. In cultures that do not have the same tradition of individualism that is prevalent in the West, tribal chieftains often make decisions for the entire tribe. Seemingly the only way to apply the ethics of respect for persons to people in such cultures is to assume that when a person's representative gives consent, he gives his consent. With these considerations in mind, the rule presupposed by the practice of Plasma International might be stated in this way:

    A firm may buy blood from donors at prices that allow it to enjoy an unusual profit margin on the resale of the blood, even though the donors are not aware that they could sell the blood for more, as long as safe methods of blood extraction are used and the donors or their representatives give consent.

2. The practice of Plasma International provoked a considerable protest in Tampa. If similar practices were widespread, it stands to reason that the objections would be much more vehement, so much so that action might be taken to prevent them. Therefore, we have some reason to think that the practice might be self-defeating if it were widely employed. However, this conclusion is not certain, so we must conclude that there is only a probable violation of the self-defeating test.

3. The negative test of the means-ends principle asks whether the action of Plasma International overrides the freedom or well-being of the donors. The donors' well-being was not overridden in any obvious way. Because the methods they used were safe, their health was not being threatened. Furthermore, the donors, as far as it can be determined, were not coerced into making the decision to give blood. Even if their tribal chieftain in effect made the decision for them, in a nonindividualistic culture this must

---

[9] This case was prepared by T. W. Zimmer and P. L. Preston, Florida Atlantic University, from *Business and Society*, eds. Robert D. Hay, Edmund R. Gray, and James E. Gates (Cincinnati, OH: South-Western, 1976). Used with permission.

be considered a noncoerced decision. Nevertheless, it is probably not fully informed, in the sense that the chief and the donors may not have realized that the price for which they were selling their blood was so far under the market price. Even though the action of the chief and his tribespeople was not coerced, therefore, it was not fully informed and therefore not completely free. So we must conclude that there was a violation of the negative test, although not a severe one.

4. The positive test of the means–ends principle asks whether the practice of Plasma International, as described in the rule, assists the donors in achieving their freedom and well-being. The well-being of the tribespeople is promoted in some way by the fact that they are given something for their blood. However, it is not clear that the relationship between buyer and seller is one in which either side has an obligation to promote the freedom or well-being of the other. So we shall conclude that this test is not relevant.

5. The alternative version of the rule might be stated as follows:

A firm may not buy blood from donors at prices that allow it to enjoy an unusual profit margin on the resale of the blood if the donors are not aware that they could sell the blood for more, even though safe methods of blood extraction are used and the donors or their representatives give consent.

This rule does not violate the self-defeating test of the universalization principle: if every firm followed such a rule, there would be no problem with Plasma International's following it. It does not violate the negative test of the means–ends principle, because it would not allow firms to take advantage of ignorant people by buying blood at below-market prices. Finally, if the positive test is not applicable in the first rule, it is not applicable in this one, either.

Because the first rule fails to pass the negative test of the means–ends principle, and because the second rule passes all of the tests, we must conclude that Plasma International's practice was impermissible from the standpoint of the ethics of respect for persons.

Two final comments should be made. First, the first rule violates the self-defeating test and the negative test of the means–ends principle in a relatively innocuous manner. It is not entirely clear that a universalization of the rule would be self-defeating. Although the donors may not be fully informed that they are selling their blood at below-market prices, the decision to sell a pint (or even several pints) of blood was probably not a decision with far-reaching consequences on their lives. It is important to see that some cases should probably be considered borderline, and this may be one of them. In fact, perhaps the considerations from the standpoint of the ethics of respect for persons could be legitimately overridden from a utilitarian perspective. Second, the morality of selling blood to people under conditions of great need has not been considered. The moral problems raised by selling blood might be more serious than the ones raised by buying it.

EVALUATING THE ETHICS OF RESPECT FOR PERSONS AS A MORAL THEORY

Now we are ready to evaluate the ethics of respect for persons with our four criteria. Remember that a subjective element is always present in evaluating moral theories. The following evaluations are my own, although they reflect widely held positions among moral philosophers. These evaluations are for your own consideration rather than for uncritical acceptance.

Criterion 1: Consistency

The fact that this moral philosophy has two moral standards rather than one might be considered a source of inconsistency, because the two standards sometimes yield different conclusions. But the stipulation that an action must pass the tests of both standards before it is considered morally acceptable rules out this problem. Besides, the two moral standards taken together express a common moral theme—namely, the equal respect due all persons.

Another possible source of inconsistency is the two principles used in applying the means–ends principle. These principles are (1) that a person can forfeit his rights to freedom and well-being by violating the rights of others and (2) that the rights of others should be respected equally. If they are not derivable from the theory itself, a problem of consistency arises. But because both of these principles can be derived from the idea of equality embodied in the universalization principle, they are not inconsistent with the theory.

Criterion 2: Justification

Evaluating the justifications of the two moral standards of the ethics of respect for persons presents special difficulties. Kant's arguments are too complex and controversial to be discussed here. We shall therefore evaluate arguments by contemporary writers who advocate principles at least analogous to the universalization principle and the means–ends principle, beginning with a consideration of the universalization principle.

The universalization principle is primarily a requirement of equality. It states that everyone must be able to adopt the rule underlying an action. The idea underlying this requirement is that rules applicable to me must be applicable to others in similar situations. If the rules cannot be universally applied without undermining my own ability to use them, then I must not act in accordance with them, either. But in what sense must I be willing for others to adopt the same rules of behavior I adopt? In other words, how would I justify the universalization principle?

One answer to this question is that the force behind the universalization principle is derived from the nature of morality itself. Some philosophers have maintained that the plausibility of the principle is derived from the term *moral.* To see the force of this claim, consider the case discussed in Chapter 5 of John Zimmerman, an attorney whose physician discovers an aneurism in his adversary's client. Suppose Zimmerman refuses to reveal the information and the boy dies. Suppose, also, that a few months later his own daughter is in an accident, and the attorney for the other side discovers information about his daughter's medical condition that could save her life if he revealed it. Instead, he conceals the information, and Zimmerman's daughter dies. When Zimmerman discovers what the lawyer has done, he is enraged and tries in every way possible to have the attorney disbarred or otherwise punished. He calls the lawyer's conduct immoral, an outrage to society, and a disgrace to the legal profession.

Most of us would say that, by this reaction, Zimmerman has conceded that his own conduct in concealing similar information was immoral. But suppose Zimmerman insists that his conduct was not immoral, even though he admits that the only significant difference between the two cases is that in this case he is related to the deceased person. At this point, we would probably severely criticize Zimmerman's behavior. One way of stating our criticism would be to say that Zimmerman does not know how to use the words *moral* and *immoral*. If he is going to use moral language correctly, he must apply the same rules to himself that he applies to others.

How could Zimmerman respond to this agreement? On the one hand, he could deny that he is violating the rule that governs the use of the words *moral* and *immoral*. He could say that he is just an ethical egoist who is unwilling to universalize his egoism. And surely one would want to call such egoism either moral or immoral, not amoral as one would have to do if egoism were outside the boundaries of morality altogether. On the other hand, Zimmerman could say that, although his position may not be "moral" in the proper sense of that term, he does not care. "Why should I be moral if it is contrary to my self-interest?" he might ask. At this point, we must then show why a person should govern his actions by moral principles. We shall not pursue this issue further here. The justification of the universalization principle is a complex issue that still provokes controversy. But the implausibility of Zimmerman's replies to criticism of his behavior indicates that the universalization principle is deeply rooted in our moral thinking.

The justification of the means-ends principle is, if anything, more controversial.[10] One of the most plausible arguments is that refusal to respect the essential nature of personhood in oneself or others involves a contradiction.

---

[10] One of the most interesting attempts to justify a principle like the means-ends principle is Alan Gewirth's *Reason and Morality*. I am indebted to his book for the basic ideas presented here, although this particular version is my own and differs in important aspects from Gewirth's. I am also indebted to Henry Veatch's review of Gewirth's book in *Ethics* 89 (July 1979) for my presentation and criticism of these ideas. For other discussions of this issue, see Marcus Singer, "On Gewirth's Derivation of the Principle of Generic Consistency," in *Ethics* 95, No. 2 (January 1985), pp. 297–301; and Alan Gewirth, "From the Prudential to the Moral: Reply to Singer" in *Ethics* 95, No. 2 (January 1985), pp. 302–304. For the most recent and thorough discussion of Gewirth's arguments, see Deryck Beyleveld, *The Dialectical Necessity of Morality* (Chicago: University of Chicago Press, 1991).

The first step in exposing this contradiction is to maintain that if we cannot be personal agents without having our freedom and well-being respected, we will necessarily claim the right to have these aspects of our personhood respected. This claim is not merely a matter of the intellect but primarily embodied in our action. That is, we must act as if we have the rights to the freedom and well-being we need to accomplish our purposes. But if the implicit assumptions of our action are based on nothing more than the fact that we are moral agents, we are forced by the constraints of consistency to acknowledge that any other person who is a moral agent like ourselves has exactly the same rights. To deny this respect to other agents while claiming it for ourselves is inconsistent.

Even though this argument is impressive, we can still ask how the fact that we implicitly claim certain rights by our action justifies the claim. And perhaps there are no implicit moral claims behind certain types of action; perhaps we just act in our self-interest. A successful justification of the means-ends principle must answer these questions.

Criterion 3: Plausibility

Many people, especially those strongly influenced by traditional moral ideas, would maintain that the ethics of respect for persons is more compatible with their previously held moral beliefs than utilitarianism or egoism. They might well hold that it is closer to their moral beliefs than natural law, although the version of the theory presented here may not suggest traditional positions on such issues as premarital sex or suicide.

Perhaps the most general criticism of the ethics of respect for persons, from the standpoint of agreement or disagreement with our previously held moral beliefs, is that the theory does not sufficiently account for an action's consequences. In many issues of public policy, for example, utilitarian considerations seem relevant. Sometimes it seems justifiable to sacrifice some innocent lives to save the lives of a larger number of people. If killing some civilians is necessary to end a war and ultimately save many more lives, is it wrong to do so? Is it wrong to adopt policies that increase unemployment somewhat but reduce the inflation rate? It sometimes seems morally permissible, if not obligatory, to engage in an action that involves wrongs to individuals because the overall consequences justify it.

Criterion 4: Usefulness

Applying the ethics of respect for persons can be difficult for three reasons. First, the rule describing an action can be stated in many different ways, which means that different conclusions will be drawn depending on which rule is used. Usually this problem is not too severe, because the most adequate rule is reasonably obvious. However, the rule sometimes must be stated in an ambiguous or open-ended way to be acceptable. At other times, the proper rule may be difficult to determine, and the way in which the rule is stated may decisively influence the outcome of the ethical analysis. When these problems arise, they diminish the usefulness of the theory in providing a clear indication of what should be done.

Consider the case of the physician who does not believe in sterilization but who is asked to perform a sterilization on a man for whom he is the only available physician. We would probably not want to consider a rule that reads, "Physicians should always follow their patients' wishes." Nor would we want to consider a rule that states, "Physicians should always follow their own conscience, even if it means denying their patients' wishes." Perhaps a better rule is the following: "Physicians should always follow their patients' wishes, even if it involves violating the physician's own strongly held moral beliefs, as long as a patient's request is within the bounds of ordinary morality." This rule is still open-ended, because the phrase "within the bounds of ordinary morality" has various interpretations. But there does not appear to be any way to eliminate the open-ended character of a rule covering this situation.

A second difficulty is that we sometimes find it hard to determine whether an action passes the tests of the two moral standards. Sometimes the self-defeating test is hard to apply. For example, suppose we are attempting to determine whether the self-defeating test is passed by a rule allowing physicians to lie to their patients when the physician believes it is for their good. If it were generally accepted that physicians will sometimes lie to their patients, would patients no longer trust physicians? If patients generally lost confidence in the word of physicians because this rule was followed, then physicians could still lie to their patients, but they could not achieve the purpose they had in lying. The rule would thus be self-defeating. However, physicians' lying in such special circumstances as the rule describes might not be enough to undermine a general confidence in the word of physicians, so the rule would not be self-defeating. At any rate, the application of the self-defeating test of the universalization principle sometimes depends on factual assumptions about the consequences of actions that are often little more than speculation.

We have also seen that the means-ends principle is difficult to apply in many ethical controversies. It is not always easy to determine how the negative test applies or whether the positive test is relevant.

A third problem with this theory is that we sometimes find that both an action and its alternative have difficulties with one or more of the tests. The sterilization case mentioned previously might well be one in which both the rule and its alternative would violate the negative test of the means-ends principle. The rule requiring physicians to honor patients' wishes would violate the moral agency of physicians, and the alternative rule requiring physicians to honor their own consciences would violate the moral agency of patients. In such situations, we are forced to make a judgment as to which violations are more serious, and this judgment makes the solution to the problem controversial. Any moral theory will yield ambiguous conclusions in some instances, so this state of affairs is not a refutation of the ethics of respect for persons. Nevertheless, this limitation, which should be noted in any evaluation, is especially prominent in respect-for-persons morality.

CONCEPT SUMMARY

The ethics of respect for persons has no obvious inconsistencies. An argument for the universalization principle is that it is required by the meaning of the word *moral*, but some people might argue that an action guide need not meet the requirements of morality. An argument for the means-ends principle is that as agents, we necessarily claim that our purposes and the conditions necessary for their realization should be respected. If we make this claim simply because we are agents, we must respect an equal claim on the part of other agents. But the fact that we make a claim to certain rights does not necessarily mean the claim is valid, and we may not necessarily even have to make this claim.

The ethics of respect for persons is generally consistent with most people's prior moral beliefs, although its lack of emphasis on consequences leads to some conclusions that many people find implausible. However, respect-for-persons morality sometimes cannot produce a clear resolution of moral dilemmas. Possible problems are that the rule describing an action can be stated in more than one way, it is difficult to know whether an action passes the tests of the two moral standards, and the action and its alternative are equally justifiable or unjustifiable.

Applying the
Four Theories

Our evaluations of moral theories do not allow us to say that one moral theory is clearly more rationally defensible than all the others. Thus, we have not arrived at a complete answer to moral subjectivism. Nevertheless, the following points should be kept in mind.

First, we have shown that argument about moral principles and theories is possible. Extreme forms of subjectivism, which hold that ethics is an area in which we merely express our feelings, are thus implausible. You cannot say just anything you please in ethics without rational analysis or argument. Even if complete agreement on the proper moral principles is unlikely, ethics is still a rational activity. There are constraints on what moral principles can be defended.

Second, the four moral theories tend to come to similar conclusions in many areas. All of the theories would agree that murder, lying, theft, slavery, rape, assault, slander, and fraud, for example, are generally wrong. Even the egoist would probably prefer to live in a society in which these acts were forbidden, provided others would agree to the prohibitions. The four theories converge, then, on a core area of morality.

This convergence is obscured by the types of cases usually discussed in ethics texts, including this one. The cases presented for analysis, in both the text and Appendix II, are usually the more difficult and controversial ones, not the core cases on which most people (and most moral theories) would agree. For example, no cases pose the question of whether murdering a parent to collect an inheritance is morally permissible. All of the theories (with the possible exception of act egoism) would agree that it is not morally permissible. On the other hand, there might be cases that ask the question of whether it is wrong to administer a lethal dose of an analgesic to a person who is suffering from terminal cancer, is in great pain, and wants to die. These latter cases are the kinds that are morally troublesome and intellectually interesting. However, exclusive focus on them can convey the false impression that all moral evaluations are difficult and controversial.

Third, some theories do come out better in our rankings than the others. Using the criteria for evaluation we developed, utilitarianism and the ethics of respect for persons seem to be more acceptable theories, all things considered. This conclusion is widely accepted among moral philosophers. Thus, although a single theory has not yet gained universal acceptance, utilitarianism and the ethics of respect for persons are widely thought to be the most rationally defensible moral theories. So the moral principles that are justified by these theories would be the most rationally defensible moral principles.

Fourth, moral philosophers have reached some degree of consensus about what should be done when utilitarianism and the ethics of respect for persons disagree. In general, the ethics of respect for persons should prevail except when utilitarian considerations are very strong. Thus, killing a person and using his organs to save the lives of several other people would not be morally permissible, even though greater overall utility might be produced. But suppose a small number of people are carriers of a plague that will kill 99 percent of the people who contract it. Suppose further that these individuals became carriers of the plague through no fault of their own and that they will not themselves die of it. Suppose that, because of unusual conditions, such as those that would prevail after a nuclear war, it is not possible to isolate the individuals from other humans. Would it be permissible to kill them to prevent massive deaths? Many moralists would say yes, even though the disease carriers have done nothing worthy of death and would not die of the plague themselves.

After making these points, however, we must still concede that morality has a place for personal judgment and even personal commitment. Moral theory can provide enormous insight into moral problems and their solutions. Even apart from resolving moral controversies, it can help us understand more clearly the moral issues at stake in a controversy. For example, case 5 in Appendix II, "The Use of Cadavers for Crash Testing," seems to involve a conflict between utilitarian and respect-for-persons considerations.

In analyzing the cases in Appendix II, you should keep several things in mind. First, you must decide which moral theories to use. Although it might be desirable to use all of the theories in analyzing every case, sometimes some theories will obviously be more relevant than others. For example, we have suggested that utilitarian and respect-for-persons theories are especially relevant to case 5.

Second, you will have to decide what factual issues are raised by a case. Sometimes a so-called "moral" controversy turns out to be a disagreement over the facts and not a disagreement over moral principles at all. When the factual disagreement is resolved, the controversy ends. For example, a disagreement over whether an engineer should object to a new chemical process that results in emitting a substance from a smokestack might depend entirely on whether the substance is harmful to people or the environment.

The case descriptions will not always present all the facts you need to resolve the issue. If you were in an actual situation, you would be able to investigate the issue and perhaps resolve the factual uncertainty. Because you do not have this option here, you will have to make certain factual *assumptions* and clearly *state* what they are. As we all know, however, investigation will not always resolve factual uncertainties. If you have reason to believe that investigation would not resolve a question about the facts, it is better to attempt to decide how the ethical issue should be resolved in the face of factual uncertainty.

Third, in analyzing cases, you should always keep an eye out for issues involving the meanings of crucial terms. Sometimes a so-called "moral" controversy is actually a disagreement over the meanings of certain terms and whether the terms apply in a given situation. Once these debates are settled, there may be no further disagreement. Two people might disagree about the definition of *lie* or *breaking confidentiality* or whether using another's intellectual property is extensive enough to be called "theft." Most people agree that lying, breaking confidentiality, and stealing are wrong, at least under most circumstances, so the question hinges on the problems in applying the moral principles involving lying, breaking confidentiality, and stealing. If two people disagree over the definition of a "lie," for example, they may also disagree over whether a statement is really a lie, and so over whether the moral principle "Don't lie" is relevant.

Fourth, keep in mind that deciding whether a principle applies (a relevance problem, in our terminology) is not always sufficient to resolve a moral issue. Sometimes more than one moral principle is relevant in a situation, producing a conflict problem. The circumstances may be such that, even though a course of action may involve lying, breaking confidentiality, or stealing, for example, it still might be the right thing to do. Suppose a physician believes that breaking patient-physician confidentiality is justified to expose a case of child abuse. In this case, he believes that the moral principle requiring us to keep confidentiality overrides the moral principle requiring us to protect the innocent.

Fifth, in attempting to resolve the cases in Appendix II in which there is a conflict problem, remember to look for creative middle-way solutions. That is, if the competing moral considerations seem roughly equally important, look for solutions that attempt to do justice to all of the competing considerations. For example, Martin Luther King developed a policy of nonviolent resistance. The policy enabled him to resist injustice but to do so in a way that did not involve violence (at least on his part) and accepted the legal consequences of breaking the law. Thus, he was able to honor his desire both to promote social justice and to do so in a way that respected the basic institutions of the United States. Of course, if one obligation is far more important than the other, the creative middle-way solution is inappropriate. The more important obligation must be honored at the expense of the less important one.

Sixth, it is worth emphasizing again that in some cases rational people can disagree, over both which moral theory is most appropriate and what conclusions a given moral theory yields. Moral theory has its limits. It cannot provide automatic answers in all moral problems, nor can it take the place of the morally sensitive and discerning individual. It is not a dictatorial master but a helpful guide in the moral life.

Cases for Analysis

Case 1: The Patient Wants to Die

A thirty-six-year-old accountant, whom we shall call Charles Johnson, married and the father of three young children, is diagnosed as having immunoblastic lymphadenopathy, a fatal malignant tumor of the lymph nodes. He has been receiving a variety of treatments, yet his condition has steadily worsened. Charles knows that all surgical and medical measures have been exhausted. He suffers daily from excruciating nerve-root pain; he must take addicting doses of narcotics but still is not free from pain. The expenses of his treatment are rapidly exhausting his family's financial resources. Charles's wife and family are beginning to withdraw from him emotionally, in anticipation of his inevitable death. Having reconciled himself to his death, he asks the doctor for the means of killing himself to end his pain, the suffering of his family, and the depletion of the funds that are so important for his family's future well-being. Is it morally permissible for the physician to acquiesce in this request?[1]

Case 2: A Lawyer's Dilemma

In July 1973, Robert Garrow, a thirty-eight-year-old mechanic from Syracuse, New York, killed four persons, apparently at random.[2] The four were camping

---

[1] This case was supplied by Harry S. Lipscomb, M.D. Used with permission.

[2] Reported in several sources, including "Slayer's Two Lawyers Kept Secret of Two More Killings," *New York Times*, June 20, 1974, p. 1.

in the Adirondack Mountains. In early August, following a vigorous manhunt, Garrow was captured by state police and indicted for the murder of a student from Schenectady. At the time of the arrest, no evidence connected Garrow to the other deaths; in fact, two of the people were not even known to be dead. One was a young Illinois woman, the other a Syracuse high school girl listed as a runaway. The body of the third, a camping companion of the Illinois woman, was found on July 20, before Garrow's capture. The court appointed two Syracuse lawyers, Francis R. Belge and Frank H. Armani, to defend Garrow.

Some weeks later, during discussions with his two lawyers, Garrow told them that he had raped and killed a woman in a mine shaft. Belge and Armani located the mine shaft and the body of the Illinois woman but did not take their discovery to the police. The body was finally discovered four months later by two children playing in the mine. In September, the lawyers found the second body by following Garrow's directions. This discovery, too, went unrecorded; the girl's body was uncovered by a student in December.

The Illinois woman's father read that Belge and Armani were defending a man accused of killing a camper in the Adirondacks. Knowing that his daughter's companion had also been found dead there, he journeyed to Syracuse to talk to the lawyers. He asked whether they knew anything about his daughter, but they denied having any knowledge that would help him. Belge and Armani maintained their silence until the following June. Then, to try to show that he was insane, Garrow made statements from the witness stand that implicated him in the other three murders. At a press conference the next day, Belge and Armani outlined for the first time the sequence of events.

The local community was outraged. The lawyers, however, believed they had honored the letter and spirit of their professional duty in a tough case. "We both, knowing how the parents feel, wanted to advise them where the bodies were," Belge said, "but since it was a privileged communication, we could not reveal any information that was given to us in confidence."

Their silence was based on the legal code that admonishes the lawyer to "preserve the confidence and secrets of a client." The lawyer-client "privilege" against disclosure of confidences is one of the oldest and most iron-clad in the law. If the defendant has no duty to confess his guilt or complicity in a crime, it can make no sense to assert that his lawyer has such a duty. Otherwise, the argument goes, the accused will tell his lawyer at best a deficient version of the facts, and the lawyer cannot as effectively defend the client. This argument frequently seems unconvincing; it certainly did to the people of Syracuse. Should the lawyer have revealed the whereabouts of the Illinois woman's body to her father?

Case 3: The Use of Fetal Tissue

Although researchers have not publicized the fact, they have for decades used fetal tissue for a wide variety of medical research in many areas, from birth defects to Parkinson's disease. Fetal tissue is widely used because it grows quickly and easily in the laboratory and resembles cancer cells in some ways, enabling scientists to investigate what controls cell growth. Scientists hope that fetal tissue transplants might soon cure diabetes and Parkinson's disease and perhaps other diseases such as Alzheimer's.

In November 1989, the Bush administration announced that it would extend a twenty-month ban on federal financing of fetal tissue transplants, intending to head off what abortion opponents feared might be an enormous market for fetal tissue.

"The sleazy, scummy world of fetal tissue procurement cries out for federal regulation," said Dr. Arthur Caplan, a codirector of the Center for Bioethics at the University of Minnesota. Caplan and James Bopp, general counsel for the National Right to Life Committee, said informed consent from women is virtually unheard of in the fetal tissue business. "You want to be sure there is no cutting of corners, no risk to the mother, no encouragement to have an abortion," Caplan said.

The largest supplier of fetal tissue is a nonprofit company, the Institute for the Advancement of Medicine, in Effington, Pennsylvania. President James W. Beardsley said he provides scientists with 300 to 600 specimens a month from 150 to 300 fetuses. Caplan said 90 percent of researchers get fetal tissue through private arrangements with abortion clinics or gynecologists.[3] Is the use of fetal tissue justified?

Case 4: Is AZT Overpriced?

AZT (azidothymidine) is one of the most effective drugs used in the treatment of AIDS.[4] It stops the multiplication of the virus that causes the disease and lengthens the life of AIDS patients, although it does not cure the disease. It is also one of the most expensive drugs ever sold for daily use over a long period, often costing the patient $8,000 a year.

The prospect of huge profits from the sale of AZT has brought a wave of protests against the Burroughs–Wellcome Company, manufacturer of the drug. Advocates for people with AIDS have organized boycotts of other company products. One form of protest would be sending letters to all physicians in the country, asking them to substitute another antibiotic for one made by Burroughs–Wellcome.

Government lawyers have considered whether to invoke a 1910 law that would allow federal officials to override the company's patents to make larger supplies available. The law was last invoked in the 1950s when military officials sought a lower price for tetracycline than that offered by drug companies in the United States. The law provides that the government may override

---

3 Gina Kolata, "More U.S. Curbs Urged in the Use of Fetal Tissue," *New York Times*, November 19, 1989, p. A1.

4 See Philip J. Hilts, "Wave of Protests Developing on Profits from AIDS Drug," *New York Times*, September 16, 1989, p. A1.

patent protection if the action is important for the welfare of the nation. The company whose patent is negated cannot sue the government under normal patent law but can recover a "reasonable compensation" in the Court of Claims, a special court that considers claims against the federal government.

An article in the *Journal of the American Medical Association* called the high cost of AZT unnecessary, and the authors of the article said in a press conference that the company is guilty of "price gouging." John A. Folkenberg, an analyst with the British investment bank of Barclays, Dezoete, Wedd, Inc., in New York, said pharmaceutical companies assume a worst-case scenario: the product will have a short life, few patients, and other problems. Dr. Leonard Schifrin, a health care economist at the College of William and Mary, said, "The company wants to build up a very nice nest egg to recover costs, and so the price of drugs like AZT seems very, very high. Then, when the worst cases do not happen, but instead there are more patients and a longer life in the market, it can turn those worst cases into billion-dollar bonanzas." Recent findings indicate that the number of people who could benefit from AZT has increased from about 45,000 people with AIDS to 600,000 people who are infected but show no symptoms.

The argument of Burroughs-Wellcome is that the price is high because research and development costs are high and the market is relatively small. It also says that it began research and manufactured the drug when other companies did not want to take the risk.

Industry analysts estimate that the cost of bringing the drug to market was $80 to 100 million. Sales of the fiscal year ending in August 1989 alone were $220 million, translating into estimated profits of $100 million before taxes. Estimates of the cost of producing an AZT capsule range from 7 to 53 cents per capsule, whereas patents pay about $1.75. Was Burroughs-Wellcome morally justified in charging these prices for the drug?

Case 5: The Use of Cadavers for Crash Testing

Germany's Heidelberg University used more than two hundred corpses, including those of eight children, in automobile crash tests.[5] The university claimed it received relatives' permission. The research ministry of Baden-Wuertemberg (the state in which the university is located) ordered the university to document these permissions. The revelation of these tests drew immediate protests in Germany. Rudolph Hammerschmidt, spokesman for the Roman Catholic German Bishops' Conference, objected, "Even the dead possess human dignity. This research should be done with mannequins." ADAC, Germany's largest automobile club, issued a statement saying, "In an

---

[5] This case is based on Terrence Petty, "Use of Corpses in Auto-Crash Tests Outrages Germans," *Kalamazoo Gazette*, November 24, 1993, p. A3. The case was prepared by Michael S. Pritchard and originally printed in Charles E. Harris, Jr., Michael S. Pritchard, and Michael J. Rabins, *Engineering Ethics: Concepts and Cases* (Belmont, CA: Wadsworth, 1995), pp. 183–184. Used with permission.

age when experiments on animals are being put into question, such tests must be carried out on dummies and not on children's cadavers."

German law permits the use of cadavers for research if relatives grant permission. In the crash tests, the bodies are strapped into cars that are smashed into other cars, walls, and barriers. The impact on humans is measured with cameras and electronic sensors. Heidelberg's Dr. Reiner Mattern, head of the forensic pathology department, indicated that children's cadavers had not been tested since 1989 but that testing of adult cadavers is continuing. He added that the tests have saved lives, including those of children.

Clarence Ditlow, head of the Center for Auto Safety, a public advocacy group in Washington, D.C., reported that tests with cadavers were conducted by at least two research teams in the United States during the 1980s, including Detroit's Wayne State University. Ditlow said that the center advocates three criteria for such testing: (1) prior consent by the deceased person, (2) informed consent of the family, and (3) assurance that the data sought by the tests cannot be gained from using dummies.

Robert Wartner, a Wayne State spokesman, said the university's Bioengineering Center conducted tests as apart of a study by the federal government's Centers for Disease Control. However, he added, "Cadavers are used only when alternatives could not produce useful safety research."

Time magazine (December 6, 1993, p. 70) reported that German parents were initially upset when asked whether their children's bodies could be used in auto crashes. However, nearly all, said *Time*, granted permission when they were told that data from the tests are "vital for constructing more than 120 types of instrumented dummies, ranging in size from infants to adults, that can simulate dozens of human reactions in a crash." In addition, despite a 75 percent increase in the number of cars on the road over the last twenty years, the fatality rate decreased more than 50 percent. "Much of that improvement," *Time* said, "is due to the introduction of such devices as seat belts, air bags, safer windshields and stronger doors—all of which were developed with the aid of crash dummies. Is the use of cadavers in crash testing morally justified?

Case 6: Highway Safety Improvements

Tom Byrne, a young civil engineer, is assigned the task of spending $25,000 for highway improvements.[6] Option A is to spend the money for improvements at an urban intersection, which 24,000 vehicles use each day. The intersection averages two fatalities and six injuries each year at the intersection. Option B is to spend the money for improvements at a rural intersection, which 6,000 vehicles use each day. The intersection averages one fatality and two injuries each year. Government figures at the time placed a value of $235,000 on each human life and $11,200 on each injury. Byrne sees that he

---

[6] This case is based on one developed by James Taylor of Notre Dame University.

will prevent more deaths and accidents by choosing option A. He also sees that the chance of a person's getting killed or injured is greater at the rural intersection. Which option should he choose?

Case 7: The TV Antenna

Marsha Johnston works for Antenna Engineering, which has designed the antennas and a thousand-foot TV antenna tower for a local TV station.[7] The tower has been put in place, except for the last section containing the antenna baskets. Because the antenna baskets are attached to the top section, it cannot be lifted in the same way as the other sections. To hold the last section away from the tower as it is hoisted so that the antenna baskets will not be damaged, the construction workers, none of whom are engineers, bolt some lifting arms to the section. These arms, which extend beyond the edge of the tower section, would allow the section to be held far enough away from the tower to prevent damage to the antenna baskets. Not being confident that this method of lifting the final section is sound from an engineering standpoint, the construction workers call Johnston, asking, "Can you look at our proposal for lifting the last section to be sure it is safe?"

Johnston calls her boss, Bill Mason, the president of the design firm, to relay the request. His response was emphatic:

No way! If we are involved in construction in any way and there is an accident, we are liable. Our contract was only to design the tower and the baskets. We have no responsibility for construction. We tried to be the nice guys once before and ended up being sued for $250,000. We are a small company and cannot afford to lose our insurance.

Johnston knows enough about the contractor's proposed way of lifting the last section to suspect that it is indeed unsafe and that there is a real possibility that the section could fall, killing the construction workers who will be riding the section to the top of the tower. Unfortunately, she also knows that Mason's fears for the welfare of his company are legitimate and that she will probably lose her job if she gives the contractors any advice. What should she do?

Case 8: Violent Lyrics

A rap CD contains lyrics that appear to advocate violence against women. The lyrics suggest that women are sexually excited by being slapped and receiving other forms of physical and verbal abuse. The lyrics also suggest that men can take a woman's protest as a way of actually giving consent to sexual intercourse and that rape is a myth. In response to criticism, members of the

[7] This case is a modification of a real case. It is described in more detail in R. W. Flumerfelt, C. E. Harris, M. J. Rabins, and C. H. Samson, eds., *Introducing Ethics Case Studies into Required Undergraduate Engineering Courses*, final report to the National Science Foundation on Grant No. DIR-9012252, November 1992, pp. 231–261.

rap group respond that they have a right to advocate their views and that they sincerely believe males in our society need to reclaim their masculinity.

Critics of the group argue that the group encourages rape and abuse of women. Defenders of the group either agree with the group's philosophy or argue that freedom of expression should override other considerations. Which side has the stronger moral argument?

Case 9: The Eye Test

Cosmetics manufacturers often test products, such as shampoos, by dropping them in the eyes of rabbits. At Cosme-Tech, this practice often results in the rabbits' going blind. The practice also causes considerable pain to the rabbits. When the rabbits go blind or are otherwise no longer suitable for the tests, they are killed in a painless way.

Recently, animal rights activists have begun protesting this practice at Cosme-Tech and similar firms, blockading the entrance to the plant and advocating that customers no longer buy the products. Industry advocates argue that this method of testing products is common and that testing on animals has prevented releasing some seriously harmful products to the public: better blind animals than humans. Who has the moral high ground in this argument?

Case 10: Spiking Trees

Protect the Trees (PT) is an environmental group determined to protect an old-growth forest that loggers are about to destroy. Having exhausted legal remedies, they resort to "spiking" some of the trees. In this practice, large iron spikes are driven into the trees. When the loggers' saws hit the spikes, they often inflict serious injuries on the loggers. In a few instances, loggers have even been killed. Critics of PT's tactics argue that human life is being endangered to protect trees. Defending their practice, PT members argue that trees, especially of the age and majesty of those they are trying to protect, deserve respect and that the danger to human life is small. Furthermore, they argue, we have an obligation to future generations to protect what old-growth forests remain. Disregarding legal questions, which side has the stronger moral argument?

Case 11: Development versus Preservation

During the 1960s, a controversy erupted over the proper use for the Mineral King Valley, a wilderness area adjacent to Sequoia National Park in California. On the one hand, Walt Disney Enterprises wanted to develop the valley as a ski resort that would bring an estimated 14,000 visitors to the valley each day. The development would involve building ski slopes, hotels, restaurants, parking lots, and other facilities. The Sierra Club argued for keeping the area in an undeveloped state and allowing only hiking, camping, hunting, and fishing.

Making its decision in favor of Walt Disney Enterprises, the U.S. Forest Service argued that the Disney proposal would serve more people and that the higher prices people were willing to pay for skiing showed that people wanted to ski more than they wanted to camp, hunt, and fish. The Sierra Club argued that this economic approach failed to give due consideration to the aesthetic and ecological factors, as well as the animals, plants, rivers, and mountains. Which side was right in this debate?

Case 12: An Unusual Request

James Harrison is a seventeen-year-old high school senior and an honors student. He has been studying the world population problem and is convinced that the explosive growth of the human population must be stopped. In an attempt to do his part to slow population growth, he asks his local physician for a vasectomy. His physician refuses, arguing that Harrison is not mature enough to make such a decision. Harrison argues that people his age are not prevented from climbing mountains, racing cars, engaging in risky sexual practices, and doing many other things that can affect their lives in even more serious ways. Therefore, he should be allowed to have a vasectomy if he wants one. Was his physician morally justified in her decision?

Case 13: Should the Physician Tell?

While seventy-five-year-old Ethel Morgan is undergoing a routine hernia operation, the surgeon discovers that she has one undescended testicle. The surgeon informs Morgan's family physician, who orders a genetic analysis. The analysis shows that she is genetically male. The family physician knows that Morgan was never able to have children and that she has one adopted daughter. He also knows that she is happily married and that both she and her husband would be deeply disturbed if they knew about the undescended testicle and the genetic analysis. Should the physician reveal the information? Should he have ordered the genetic tests? What if Morgan were twenty-one instead of seventy-five?

Case 14: Mothers and Fetuses

Big Chemical has learned that some of the substances to which their employees are exposed pose considerable risks for fetuses, although they appear to pose no risk to the adult employees of the plant. To remedy this problem, Big Chemical announced a policy of laying off pregnant employees, with written assurance that their jobs would be restored after delivery. The company also required female employees to sign a statement that they would notify the company as soon as they were pregnant. Complaining that the policy is discriminatory, the female employees asked that it be revoked. What should plant managers do?

Case 15: Killing Pain

Mike Brown has terminal throat cancer, which produces excruciating pain. His physician knows that the analgesic necessary to eliminate the pain will itself be life shortening. The physician believes that such practices are wrong. Should she administer the analgesic anyhow, because her patient requests it?

Case 16: Amish Schools

Zachary Yoder wants his children to attend Amish schools rather than the public schools in Pennsylvania. Others argue that the Amish schools are inferior in quality and will make it virtually impossible for the children to leave the Amish community, because they will not have a sufficient education to find jobs elsewhere. They also maintain that the children cannot gain sufficient information about the larger American society from Amish schools, so they cannot make an informed decision as to whether to leave or stay in the Amish community. Thus, the free choice of the children cannot be preserved if they attend Amish schools.

Yoder argues that if his children go to public schools, they would not have a sufficient knowledge of Amish culture to make an intelligent and genuinely free choice about whether to remain a part of it. He also states that they will be alienated from their culture by peer pressures and the influence of secular American society. Finally, he says that he has the right to determine the education of his children. Members of the local school board are considering going to court to force Yoder to send his children to the public schools. Would they be morally justified in doing this?

Case 17: Allowing to Die?

Tom Allen, a thirty-year-old Jehovah's Witness and father of two small children, believes that blood transfusions are contrary to God's law. He is brought to the hospital with injuries and internal bleeding, caused by a tree falling on him. He does not want a blood transfusion, which is probably necessary to save his life. His wife concurs in his decision to refuse the transfusion. The physician must make a quick decision, and he knows that he will not face legal problems, whatever decision he makes. Should he give the transfusion?

Case 18: Taking Care of Your Own

Louise Lax, twenty-five years old and married for four years, has just discovered that she has a genetically based disease and that she has a 50 percent chance of passing it on to any offspring. She and her husband have not had any children, but they very much want to have a family, even if she is not alive to care for them until maturity. She wants to take the risk of having a child. However, the state has just passed a new law stating that if a woman gives birth to a defective child after learning that she or her husband is a carrier of this disease, the husband and wife must pay for the upkeep of the child. Such children cannot usually be cared for at home. If the parents cannot pay for the child's care, usually about $40,000 a year, the state will take over, but the parents will have part of their salary deducted to pay for the child's care. This arrangement will continue throughout the parents' lives until the debt is paid, even if the child dies. The Laxes argue that this arrangement is unfair and unjustly punishes them, just because they happen to be carriers of a disease. Would such a law be morally justifiable?

Case 19: Privileged Information

Todd Bosman is a lobbyist for General Insurance, which, along with other insurance companies in the state, is promoting a bill that would make records of genetic defects available to the public. The bill is also being promoted by many employers in the state. Supporters of the bill argue that insurance companies and employers should not be burdened by people who will almost certainly have medical problems. If information about genetic defects were publicly available, insurance companies would be able to refuse health and life insurance to such people. Employers would also not have to hire people who would eventually impose heavy burdens on health insurance programs. The bill's supporters argue that the bill is also humane, because it provides that the state should take special responsibility for unemployment insurance and health and life insurance for people with severe genetic defects. Is such a bill morally justifiable?

Case 20: E-mail Exposure

Every E-mail system has a designated "postmaster," to whom undeliverable mail is forwarded. The postmaster is supposed to either send the mail (which might have an incorrect address) to the proper person or return it to the sender. In a business or governmental organization, the postmaster is usually a department head or other administrator. Although it is against the policies of most organizations in the state, postmasters sometimes read the messages before delivering or returning them.

A program has recently been invented that will automatically return undeliverable E-mail to the sender without forwarding it to a postmaster, so that the confidentiality of the messages is better protected. Unfortunately, the program is rather expensive and would be a considerable burden to small organizations. Many organizations would probably dispense with E-mail altogether before installing the software. Ben Rosen, a state legislator, is nevertheless proposing a law that would make installation of the program mandatory on all E-mail systems in the state. Would such a proposal be morally justifiable or even required?

Case 21: Genetic Testing in the Workplace

At the request of the Black Employees Association, Ameri-Chem tests its black employees for sickle-cell disease, which affects every 400 to 600 black Americans. The purpose of the testing is not to identify employees to be eliminated but to facilitate relocating those afflicted with the genetic disorder to parts of the plant where the disease would not be triggered. Critics of the policy say it allows the company to transfer workers instead of eliminating the conditions that triggered the disease, but company officials respond that toxic materials are well below government standards and that the levels are only a threat to those with sickle-cell disease. It would be enormously expensive and not cost-effective to reduce the levels further, and in some cases it would not be possible at all.

Some black critics of the policy have argued that the compulsory testing is invasive and that the results of the tests could harm employees' chance of getting jobs elsewhere. Even if the company refused to give out the results of the test, prospective employers could make pretty good guesses about which employees had positive results by asking what jobs the employees had at Ameri-Chem. If the employees were black and had been transferred to one of the areas of the plant known to be safe for sickle-cell disease, prospective employers could safely assume that the employees had a positive sickle-cell test. Employees could hardly refuse to answer questions about their former jobs. Is Ameri-Chem's policy morally justifiable?

Case 22: It's Our Affair

Jane Thompson, who is unmarried, has risen rapidly in the ranks of Vertex Corporation. She has now become a vice president. Recently she has been seen in the company of a young and very handsome unmarried accountant, Bill Jennings, who is also employed by Vertex. They are both very discrete about their relationship, but they have never denied that they are having an affair and have argued that such matters are their own business. The accountant is in a different division of the company that is not under Thompson's supervision.

Employees at Vertex are generally rather liberal in their views about sexual relations, and the company provides insurance to live-in partners, both heterosexual and homosexual. Nevertheless, many employees believe this relationship is improper. One major concern voiced by a number of employees is that, because of Thompson's high visibility and the fact that there is a twenty-year age difference between her and Jennings, the relationship is producing a bad public image for the company in the conservative community in which it is located. As a matter of fact, the purported affair has already been cited by one local conservative minister as an example of the immoral influence of Vertex in the community. A second argument is that, because of Thompson's influence, Jennings might receive undeserved promotions, even though the promotions would not be directly under Thompson's control. Vertex CEO, Jason Edwards, is aware of the controversy and thinks it is beginning to be an issue that demands his attention. What should he do?

Case 23: Selling Super-Kill

Super-Kill has been banned in this country, but Longwise Corporation still manufactures the product for overseas sales, especially to Third World countries. Critics point out that Super-Kill has been proven harmful to humans and the environment. They argue that it is morally wrong for Longwise to sell a product overseas that they know is harmful and that in many cases may be sold to unsuspecting customers.

Longwise CEO Rayford Hamilton argues that Super-Kill is a very effective insecticide and can be manufactured much more cheaply than other products that could be sold to Third World countries. Many farmers can thus buy Super-Kill when they cannot afford alternative products. Furthermore, using the chemical does increase crop yields, thus reducing malnutrition and starvation. Hamilton argues that more good is produced in foreign countries by selling the DDT abroad than by not selling it, to say nothing of the good produced in this country by the increased jobs and profits. Finally, other countries are also manufacturing Super-Kill, and they will sell the product if Longwise does not. Should Longwise be prevented from selling Super-Kill overseas?

Case 24: EMF Exposure

Electromagnetic fields (EMFs) are magnetic fields that result from electric current. They can be found around transmission lines, home appliances, and computer video display terminals. Since the 1950s, studies have suggested that there are human and environmental hazards associated with EMFs, including a higher risk of cancer. For example, studies published in the *American Journal of Epidemiology* in 1979 concluded that the children from homes located near high-current configurations (HCCs) had two to three times the normal incidence of cancer. In June 1982, a Swedish study confirmed that there was a higher incidence of childhood leukemia near high-voltage transmission lines. Despite these and other studies, however, many experts believe the evidence is not conclusive. Although we can no longer rule out the possibility of harm from exposure to EMFs, we do not know how great the risk is or how far humans must stay away from EMF generators to avoid risk. Thus, decisions about EMF-generating projects must be made with a considerable degree of uncertainty.

State Electric wants to build a very large and powerful transmission line connecting a generating facility with a city seventy-five miles away. The line travels through rural areas until it reaches the suburbs surrounding the city. State Electric will agree to provide a 450-foot easement around the line that, by the best estimates of impartial experts, is probably sufficient to protect the residents who live near the lines. As the experts admit, however, not enough information is available to know for sure what levels of EMF exposure are safe for humans.

State Electric officials argue that the city needs the additional power supply and that one large line would be safer and more economical than a number of smaller ones. City officials also agree with these claims. Local residents are not satisfied with these justifications. "Why should we and our children have to bear the risks of a project that benefits others as much as us?" one resident asks. He went on to emphasize that the costs and benefits of constructing the line would not be equally distributed and pleaded for the adoption of an alternative plan that called for the construction of the line through an undeveloped corridor. He also pointed out that, although the alternative would be almost fifteen times as expensive, the undeveloped land could be used as a wildlife refuge or park. He argued that, even though taxes would have to be increased to pay for this alternative, at least people would be sharing in the benefits and costs on a more equal basis. Which alternative should be chosen?

Case 25: A Plant Closing

American Textile and National Textile have recently merged. Managers of the new conglomerate have decided to close several of the most inefficient plants, and their attention has naturally turned to the Hoppersville operation. A mainstay in the local community for over seventy-five years, the plant is hopelessly outdated. It is not only less efficient than the newer plants, but the older equipment also poses many more hazards for workers. The older machines produce more noise and are less safe to operate. They also throw off a lot of particles that produce much lower air quality than can be achieved in the newer plants.

Employees of the plant, 50 percent of whom are within seven years of retirement, have organized to protest any plans to close the plant. They argue that the plant still generates a profit, even though not as great a profit as some of the newer facilities. They know that the plant cannot be economically brought up to state-of-the-art manufacturing, but they are willing to work under present conditions. They argue that the company has an obligation to the employees and the community to keep the plant open, at least for another decade, when most of the longtime employees will have reached retirement age. What should the managers do?

Case 26: Cigarette Advertising

In December 1991, the *Journal of the American Medical Association* published three surveys that found that the cartoon character Joe Camel was effective in advertising to children. Children, ages three to six, were surveyed, and

51.1 percent recognized old Joe Camel as being associated with Camel cigarettes.[8] The same survey showed that 97.7 percent of students between the ages of twelve and nineteen had seen Old Joe, and 58 percent were favorably impressed. In 1990, Camel shipments rose 11.3 percent. Critics of tobacco advertising say that this is hard evidence that tobacco companies are targeting children and reason to increase regulation of tobacco advertising, especially to children. Some even advocate a ban on cigarette advertising altogether.

Spokespersons for R. J. Reynolds, manufacturer of Camels, respond that the average Camel smoker is thirty-five years old and that it is not even in their interest to promote cigarette smoking among children, because it would invite increased government regulation. But they refuse to stop the Joe Camel advertisements.

Even those who find the Joe Camel ads offensive and believe they are not in the best interests of children could argue that the government should not prevent cigarette advertising. They might hold that such a prohibition would violate the rights of cigarette manufacturers and assume responsibilities for directing the behavior of children that rightfully belong to parents. They might also maintain that excessive regulation of the free-market system is not good for the economy and hence contrary to the public's well-being. Should cigarette advertising to children be forbidden?

Case 27: Carrying Ideas from Company A to Company B

While an employee of Company A, Joel Morelli developed a computer program that he thought would enable a firm to keep track of large inventories more efficiently. It turned out that the program was not as useful as Morelli had thought, and the company never marketed the product or patented it. Company A was a small firm that had close but informal relations with its employees, so that it did not require its employees to sign an agreement that employees must not take "intellectual property" developed at company A to a new employer.

Two years later, Morelli moved to company B. He quickly found that a modification of the program he had developed at company A would enable company B to keep track of its own inventory more effectively than any other program, so he began using it in his own work. Company B does not intend to market the product. Was Morelli's action "theft"? Was it wrong?

Case 28: Executive Compensation

Chief executive officers in American companies earn 160 times more than the average American employee, whereas similar executives in Japanese companies earn only 16 times more than the average Japanese employee.[9] The American

---

[8] K. Deveny, "Joe Camel Ads Reach Children, Research Finds," *Wall Street Journal*, December 11, 1990, p. B1.

[9] Jill Abramson and Christopher J. Chipello, "High Pay of CEO's Traveling with Bush Touches a Nerve in Asia," *Wall Street Journal*, December 30, 1991, p. A1.

executives might argue that these salaries are justified to attract qualified people to the high-stress positions. "If highly qualified people occupy these positions," the argument goes, "everyone will benefit: even the lowest-paid worker will be better off than he or she would be otherwise, because there will be more and better-paying jobs." Others argue that corporations have the moral right to allocate the resources as they wish, and so there is no moral problem, even if the previously mentioned claim is invalid. What are the moral and factual issues in the debate over justified executive salaries?

Case 29: Billing for Medical Services

Physicians can "fudge" on insurance claims in various ways. For example, physicians can code the removal of a mole as a larger procedure ("upcoding") or break down surgeries into smaller procedures and charge for each procedure individually. Often these practices are clear cases of insurance fraud, but sometimes the considerations are more complex.

Sophia Jackson has been Dr. Kaufmann's patient for over twenty-five years. Her financial situation is precarious, but she comes in regularly for removal of moles. Ordinary mole removals are not covered by her health insurance, but they are covered if they are coded as necessary to "rule out cancer." Kaufmann does not believe the moles he has removed during the past year were cancerous, but he also knows that Jackson worries about them incessantly. To relieve her of anxiety and not jeopardize her finances, he routinely "upcodes" the procedures as necessary to "rule out cancer." Is this ethically permissible?

Case 30: Health Benefits to Homosexual Couples

Several cities, firms, and other organizations (including the American Psychological Association) extend health insurance benefits for partners in a homosexual relationship. The controversy surrounding this issue has now spread to Mary Nielsen's hometown. The next election will contain an initiative to repeal the city's policy of extending health benefits to gay couples. On the one hand, Nielsen is uncomfortable with supporting a policy that she thinks might give legitimacy to a lifestyle she thinks is wrong. She also thinks she has a right to vote her conscience. On the other hand, she believes in individual freedom and is uneasy about placing restrictions on the lives of people whose lifestyle she condemns. Should she vote for or against the repeal?

Index